TEXTS, FACTS, AND FEMININITY

Dorothy E. Smith is one of the leading feminist thinkers in North America. Her book consists of key published and unpublished essays which illustrate the full range of her work on texts as social relations.

Included here is Professor Smith's famous essay 'K is mentally ill' which explores the concept of mental illness as a method of reading and writing, a factual account of someone becoming mentally ill. There are also some studies on femininity as discourse; the social relations of description in the context of a sociological study of news; the micro-politics of a meeting; the 'structuring' of power through texts telling different versions of a confrontation between police and street people. The book concludes with a discussion of the distinctive properties of social organization and relations mediated by texts.

Discursive and exhaustive, *Texts, Facts, and Femininity* will be of interest to students of women's studies, sociology, social theory, cultural theory, communications, and psychology.

TEXTS, FACTS, AND FEMININITY

Exploring the relations of ruling

DOROTHY E. SMITH

LONDON AND NEW YORK

First published 1990
Paperback published 1993
by Routledge
2 Park Square, Milton Park, Abingdon, Oxon, OX14 4RN

Transferred to Digital Printing 2005

Simultaneously published in the USA and Canada
by Routledge
270 Madison Ave, New York NY 10016

Typeset in Baskerville by LaserScript Ltd, Mitcham, Surrey

British Library Cataloguing in Publication Data

A catalogue record for this book is available from the British Library

Library of Congress Cataloging in Publication Data

Smith, Dorothy E., 1926–
Texts, Facts, and Femininity: Exploring the relations of ruling/
Dorothy E. Smith.
p. cm.
Includes bibliographical references.

1. Sociology – Methodology.
2. Discourse analysis. 3. Feminist criticism.
I. Title.
HN28.S56 1990
301'01 – dc20
89-10961
CIP
ISBN 0–415–03231–8
0–415–10244–8 (pbk)

CONTENTS

ILLUSTRATIONS

ACKNOWLEDGEMENTS

As is necessarily the case, I am indebted to many in the writing of this book. There are two, however, whose contributions have been of special importance. They are Nancy Jackson and George Smith. I would also like to thank the following publishers for permission to reproduce copyright material: Basil Blackwell Ltd for permission to reprint 'Textually mediated social organization' (Chapter 7), which appeared originally in the *International Social Science Journal* 36 (1) 1984: 59–75; Falmer Press for permission to reprint portions of the abridged version of 'Femininity as discourse' (Chapter 6) which appeared in Leslie Roman and Linda Christian-Smith (eds) *Becoming Feminine: The Politics of Popular Culture*, 1988, 37–59; Kluwer Academic Publishers for permission to reprint 'On sociological description: a method from Marx' (Chapter 4), which appeared originally in *Human Studies* 4, 1981, 313–37; BSA Publications Ltd for permission to reprint 'K is mentally ill: the anatomy of a factual account' (Chapter 2), the English version of which appeared originally in *Sociology* 12 (1) 1978, 25–53.

Chapter One

INTRODUCTION

The papers making up this book build on the two lines of inquiry I have been exploring for a number of years. It seemed, for a long time, that they traveled on parallel tracks and would not meet. Gradually I came to see them as aspects of one unfolding inquiry into contemporary history and society and, indeed, that the underground grubbing and molework that went into bringing them into coherent relation to one another was foundational to an ability to engage properly with either. These two lines of inquiry are, first, into what it means to explore the social from the site of women's experience and beginning therefore with an experiencing and embodied subject, and second, into the social organization of the objectified knowledges that are essential constituents of the relations of ruling of contemporary capitalism. The methods of inquiry developed and used in these chapters have emerged from conjoining these lines of inquiry.

I began thinking through how to develop sociological inquiry from the site of the experiencing and embodied subject as a sociology from the standpoint of women. In the women's movement, we began to discover that we lived in a world put together in ways in which we had had very little say. We found that we had participated unknowingly in a culture and an intellectual life in the making of which we had had little part. We discovered that we had been in various ways silenced, deprived of the authority to speak, and that our experience therefore did not have a voice, lacked indeed a language, for we had taken from the cultural and intellectual world created largely by men the terms, themes, conceptions of the subject and subjectivity, of feeling, emotion, goals, relations, and an object world assembled in textually mediated discourses and from the standpoint of men occupying the apparatuses of ruling. We came to understand this organization of power as 'patriarchy', a term that identified both the personal and the public relations of male power.

When women, in this phase of the women's movement, entered the public process as speaking subjects, we found we lacked a language with which to identify ourselves and to speak of what it was we have in common as women. Our discoveries of a language, political, cultural, artistic, philosophic, were grounded in the practice called 'consciousness raising'. It has had many uses, but its early uses were to work on how to speak from what we knew that had no names, that had to be expressed in any kind of language we could lay hold of that would do the job. Speaking from experience was a method of speaking; it was not a particular kind of knowledge, but a practice of telling wherein the particular speaker was authority in speaking of her everyday life and the world known to her as she was active in it.

The ruling apparatuses are those institutions of administration, management, and professional authority, and of intellectual and cultural discourses, which organize, regulate, lead and direct, contemporary capitalist societies. The power relations which come thus into view from the standpoint of an experience situated in the everyday world are abstracted from local and particular settings and relationships. These forms of communication and action are distinctively mediated by texts. The textual mediation of its forms of organization are fundamental to its characteristic abstracted, extra-local forms, and its curious capacity to reproduce its order in the same way in an indefinite variety of actual local contexts.

Sociology did not know how to develop inquiry from the standpoint of a subject situated in the local actualities of her life. Indeed it abjured such a standpoint. Sociology created and creates a construct of society that is specifically discontinuous with the world known, lived, experienced, and acted in. The practice of sociology in which we were trained as graduate students was one that insisted that the sociologist should never go out without a concept; that to encounter the raw world was to encounter a world of irremediable disorder and confusion; to even begin to speak sociologically of that world required a concept, or concepts, to order, select, assemble, a sociological version of the world on paper.

But of course the world is full of order even when disorderly and disorganized. For people are forever at work coordinating and co-ordering their activities, latching on and operating the coordinative schemata built into language, taking direction, managing the deployment of a steel girder on a construction site, entering a classroom and activating the programs and forms of a lecture, recognizing and coordinating activities with the social organized properties of things (tables, chairs, sidewalks, and so on indefinitely), ad libbing, extrapolating – the irremediable disorder and confusion threatening the sociologist is a problem of the richness of the material to be mined rather than its instrinsic lack of order. For people themselves are continually bringing into being in their daily/nightly activities the co-ordering that is the object of her inquiry.

The break I experienced between a world known, acted, and lived directly in particular local sites in relation to particular others, and objectified knowledges built into the relations of ruling is itself socially organized. Such social organization is necessarily a specific organization of practices through which subjects always and ineluctably located in the actualities of their bodily being participate in and accomplish those objectifications. It is an organization within local actualities accomplishing an operative world transcending it. Its organization, as such, is examinable only from the standpoint of actual subjects. The sociologist here works as an insider, as one who is a practitioner of that organization, explicating and analyzing its properties as she knows and discovers them as actual practices. Her sociology, rather than re-enacting the objectifying break, explores and explicates the actual determinations and organization of the actualities of people's experienced worlds – not, of course, as to the particularities of their experience, but as their experiencing participates in and is shaped by that organization. Such a sociology speaks of the same world as that in which it is written and read.

These chapters, with the exception of the last, are all pieces of inquiry and all work with and contribute to the development of such a method of inquiry. The latter relies on the insider's knowledge of how the social relations and organization in which she participates work, how they are put together. Texts are not seen as inert extra-temporal blobs of meaning, the fixity of which enables the reader to forget the actual back and forth work on the piece or pieces of paper in front of her that constitute the text as a

3

body of meaning existing outside time and all at once. Writing an insider's sociology,[1] that is, an exploration and analysis of the social as it is known from the inside (as indeed it must be known) displaces the surface of the text as focus. The text is analyzed for its characteristically textual form of participation in social relations. The interest is in the social organization of those relations and in penetrating them, discovering them, opening them up from within, *through the text.* The text enters the laboratory, so to speak, carrying the threads and shreds of the relations it is organized by and organizes. The text before the analyst, then, is not used as a specimen or sample, but as means of access, a direct line to the relations it organizes. It is in the same world as she is.

The proposal and practice are to investigate the social relations and organization of consciousness. It is a terrain of investigation that intersects with the focus and site of major contemporary explorations of culture, language, and discourse. Clearly, however, it works from a site that transgresses foundational principles of these explorations, notably the displacement or cancellation of the presence of actual subjects as integral to inquiry and analysis and the recuperation of the subject within textually mediated discourse. Foucault's insistence on an exploration of discourse, and hence of working within the textual and from the textual, but by implication only, to the actualities of people's lives, has offered an important alternative to that of simply going ahead and writing it anyway (any way). Cultural theory following from his work and the work of other structuralists and post-structuralists in this area has also adopted the strategy of working from within the textual, from this side, the reading and writing, seeing, hearing side of textual surfaces, where the sociologist, cultural theorist, or other inquirer works in her analysis in the same medium, meaning, that is the object of her investigation. The old ontological problem raised by giving presence to subject–object relations of which the text speaks is bypassed altogether. The method presupposes the textual and works within it, reading off the actualities of people's lives, as Foucault does with sexuality, from the textual. The ideology of post-modernism permanently seals off any attempt to find an escape hatch for inquiry beyond the textual surface of discourse.

But as I have addressed it, the standpoint of women has already provided such an escape hatch, emerging at a point in women's contemporary struggles when we had to place a radical reliance on our experience in learning with each other how to speak together as women. The method of experience returns us always to the subject active in remembering, in finding out how to speak from the actualities of her life, bringing forward what was into a speaking for which she is the only authority. It is a method that feminists have taken up in a variety of ways. For me, it established a place to situate a subject as knower of a sociology that might explore how her life is put together by relations and forces that are not fully available to her experiencing.

This knower as subject is always situated in the actualities of her experiencing. Therefore inquiry into the social organization of knowledge is positioned prior to and including the moment of transition into the textually grounded world. There is an actual subject prior to the subject constituted in the text. She is active as reader (or writer). Inquiry begins there and not on the already written side of the text. Ethnomethodology for a time used what seemed the rather irritating device of preceding every social given with a participle expressing the accomplished character of what was named. I am uncomfortable with the device, but I want to use it. I am investigating 'doing knowing' as an accomplishment of text and reading subject. I explore the reader doing knowing where knowing is specifically a practice of reading. In so doing, I rely on experiences of reading, of what I know how to do as reader. The method explicates practices within which what might be recuperated as experience arises. Texts are analyzed to display what the subject knows how to do as reader and what the subject knows how to do in reading, and in so doing also displays the organizing capacity of the text, its capacity to operate as a constituent of social relations.

The project, however, is not simply to elucidate the encounter of text and reader. This is not a version of the 'reader-response' (Tompkins 1980) method of literary exploration deployed for non-literary texts. Rather I see working with the texts and topics I have chosen as exploring of the intersection of the extended social relations of ruling through an actual experience of reading. Hence analysis focuses on just that intersection, on how the reader operates the text to enter the objectified modes of knowing characteristic of the relations of ruling. It is a two-way street, a

5

method of exploring relations in which we are active and which govern us.

RELATIONS OF RULING

The notion of relations of ruling has no particular theoretical intention. It names an area for examination that is explicated as the standpoint of women arises as a distinct epistemic moment. The institutional order of the society that excluded and silenced women and women's experience is elucidated from women's standpoint in the local actualities of our everyday/everynight world as they are organized extra-locally, abstracted, grounded in universalized forms, and objectified. The phrase 'relations of ruling' designates the complex of extra-local relations that provide in contemporary societies a specialization of organization, control, and initiative. They are those forms that we know as bureaucracy, administration, management, professional organization, and the media. They include also the complex of discourses, scientific, technical, and cultural, that intersect, interpenetrate, and coordinate the multiple sites of ruling. Chapter 7 describes their essentially textually mediated character.

The focus of inquiry is the textually vested versions of the world that are constituents of the relations of ruling. Of the many dimensions of textuality that mediate these relations, these inquiries, with the exception of the essay on 'femininity as discourse' (Chapter 6), explore the construction of the virtual realities that constitute the world as actionable within them. I am of course exploring a terrain that Marx identified in the preface to *A Contribution to the Critique of Political Economy* (Marx 1971) as the 'superstructure'. The method of inquiry is grounded in his materialism as described in *The German Ideology* (Marx and Engels 1976), the premises of which are not concepts or principles but the actual activities of actual individuals and the material conditions of those activities.[2] I am exploring it by an extrapolation of a materialist ontology, namely by exploring it as the actual practices of actual individuals. I have wanted to discover, to analyze what is there, and to find and refine concepts to analyze and express properties of social organization as these come into view in the course of inquiry. I have wanted to be open to how the terrain under analysis

6

is actually put together, rather than to theorize it in advance of discovery. The ontological ground of such a sociology must therefore be people's actual practices and activities as they are coordinated and co-ordered.

The approach extends to the terrain of consciousness the methods of materialism which Marx proposed as the ground of inquiry into the ways in which people produce their existence through a social division of labour acting upon nature. For though *The German Ideology* proffers an account of consciousness as united with actual individuals and inseparable from them, although ideology is analyzed as practices, and although social consciousness is given a preliminary materialist formulation as uttered, the bold ontology that enables the materialism of a political economy stops short at a materialism enabling investigation of the social relations and organization of consciousness.

Why is this so? Marx's own method suggests an answer. The social forms of consciousness also exist only in actual practices and in the concerting of those practices as an ongoing process. If consciousness appears as distinct from and determining social action and relations, that too is a product of the activity of real individuals and their material conditions. Marx's epistemology grounds the concepts and categories in and through which the nature of capitalism is disclosed in that historical mode of production itself. In capitalism, a system of economic relations emerges as a differentiated and objectified form. Capitalism itself creates the conditions of political economic analysis.[3] It abstracts relations of interdependence arising from the social division of labour from relationships between particular individuals and land, creating an independent system of relations mediated by money and commodities. It creates the category of the 'economy' as relations which can operate apart and can be seen apart from other dimensions of social existence.

Capitalism thus explicates *in practice* the properties and categories of economic relations on which a science of political economy can be founded. I suggest that in our time we see a corresponding development of a social consciousness which emerges fully only now. Marx's time lacked the developed social relations of reasoning and knowledge externalized as textually mediated forms of organization and discourse. They existed prototypically in legal institutions, early bureaucratic forms, and emerging textually mediated discourse such as that in which Marx himself participated. But the social forms of consciousness of that period had not yet found forms differentiating them from individuals as such. Although we can find adumbrated in *The German Ideology* (Marx and Engels 1976) an account of the differentiation of social consciousness with the emergence of class and 'mental production' as a specialized activity of a ruling class, the conditions for the exploration of a differentiated social consciousness, a social consciousness existing as differentiated practices and relations, did not yet exist. The forms which were prototypical in Marx's day, have in our times emerged as a complex of loosely coordinated functions of organization and regulation vested in texts and documents and increasingly in computer software and data banks. Information, knowledge, reasoning, decision making, control, etc., become properties of external organizational and technological forms. They are accomplished in a division of labour concerted discursively or hierarchically. The social relations of textually mediated discourse intersect and penetrate organizational structures constituted as complex entities with differentiated functions, corporations, government agencies, universities, and so on.

It is no mere historical contingency, nor mere progress of thought, nor the inventiveness of particular genius, that has brought us a structuralist theory of language providing the basis for semiology conceiving of signifying systems independent of particular utterances or expressions. Or a grammatology. Or the contemporary studies of culture or ideology. Or the rediscovery of Gramsci's concept of hegemony. Or Foucault's substitution of discourse and its autonomous historical movement for the analysis of thought through its authors, and his later concentration on the relations of power and knowledge. Or Baudrillard's theorizing of a textually constituted reality with no ground outside itself. Or sociological studies of formal organization and bureaucracy. Or contemporary Marxist theorizing of the state. History itself has supplied the reality of what formerly could only be arrived at by a conceptual leap. Social consciousness exists now as a complex of externalized social relations organizing and coordinating contemporary society. It exists as co-ordered practices and can be investigated as such.

A METHOD OF INQUIRY

Though these inquiries are not in general concerned with specifically feminist topics, the standpoint of women has been essential to the method used. The theorizing and exploration of the contemporary terrain of textually mediated relations have been addressed virtually exclusively from a standpoint that presupposes and forgets about its textual mediation. The working life of the intelligentsia anchors the subject in a layering of texts, signifiers, and significations, one layer yielding to another beyond. Constitutional devices such as Lacan's positing of the emergence of the subject at the coincidence of her simultaneous entry to language and the law of the father, or the cancellation of the subject and the substitution of discourse (Foucault), or Baudrillard's grounding of a hyperreality in media technology, entitle inquiry to forget the irremediable grounding of the subject, who deftly performs this forgetting, in the actualities of her daily/nightly life. This standpoint has been until very recently an exclusively male province. By contrast, women's standpoint, as I and millions of other women lived and live it, locates subject in her work with particular others, in a particular local site, her children, her partner, her neighbors, the local grocery store, and so on. It is a working consciousness addressing in daily and nightly practices precisely these particularities. Entry to the virtual realities of the relations of ruling call for her actual practice of their social organization.

This insider's standpoint is not subjective, nor is it phenomenological in the sense of an exploration from within of the constitutive moves of consciousness. It addresses from within the actual work of coordination, the ongoing co-ordering that brings into being, that *is*, the social. The practices and coordination are actual processes in time, they are done, they are accomplished. Or rather they are being done, being accomplished. The working assumptions of inquiry are in these ways close to those of ethnomethodology. They differ in three ways. One is in working with an insider's standpoint. Ethnomethodology makes the characteristic sociological shift from what we know as members to a member's knowledge that is constructed as externalized in the ethnomethodological text (Turner 1974a). The second is in having as an objective the exploration of the actualities of the society in which we live, rather than those of a generalizing science. The third is in seeking access to the extended or macro-relations organizing the society through an analysis of the micro-social.

Social scientific strategies for exploring macro-social relations depend on conceptual practices that construct a textual version of society and social relations excluding the presence of subjects (Smith 1989), hence displacing the connection between the explored and analyzed relations and the actualities of people's lives.[4] In contrast with such strategies, the move precipitated here by the standpoint of women abjures the need for a totalizing theory or master-frame[5] situating the knower outside the society she is part of and active in. Working from an insider's knowledge of the social organization of the actual practices that bring the actualities of society into being provides a route for exploration of its actualities. Here, of course, the enterprise departs from Marx. For though Marx saw concepts as expressing social relations, he had no way of seeing concepts as part of the action. Things go on inside people's heads; and they go on outside them.[6] People reflect and conceptualize. But though reflection and conceptualization might be thought of as part of the action, Marx does not conceive of reflection and conceptualization as socially organized and organizing practices. He knows, asserts, that consciousness is only and always the consciousness of actual individuals. At the same time he works in practice with a double ontology, with actual practices, actual activities of individuals on the one hand, and thought, ideology, consciousness stuck at the level of meaning on the other.

Without a totalizing theory or externalizing master-frame, the mode of inquiry begins where people are and explores the actual practices engaging us in the relations organizing our lives. The investigation of the facticity (the property of being factual) of an account of someone becoming mentally ill (Chapter 2) provides an entry, beyond the text, to relations and organization that are necessarily part of, hooked into, more extended relations. Neither 'mental illness' as a conceptual practice of writing and reading, nor facticity as a social organization of the text, begins and ends with it. To explore their textuality is to explore a segment of the relations of ruling. Chapter 3 exploring the micro-politics of a meeting does not just describe a particular meeting, but shows how a particular meeting relates a local setting into an extra-local organization, the properties of which contain and divert a local political process. Chapter 4 elucidates a problem of field method and writing ethnography by explicating properties of the social relations in which ethnography is embedded. Chapter 5 on the 'active text' examines a sequence of reading two different versions of a single event and how the social organization of the two texts in sequence recaptures the reader as a member of the institutional order. Chapter 6 examines femininity as a textually mediated discourse where discourse is addressed as an organization of intersecting local and extra-local practices. A final essay on textually mediated social organization (Chapter 7) builds outward from empirical explorations, those in this volume among others.

If this work can claim to innovate, it is as a project of inquiry that explores concepts, interpretations, ideology, knowledge, ideas, as socially organized and organizing practices. The latter are understood not as mysterious operations of the subjective hidden inside people's heads, accessible only in the same medium, interpretively, but as actual ongoing social practices integral to the social courses of action I am calling social relations. Hence they are taken as occurring/accomplishing in time and as part of specific local historical processes. These investigations of texts do not constitute them as a realm of meaning separated from the world they are written and read in. Rather, texts are taken up as constituents of ongoing social relations into which our own practices of reading enter us.

Chapter Two

K IS MENTALLY ILL: THE ANATOMY OF A FACTUAL ACCOUNT[1]

This paper analyzes an interview which tells how K comes to be defined by her friends as mentally ill. It is not just a record of events as they happened, but of events as they were seen as relevant to reaching a decision about the character of those events. This is a common feature of the kinds of records etc. with which the social scientist in the field of deviant behavior is concerned. The various agencies of social control have institutionalized procedures for assembling, processing, and testing information about the behavior of individuals so that it can be matched against the paradigms which provide the working criteria of class-membership whether as juvenile delinquent, mentally ill, or the like. These procedures, both formal and informal, are a regular part of the business of the police, the courts, psychiatrists, and other similar agencies (Cicourel 1969). A full description of the organizational practice of such agencies in these respects would be a description of one type of procedure by which a set of original and actual events is transformed into the currency of fact. A number of studies in the field of mental illness (Goffman 1961a; Scheff 1964; Mechanic 1962; Smith 1975), show that descriptions of the activities of the official agencies are far from adequate in accounting for how people come to be defined as mentally ill. In this account it is K's friends who are doing the preliminary work. K does not get so far as the formal psychiatric agencies though this is fore-shadowed. Accounts of 'paths to the mental hospital' (Clausen and Yarrow 1955) suggest that a good deal of non-formal work has been done by the individual concerned, her family, and friends, before entry to the official process. These non-formal processes may also be described as a social organization which in this case precedes the production of an interview account of the kind I am concerned with here.

The term 'social organization' is used here in a sense which leaves the question of planning or purpose open. Such a use of the concept can be compared with the economic concept of a market which makes possible the analysis of the activities of numbers of individuals buying and selling as a social organization which is unintended by its participants and which produces 'market phenomena' as an unintended consequence. It is used here analogously to include as participants in the production of this account, not just the sociologist, the interviewer, and the respondent, but also those who brought about the original events and those who tried to reach a decision about what they were. It is thus a means of making explicit the various steps and activities that intervene between the reader of the account and the original events; and of showing how the acceptability of the interview as a factual account and as an account of someone who is, or is becoming, mentally ill is provided for. I have accordingly also stressed throughout the fact that we all recognize but normally bracket, namely that the sociologist is and must be an active participant in constructing the events she treats as data.

THE ORIGIN OF THE DATA

In an undergraduate course of deviance, I worked with a few students on a research project concerned with how the lay person comes to define someone as mentally ill. The research was modeled, though loosely, on Kitsuse's paper on 'Societal reaction to deviant behavior' (Kitsuse 1962) which examines how people come to identify someone as homosexual. The interviewing approach used was less structured than Kitsuse's. The interviewers were instructed to begin with the question 'Have you ever known anyone you thought might be mentally ill?' Respondents were to be told to define mental illness and to tell the story pretty much in their own way, but the interviewer was told to get information on four points:

(a) the incident or situation in which the respondent first came to think the person might be mentally ill;
(b) what the subject was doing then or in other previous

13

situations that suggested this definition or which could later
be seen as instances of that kind of behavior;
(c) what the relationship between the subject and respondent
had been;
(d) and what others were involved in the process of definition,
who the respondent had talked to, etc.

This interview may not be a model of what such interviews
might be like. The interviewer's write-up did not include her own
questions, nor was the interview tape recorded, which is the
ideal, though at that time one not ordinarily available to under-
graduates. But my interest in analyzing is in just the account it is.
The interview was discussed in class. At that time I did not have the
written account before me. The interviewer gave a verbal presentation. Hearing her account, I took it to be an account of a
developing schizophrenic reaction of some type. I thought to
myself, 'The subject will get more and more disorganized and then
one day things will go to pot at work and she'll be hospitalized'. In
other words, I heard the interviewer's account as an account of
someone who was or was becoming mentally ill. The verbal
account differed, and differed I believe in important ways, from
the written account, in that it included some material that is not in
the written account and omitted some that is. Later, however, I saw
the typescript of the interview and it was just as clear to me that a
rather different picture of the goings-on could be drawn and that
I would have no trouble drawing it, at least as a tentative picture,
on the basis of evidence internal to the interview. The alternative
picture, very simply stated, was that what was going on was a kind
of communal freezing-out process, very like that which Lemert
describes in his paper on 'Paranoia and the dynamics of exclusion'
(Lemert 1962) and that if there was anything odd in K's behavior
(and reading the account suggested to me that there was doubt
whether anything was psychiatrically very odd) it might reasonably
be supposed that people do react in ways which seem odd to others
when they are going through this kind of process.
    The usual thing to do with this type of difficulty is to try to arrive
at some kind of decision about which interpretation is correct.
This would normally involve wanting more information, or
examining with care what is already there. In this case most likely
the decision would have to be that the interview was not adequate

14

for this purpose. But what I had been struck with was the figure–ground effect, that first I saw the verbal account as mental illness and could still see distinctly the lineaments of that in the written interview, and that now I could see the alternative. So the interview can be read for the mental illness effect and then that is what you see (and clearly that had been what the interviewer had seen and had further communicated to me and the students in class); but having seen the alternative model it is then hard to see the one where the subject is mentally ill.

RECOGNIZING MENTAL ILLNESS

The criteria of class-membership in other types of deviant categories, such as homosexual, juvenile delinquent, etc., are fairly straightforward. A definite rule must have been broken or a norm deviated from. The process of showing that something an individual has done can be properly seen as an instance of breaking the rule is not by any means simple. Nevertheless the difficulty with the category 'mental illness' is of another kind. The criteria of class-membership are not clear. It is not clear what norms are deviated from when someone is categorized as mentally ill. Yet it is clearly possible to describe behavior in such a way that people will make that definition with full confidence in its propriety. There must therefore be some set of rules or procedures for representing behavior as mentally ill types of behavior and those procedures must meet the normative conditions for recognizing individuals as members of the class of persons who are mentally ill. In the verbal account given by the interviewer in class, I, and I take it others present, recognized the behavior of the subject, K, as mentally ill behavior. The interview purports to be, and can be, recognized in the same way. Recognizing in events the 'fact' that someone is mentally ill involves a complex conceptual work. It involves assembling observations from actual moments and situations dispersed in time, organizing them, or finding that they can be organized, in accordance with the 'instructions' which the concept provides. A simple, immediate, and convincing recognition of a fact at this conceptual level implies that much of the work of providing events with the appropriate conceptual order has already been done. All that the reader/hearer has to do is to discover in those events, or rather that account of events, the model which enables her to classify them as this or that kind of social fact. The conceptual schema which is the meaning of the term 'mental illness' (as I know it) provides a set of criteria and rules for ordering events against which the ordering of events in the account may be matched, or tested. An account which is immediately convincing is one which forces that classification and makes any other difficult. And if it does, then the events of the account must already display the order giving them the shape of the fact for the reader/hearer. It is this which entitles me, I suggest, to analyze this account to discover (in a preliminary way) the lineaments of the concept of mental illness. The structure of this account with respect to how it may be seen as an account of someone being mentally ill is treated as isomorphic with the structure of the conceptual schema used to recognize it as such. In analyzing this account as an account of mental illness I am, I argue, *recovering the structure of the conceptual model which I make use of in recognizing that that is what it is.*

THE INTERVIEW ITSELF AS DATA

In this analysis the interview is not being viewed as an account from which we are trying to infer back to what actually happened. The effect of questions is not merely to generate information. The difference between questions in different forms is not merely that some yield more and others less information. The form of the question tells the respondent what sort of work she is being asked to do. It asks her to operate on her knowledge, experience, etc., in a particular way. In this interview the opening question – 'Have you ever known anyone you thought might be mentally ill?' – asks the respondent to do a matching operation, to find from her own experience an instance (presumably known only to her) which can be properly matched against criteria of class-membership assumed to be known at large. An interview of this kind is thus a process in which the respondent works up and tests the status of her experience, knowledge, and definitions of events against the knowledge etc. imputed to the interviewer as representative of the culture at large. This account therefore is a further step in establishing the propriety of the definitions made prior to the interview. Thus from the respondent's point of view the interview is a further though unanticipated step in the process of testing a

16

categorization already made. She has her uses for the interview just as the interviewer and I have ours. What actually happened – whatever that was – was something that the respondent was, and still was in the interview (I believe), working up into an intelligible form, a form in which she could find the shape and direction of those events. The actual events can be looked upon as a set of resources upon which the respondent drew in creating for herself and the interviewer an account of what had happened. Of course the actual events were much richer, much less orderly, simply much more, than those arranged into an interview of an hour or so; and indeed, might have lent themselves to being worked up in different ways from that selected by the respondent. So radical processes of selection have gone on; a lot is left out and what is left in is ordered to provide a coherence for the reader which was not present in the events. Moreover some events are brought into the foreground as elements of the picture whereas others that are also there are treated as part of the background or of the machinery of the narrative. That may be conceived to be the work of the respondent.

There is, however, a second step before the interview arrives at the reader/hearer. This is the work of the interviewer. Since the interviewer was inexperienced and did not use a tape recorder, we may suppose that this was fairly substantial and do not know precisely what it had been. Thus the interview as we have it must be regarded as a cooperative working up of a now rather distant and wholly indeterminate set of events. In addition I have myself done some very minor editing to ensure further that the subject should be identifiable. In analyzing the account and the organization of its relationship to the actual events it claims to represent, we will not be concerned with the actual character of these events. Whether K was really mentally ill or not is irrelevant to the analysis. It is important that I convey to the reader *that the data the paper is concerned with are wholly present to her – just as they are to me – in the typescript of the interview which she will find below.*

Here is the interview as I received it, plus minor alterations to conceal identities further. The punctuation is the interviewer's. The form and paragraphing are as the interviewer wrote it up.

1 Angela was interviewed about her impressions regarding a
2 friend, who will be called 'K' for the purpose of this
3 study. Angela met K about 4 years ago, during her first

4 year at university. Angela had been to the same school
5 but in a grade below K and when introduced to K felt full
6 of admiration. Here was a girl, a year older, of such a
7 good family, a good student, so nice, so friendly, so
8 very athletic, who was willing to befriend her. K sug-
9 gested outings, and they went skiing , swimming, playing
10 tennis together. In the fall they shared in a carpool,
11 so that more people were immediately involved in the con-
12 tact. Nearly every morning K would cry in the car, being
13 upset about little things, and the girls would comfort
14 her. Sometimes she would burst into tears in the middle
15 of a conversation. She began to have trouble with her
16 courses, dropped some of them and switched some.
17 ANGELA: My recognition that there might be something
18 wrong was very gradual, and I was actually the last of
19 her close friends who was openly willing to admit that
20 she was becoming mentally ill. Angela found it easier to
21 explain things chronologically, and, in retrospect, it
22 appears that this would make the observations fall
23 more easily into place.
24 We would go to the beach or the pool on a hot day, and I
25 would sort of dip in and just lie in the sun, while K
26 insisted that she had to swim 30 lengths. It was very
27 difficult to carry on an intelligent conversation with
28 her, this became apparent when I wanted to discuss a
29 particularly good movie, and she would make childish
30 inane remarks, completely off the point.
31 Slowly my admiration changed to a feeling of bafflement.
32 I began to treat her more like a child who was perhaps
33 not too bright, and I became protective of her. I real-
34 ized that this change had taken place, when a mutual
35 friend, Trudi who was majoring in English, had looked
36 over one of her essays, and told me afterwards: She
37 writes like a 12 year old – I think there is something
38 wrong with her.
39 K is so intense about everything at times, she tries too
40 hard. Her sense of proportion is out of kilter. When
41 asked casually to help in a friend's garden, she went at
42 it for hours, never stopping, barely looking up. When
43 you meet her, you are struck, by a sweet girlish
44 appearance. She will sit quietly in company, smiling
45 sweetly at all times, and seems disarmingly appealing.
46 But when there were young men in the company, she would
47 find it harder than ever to carry on a conversation, and
48 would excuse herself and leave very soon. During all the
49 time that I have known her she has really never gone out
50 with a boy, although she did occasionally share with them
51 in athletic activities. It was obvious that she was ter-

52 rified of anyone getting too near to her, especially men.
53 And yet she used to pretend to us (and obviously to her-
54 self too) that she had this and that guy really keen on
55 her.
46 During this time Angela had become more friendly with
47 Trudi mainly because she felt she could discuss things
48 with her. Her friendship with K continued, but was con-
49 fined more to athletic activities.
50 At the beginning of the next academic year Trudi and
51 Angela had found an apartment which they wanted to share,
52 but it was too expensive for two. Since K's family had
53 moved away, she was sort of on her own. And Angela par-
54 ticularly felt sort of responsible, and it was agreed
55 that K would share the apartment. Trudi had her doubts
56 that it would work out, but Angela felt confident that
57 things would work out.
58 For a few days, before the apartment became available, K
59 went to stay with Angela in her home. Angela's mother had
60 always admired the girl, K, for her politeness and gen-
61 eral good manners, and made her most welcome. Angela
62 tried to prepare her mother for any odd behaviour, but
63 found she could not bring herself to this. On the first
64 morning, Angela's mother offered to make K's breakfast.
65 K very sweetly said: Oh I don't want to give you any
66 trouble, just anything, anything that you have got. So
67 Angela's mother enumerated the things available and K
68 after much coaxing, and shy smiles, asked for tea and a
69 hard boiled egg. At that time, Angela's mother's own
70 breakfast was ready on the table, coffee and a soft
71 boiled egg. Angela's mother turned to the stove to put
72 on an egg, and water for tea and when she came back to
73 the table, there was K smiling sweetly, eating the soft-
74 boiled egg and drinking coffee. At the time Angela's
75 mother thought, well she misunderstood me. But later she
76 noticed that K was unable to put on a teapot cover cor-
77 rectly, she would not reverse its position to make it
78 fit, but would simply keep slamming it down on the pot.
79 Angela's parents are very warm and quite vocal people.
80 Angela's relationships with them is particularly good and
81 rests on mutual respect and continued expressions of
82 affection since childhood. During K's stay, she had occa-
83 sion to observe Angela's father put his arm around his
84 daughter. K turned away in embarrassment, and later con-
85 fided to Angela's mother: You know my father never put
86 his arm around me.
87 A little while after the three girls began to share the
88 apartment, they had to face the fact that K was
89 definitely queer. She would take baths religiously every

90 night and pin up her hair, but she would leave the bath
91 dirty. She would wash dishes, but leave them dirty too.
92 They would try and live within a strict budget, and take
93 turns in cooking dinner and shopping for it, each for one
94 week. K invariably overshot the budget by several dol-
95 lars. She would buy the most impractical things, such as
96 a broom, although they already one, 6 lbs of ham-
97 burger at one go, which they would have to eat the whole
98 week. She would burn practically everything. When some-
99 thing had gone radically wrong, obviously by her doing,
100 she would blandly deny all knowledge, but got very upset
101 at little things, like a blown fuse. She did not seem to
102 absorb the simplest information regarding the working of
103 the stove or other household implements. She had definite
104 food-fads, and would take condiments such as ketchup,
105 pepper to excess. Also things like tinned fruit and
106 honey, she would eat them by the jar, at one go. We grad-
107 ually began to realize that she just could not cope and
108 we began to take over more and more of her
109 responsibilities. She had begun to work in an account-
110 ant's office and we told her that she probably had too
111 much to do in her first year of working at her new job,
112 and that she could cook at the weekends only, but that we
113 would do the shopping.
114 Trudi and I found ourselves discussing her foibles in her
115 absence. I still tried to find explanations and excuses –
116 I refused to acknowledge the fact that there was anything
117 definitely wrong with K. But she'd tiptoe through the
118 apartment, when there was no need to, she would always
119 speak in a whisper, and she was always smiling, it was
120 like a mask, even when we sensed that she was unhappy. As
121 if she was trying to put on a brave front: I am going to
122 be happy, even if it kills me. We began to notice that
123 she could never do two things at once, such as: watch TV
124 and knit, or knit and talk, or eat and talk, or eat and
125 talk and listen. If she talked her food would get quite
126 cold, she would start when everyone finished. Or she
127 would ask, when is dinner ready, and when told in about
128 10 minutes, she would go and prepare something quite dif-
129 ferent for herself.
130 At a third friend's, Betty's apartment, things came to
131 sort of head. Betty is a Psychology major, and we had
132 gone there by chance, with K, had dinner and settled down
133 for a chat, when a boyfriend of Betty's walked in, an
134 easygoing friendly fellow whom K and I had not met
135 before. K wanted to go to the kitchen and wash dishes but
136 we dissuaded her. She sat down with us, and was her

137 usual retiring, sweet smiling self. Conversation was
138 lively, but she did not take part. A boy was dis-
139 cussed, but K had not him met him. However she suddenly cut
140 in: Yes, isn't he nice. Everything was quiet for a
141 moment, but I carried on talking sort of covering up for
142 her. A few minutes later she cut in again, with: Oh yes,
143 and the little black sheep and the lambs... This was
144 really completely out of touch. The young man thought K
145 was kidding him, but no doubt by our embarrassment could
146 tell something was wrong. K was upset and we suggested
147 that she went home, because she must be tired. Our apart-
148 ment was very near by.
149 At this point Betty suggested that something should be
150 done. It seems that all the girls involved were of a par-
151 ticular social stratum, the parents business people and
152 acquainted with each other. A woman friend of the family
153 was 'phoned and her advice was asked: Did you know that
154 K is not well, that she needs help, her behaviour is not
155 as it should be. The woman was willing to talk about
156 it, and admitted that this had been silently acknowledged
157 by the social circle for some time that K had seen a
158 psychiatrist some while back. This man had been recom-
159 mended by the family doctor, and although he had not
160 really been of much help, it was inconceivable that
161 anyone else could be approached, because of etiquette
162 etc. It was arranged that K should go back to the
163 psychiatrist.

DEFINITIONS

In talking about the interview material I make use of a set of terms
which are defined below:

(a) *The reader/hearer* I or anyone else who reads or hears read
the text of the interview.

(b) *The interviewer* The student who did the interview and who
with the respondent constructed the text now available to
the reader/hearer. The presence of the interviewer is
identifiable in the text in the occasional use of the
impersonal mode.

(c) *The respondent* The person who was interviewed by the
interviewer and who co-operated with her in constructing
the text. The respondent is represented in the text as the

'teller of the tale', but is not methodologically equivalent since the teller of the tale is internal to the text and is therefore the joint product – as a personage – of the interviewer and the respondent.

(d) *The teller of the tale* has in part already been defined in the above definition of the respondent. The teller of the tale is the 'I' of the account who is represented as telling the story of what happened.

(e) *Angela* et al. The sub-set personages who are represented as being actively involved in the process of categorization. This includes – Angela, Trudi, Angela's mother, Betty, and 'a woman friend of the family'. It excludes K, Angela's father, and Betty's boyfriend. This term is given further specification in the discussion of the construction of a factual account below.

(f) *The personages* Those persons internal to the account who are referred to as being in any way active in moving the events along, in however trivial a way. So that it includes all the main characters designated by the term Angela *et al.* It also includes K, Angela's father, and Betty's boyfriend. It does not, however, include persons who are reference personages only and not participants – i.e. K's family, and the psychiatrist.

The attentive reader will have noticed that this has a kind of Chinese box structure. The definitions identify different levels of responsibility for making the account and the contributions of various persons at each. In effect they yield a role structure for describing the social organization of the account. At the point where I am and where other readers of the interview are (the reader/hearers), there is the complete text. In the making of the text (apart from the slight intervention of the editor which I have neglected here since it is so minor) there is the concerted work of interviewer and respondent. The respondent is identified in the text as the 'teller of the tale'. The teller of the tale is telling a tale about a set of personages, one of whom is herself. Internal to the account as it is told is the personage 'Angela' and the sub-set of personages who cooperate in working up the raw material of the events as they happened into a form which was then available to be transformed into the text we have before us. Then, at the level of personages at large, are those who were active in generating the original set of events, who were doing what happened and what constituted the raw material out of which Angela *et al.* constructed a view of K as mentally ill. Note, then, the one term which is common to all levels of the account, namely Angela. Within the conventions of the account, she is entered as one of those active in doing the events; she is entered as one of those conceptualizing the events (the Angela *et al.* level); she is entered as teller of the tale; and she is also, as one of the members of the text, entered as the respondent. The above set of definitions is thus not merely a convenience, it also lays bare the structure which related the text you and I have to the original events as they happened. You, as reader of what I now write, may also wish to add the penultimate if not the ultimate level, namely my analysis of the text.

PRELIMINARY INSTRUCTIONS

The first part of the interview, lines 1–16, is written as the interviewer's account of what Angela, the respondent, told her. At line 15, the mode changes to the tale as told by Angela with the interpolated explanation by the interviewer (lines 20–23) that Angela found it easier to tell the tale in chronological form. In lines 17–20 the reader/hearer is provided with a set of instructions about how the interview is to be read, what it is an account of, as follows:

> My recognition that there might be something wrong was very
> gradual, and I was actually the last of her close friends who
> was openly willing to admit that she was becoming mentally ill.
>
> (17–20)

I want to draw attention to two effects which are announced at this point and which in important ways provide a set of instructions for how the account is to be read. They are as follows:

1   That K is 'becoming mentally ill' is asserted as a fact at the outset and is preserved as such throughout. The same construction is offered at various other points in the text: they had to face the fact that K was definitely queer;

(88–9)

23

> We gradually began to realize that she just could not cope;
>
> (106–7)
>
> I refused to acknowledge the fact that there was anything definitely wrong with K.
>
> (116–17)

Such constructions establish that K's state is to be treated as something which (a) is a fact and (b) is therefore already there prior to, and independently of, its being 'admitted', 'realized', 'faced', or 'acknowledged' by Angela or others.

2   We are also provided with a preliminary set of instructions for how to read further descriptions of K's behavior. These are to be read as the behavior of someone who is 'becoming mentally ill' (this has important effects for the authorization of the version which I shall elucidate below). The instructions to read the behavior as 'odd', 'wrong', etc., are repeated at intervals throughout the account. Indeed sub-collections are distinguished by markers consisting of some summary statement, the conclusion of a member of Angela *et al.* or the like, that K's behavior is definitely queer etc. These can be viewed both as summary conclusions of the previous sub-collection and as renewing or reminding the reader/hearer of the instructions for how to read what comes next (these may be found at lines 35–7, 61–3, 87–9, 115–17).

THE AUTHORIZATION OF THE VERSION

I take it as axiomatic that, for any set of actual events, there is always more than one version that can be treated as what has happened, even within a simple cultural community. This is because social events or facts at the level of those I am analyzing here involve a complex assembly of events occurring in different settings, at different times, sometimes before collections of persons. Further, the moment of actual observation is at that point where the consciousness of the individual is, and any process of assembly from the past can no longer draw on the total universe of resources which were at successive 'moments' present to the observer. For these reasons, an endemic problem must always be how a given version is authorized as that version which can be treated by others as what has happened. Accordingly an important set of procedures concern who is allocated the privilege of definition and how other possible versions or sources of possible disjunctive information are ruled out.

Here I think these authorization procedures are at work:

1   Durkheim's (1960:102) rule that the definition of an act as deviant serves to sanction and legitimize a social order can be extended to authorize as representatives of that order those who make that judgement. Their rules or norms are to be recognized as rules and norms against which the behaviͻ of the deviant is defined as deviant. Thus that we are told at the outset that K is mentally ill authorizes the version of those who realized or came to admit the fact of her illness. It authorizes or assigns to Angela the definitional privilege and – internal to the account – it authorizes also the version of Angela's friends at those points when Angela is still 'unwilling to admit' the fact. The circularity of this process is a feature of the account. Its logical impropriety does not obstruct the effect. K's illness is present as a fact independently of the wishes of the 'observers'. Her deviance serves therefore to authorize the account of her deviance which is provided and the 'rightness' of the judgement of those who defined her as such. In particular, the authorization of the judgement of the 'teller of the tale' (Angela) and her associates requires the reader/hearer to treat as the proper collection of events, the collection we have before us. Their selection procedures are implicitly sanctioned even though it is not made clear what they are.

Possibly there is a further and more general process at work here not directly linked to Durkheim's rule (Durkheim 1960). Angela is presented as having been present as an observer of the events recounted. Recollected introspection of how I read the account suggests that something like a 'willing suspension of disbelief' effect is operating – that is, I tended to suspend or bracket my own judgemental process in favor of that of the teller of the tale. The reader/hearer is always open to the challenge 'How do you know? You weren't there.'

25

2   Categorizations of deviance of the same family as mental illness serve to circumscribe the area of intelligible and warrantable behavior and belief. Since K is defined at the outset as becoming mentally ill and other members of the account are not, the boundaries in this instance are drawn so that K is excluded. This has the following consequences:

(a) Between K and Angela *et al.*, K's behavior may not be treated as a source of normative definition whereas Angela *et al.*'s may be so treated. Here is an instance where this stipulation clearly decides how the normative accent should be assigned:

> We would go to the beach or the pool on a hot day, and I would sort of dip in and just lie in the sun, while K insisted that she had to swim 30 lengths.
>
> (24–6)

Angela's beach behavior provides the norm in terms of which K's behavior is to be recognized as deviating.

(b) K is by this rule disqualified from participating in the construction of social facts. Hence any version that she might have presented is discounted from the outset. The definers are privileged to present their version without taking hers into account. This procedure cuts off a possible set of resources which might otherwise be available in making interpretations of what is happening – namely that set of resources available only to K. This legitimates the restriction of resources used in interpreting K's behavior to what is available to Angela *et al.* Here is an instance of this effect:

> Nearly every morning K would cry in the car, being upset about little things, and the girls would comfort her.
>
> (12–14)

In this instance, the reasons for K's crying are taken to be those immediate occasions which were directly observable to 'the girls' and which were 'little things', not sufficient to warrant her weeping. Angela does not raise the possibility that there might have been features of K's biography unknown to her and the others which would provide adequate reasons for K's disposition to cry so readily.

(c) Accordingly also it is not a problem or ought not to be a problem for the reader/hearer who properly follows the instructions for how the account is to be read, that no explanation, information, etc., from K is introduced at any point in the account. And it is not or ought not to be strange that at no point is there any mention of K being asked to explain, inform, etc. In sum then, the rules, norms, information, observations, etc., presented by the teller of the tale are to be treated by the reader/hearer as the only warranted set.

THE CONSTRUCTION OF THE ACCOUNT AS FACTUAL

The actual events are not facts. It is the use of proper procedure for categorizing events which transforms them into facts. A fact is something that is already categorized, already worked up to conform to the model of what that fact should be like. To describe something as a fact or to treat something as a fact implies that the events themselves – what happened – entitle or authorize the teller of the tale to treat that categorization as ineluctable. 'Whether I wish it or not, it is a fact. Whether I will admit it or not, it is a fact.'

If something is to be constructed as a fact, then it must be shown that proper procedures have been used to establish it as objectively known. It must be seen to appear in the same way to anyone. Here are some of the relevant procedures in this account:

1   The teller of the tale, Angela, is K's friend. Others involved are also described as her friends, or as having a definitely positive attitude towards her. This structural frame is continued throughout. Since the 'fact' to be realized or established is a negative one and the structural frame declares for only positive motives towards K, there are no grounds for suspecting Angela's motives. The rhetoric of the fact is here that Angela is constrained to recognize it. It is a fact independently of her wish; she does not wish it and

yet she is 'forced to face' it. This provision tends only to remove a possible difficulty. There are others more fundamental to the construction of objectivity. The construction of a fact involves displaying that it is the same for anyone and that their recognition of it as a fact is based on direct observation, is constrained by the nature of the event itself and is not determined by a hearsay construction.

2 The following structure establishes a succession of independent witnesses. A series of steps can be identified, defined by the addition of one person to the circle of those who recognize or know that something is wrong:

(a) at lines 24–33, Angela alone;
(b) at lines 34–38, Angela and Trudi;
(c) at lines 58–78, Angela, Trudi, and Angela's mother;
(d) at lines 130–48, Angela, Trudi, Angela's mother, and Betty;
(e) at lines 152–8, Angela, Trudi, Angela's mother, Betty, and a woman friend of the family.

The last step in this account breaks out of the local circle of those personally known to Angela by disclosing that this same 'fact' is known to others independently – it 'had been silently acknowledged by the social circle for some time' (156–7); and also that it had the formal sanction of a psychiatrist. This simple additive formula is a familiar one from children's stories – e.g. that of Henny-penny who went to tell the king the sky was falling. A cumulative effect is established. At each step a new member is introduced. This construction is particularly striking because it overrules indications present in the interview that some of those personages had been around before. For example, there was a carpool – who was in it and saw K cry (10–12)? Angela was 'the last of her close friends' who admitted etc. Did those friends include or exclude Trudi and Betty (18–19)? Trudi was a mutual friend of Angela and K (34–5); Betty's apartment is just 'nearby' the apartment of Angela, Trudi, and K and the account of the encounter suggests a casual dropping in ('we had gone there by chance' – 130–3) characteristic of a continuing friendship. The phone call to a woman friend of the family (152–3) is apparently to someone hitherto unconnected, and apparently taps a social circle independent of those personally known to Angela. Yet it is also said that 'all the girls involved were of a particular social stratum' and their parents were 'business people and acquainted with each other' (151–2). The inference is possible that the two social circles were in fact not independent of one another. The additive structure establishing textually the independence of witnesses overrides other possible principles governing the recognition of new presences in a narrative. Introducing new ch.· racters as members of circles of friendship would generate quite a different order. The items I have referred to above are present merely as parts of the connecting machinery of the story; it is the order of witnessing that occupies the foreground.

3   This structure makes possible the treatment of each additional witness as independent of the others. The judgement of each is based on direct observation or by inference an opportunity for such observation:

(a) Angela: in the course of ordinary interpersonal encounters with K, her admiration changes to bafflement;

(31)

(b) Trudi looks over one of K's essays and comments afterwards, 'She writes like a 12 year old. I think there is something wrong with her';   (36–8)

(c) Angela's mother observes two instances of K's odd behavior;
(63–78)

(d) Betty is present at a conversation during which K's contribution shows her to be 'completely out of touch';
(130–44)

(e) 'The woman friend of the family' may be taken to have opportunities of personal observation independently of those made by previous witnesses.   (152)

These features of the account establish the judgements as arrived at independently by each witness and on the basis of direct observation (or a reasonable basis for inferring the same) uncontaminated by previous prompting or definitional work which might be interpreted as a source of bias. Note in this connection that Angela specifically mentions that she did not

29

prepare her mother for any 'odd behavior' on K's part. The ordering of events in the narrative constructs the objectivity of the fact, the items which might serve to suggest the opposite are not only relegated to the background, they are also not constructed in the same way. They are merely, as it were, lying about. A careful search may identify them, but the work of bringing them into an order must all be done by the reader/hearer.

THE CONSTRUCTION 'MENTAL ILLNESS'

The account provides the reader/hearer with an itemized and specific account of K's character and behavior. The reader/hearer is thus appai ently given an opportunity to judge for herself on the basis of a collection of samples of the behavior from which Angela *et al.* constructed the fact of K's mental illness. The instructions for reading the account contained in lines 18–20 of the interview ('I was actually the last of her close friends who was openly willing to admit that she was becoming mentally ill') are that the collection is to be read as the behavior of someone who is becoming mentally ill. Thus the items are to be tested against a concept of mentally ill behavior (which I shall abbreviate hereafter to m.i. type behavior). The reader/hearer thus knows at the outset how this collection of characterological and behavioral descriptions is to be interpreted. If the collection is viewed as a problem, then we have been told what the solution is. The problem presented by the account is not to find an answer to the question 'what is wrong with K?', but to find that this collection of items is a proper puzzle to the solution 'becoming mentally ill'.

Earlier when I was discussing how the account is authorized, I pointed out that defining K at the outset as 'becoming mentally ill' removes her from the circle of potential witnesses to the events. The collection of items must therefore establish or justify this exclusion. K must be construed as a person who does not recognize what anybody else would recognize, who does not share the same cognitive ground as others. The description of her character and behavior must be worked up as a 'cutting out' operation (the *OED* gives for 'cutting out' 'to detach (an animal) from the herd'), which serves to draw the boundaries of the circle to exclude her. The final moment when things 'come to a head', i.e. when K is seen to be 'completely out of touch' (lines 143–4), is the point at which the cutting out operation is completed. This is its conclusion.

A strategy usually identified with the 'medical model' (see Scheff 1966: 19–22) of mental illness views m.i. type behavior as symptoms of a 'disease' or 'illness'. Thus behavior is treated as arising from a state of the individual and not as motivated by features of her situation. Though the medical model is not explicit here, the same fundamental strategy is used. Constructing K's behavior as m.i. type behavior involves showing that it is not adequately motivated by K's situation of action. Her actions are shown as not fully provided for by the instructions which follow from a rule or from how a situation is defined.

We have established already that it is the teller of the tale's privilege both to define the rule or situation and to describe the behavior. A rule or a definition of the situation yields a set of instructions for selecting those categories of action which are appropriate as 'responses'. We (the reader/hearer) must take on trust that the coding procedures for going from the original and actual behavior to such descriptive categories have been properly done. This definitional privilege and the use which the teller of the tale makes of it are of considerable importance in the cutting out operation. Behavior which is properly responsive to a rule or situation shows that the actor recognizes that rule or situation in the same way as it is defined by the teller of the tale. If it is not properly responsive, the reader/hearer may find an alternative rule or situation to which it is; or she may decide to sanction the teller of the tale's definition. The authorization rules direct the reader/hearer to select the second of these alternatives. So when we find in this account instances of a lack of fit between behavior and a rule or situation, these work as part of the cutting out strategy.

By a lack of fit I do not mean, for example, what Austin (1962:14) means by infelicitous or 'unhappy' behavior. I want to find something closer to what could be meant by 'anomalous' behavior, i.e. behavior for which no rule or set of instructions can be found. I am suggesting that social rules and definitions of situations can be viewed as if they provide a set of instructions for categorizing responses. (I should emphasize that the notion of instructions here is a metaphor at this moment, but I find it helpful.) Any such set of instructions provides for categorizing responses in two main ways: (1) by selecting a set of categories for describing behavior complying with the instructions; and (2) by selecting a set of categories for describing behavior which does not comply. So any set of instructions which might be written in the form 'do such and such' can also be written by a simple trans-formation rule in the form 'do not do such and such', where the negation is not just logical exclusion but is antonymous – i.e. the contrary or opposite of the behavior required by the instructions. In this sense, then, non-compliance or infractions of a rule are fitting. The instructions do provide for them (there are, I think, some types c f instructions where the deviant option is not available at all).

Behavior which does not fit is behavior which is not provided for by the instructions either way. It is then anomalous, and anom-alies, I suggest, are what we have to find in the descriptions of K's behavior. The cutting out operation thus involves showing how K's behavior is not properly instructed by the definitions of the rules or situations which are provided. The instructions to read K's behavior as m.i. type required that the search go from the behavior described to find the relevant rule or definition of the situation under which that behavior can be seen not to fit, or rather to be anomalous. If it does not fit, then it can be taken that K does not recognize the rules or situations as anyone else would recognize them. The procedure is analogous to the lay identification of color blindness. Anyone (given that she knows the coding rules) can identify colours in the same way. If you find someone who cannot distinguish between red and green, you do not raise questions about whether red and green can be discriminated; you rather identify as a special state of that individual her being unable to make that discrimination. You say she is color blind. The attribution of mental illness behaves in the same way. It is the state of not being able to recognize the social reality which is there for anyone else and it is effectively defined in the process of that individual having been found not to do it. The process of finding that out is what I have designated the 'cutting out operation'.

The collection of items in this account is not grandly convin-cing. There are few if any items that stand up as immediately convincing. The teller of the tale has to do a good deal of working up in order to display K's behavior as m.i. type. This visibility of the work is one of the things that makes the account worth analyzing in such detail. There are descriptions of K's behavior which, deprived of the contextualizing work put in by the teller of the tale, would not look particularly out of the way. There are even some that might be viewed as positive characteristics if the perspective were shifted just a little – e.g. K's insisting 'that she had to swim 30 lengths' (25–6) on a hot day at the pool is entirely appropriate for someone with a concern for fitness; or her working so devotedly in her friend's garden might be a particularly creditable interpretation of the obligations of friendship. So we can begin looking at this collection with the hunch that the teller of the tale has to do rather a lot of contextual work to show how the behavior can read as m.i. type.

The contextual work at the level of individual items is most apparent in a device which I will call a contrast structure. A contrast structure would be one where a description of K's behavior is preceded by a statement which supplies the instructions for how to see that behavior as anomalous. Here are some examples:

When asked casually to help in a friend's garden, she went at it for hours, never stopping, barely looking up

(40–2)

She would take baths religiously every night and pin up her hair, but she would leave the bath dirty

(89–91)

When something had gone radically wrong, obviously by her doing, she would blandly deny all knowledge,

(98–100)

The first part of the contrast structure finds the instruction which selects the categories of fitting behavior, the second part shows the behavior which did not fit. The first part may define a social rule, or a definite occasion, or some feature of K's behavior. I have counted twenty-three discrete items of behavioral description. Of these, eleven are contrast structures. I have defined this category very loosely since I am using it only to identify what seems to be a typical procedure. Other items which are not constructed as contrast structures at the level of individual items, can be shown to be contrastive with reference to larger segments of the account. And of course there are other things going on, some of which I shall try to analyze later.

ANALYSIS OF SOME CONTRAST STRUCTURES

Contrast structure type one: paradoxes of pretending

The parts of the c-structure are separated and identified by the numerals i and ii:

(i) It was obvious that she was terrified of anyone getting too near to her, especially men.

(ii) And yet she used to pretend to us (and obviously to herself too) that she had this and that guy really keen on her.

(53–5)

Embedded in this structure are two statements about K's behavior. Both describe mildy deviant behavior. K is described as being terrified of anyone, especially men, getting close to her (i); and as pretending that some man is keen on her (ii). The first is a description of a presumably stable feature of K's personality and the second a description of a kind of behavior she used to engage in. The contrast structure packages them as a unit linked by 'It was obvious ... and yet...'. What is the effect?

In part ii of the c-structure, K is said to 'pretend'. To be pretending, the actor must be trying to make others believe, or to give them the impression, by means of a current personal performance in their presence, that the actor is *abc*, in order to disguise the fact that she is really *xyz*.[2] This, I think, is how this contrast structure works to represent K's behavior as m.i. type:

1 Part ii makes clear what information was available to the teller of the tale at the time the events referred to took place. The 'It was obvious ...' establishes that the teller of the tale and others knew at that time what it was that K was trying to dissemble. Lacking the modifier 'it was obvious', the reader/hearer could infer no more than that at some time or another the teller of the tale knew that K was pretending. But the effect of 'it was obvious' goes beyond this.

34

2   What is obvious is what may be plainly seen or understood by anyone. It is available to anyone and *therefore available to K.* Part ii also has a retroactive effect on part i of the c-structure, so that the part i statement is both what is obvious and what K is concealing. But if it is obvious, then it is not only known to K but *she must also know that it is known.*

3   'Pretending' is intentional. The actor is trying to conceal *abc* by doing *xyz.* The term thus assigns to K a plan or at least a prefiguring of what the teller of the tale tells us she was doing. It also implies the following distribution of information so far as the actor is concerned:

> The actor knows that she is really *abc.* She believes that those she is trying to deceive do not know that she is really *abc.*

These are the 'belief conditions' of pretending.

4   The inference from 'It was obvious' – namely that others know and that K knows they know – removes one term of the required belief conditions, namely that the actor believes that those she is trying to deceive do not know what it is she is trying to conceal. So this c-structure yields a paradox as follows. Pretending gives the following 'proper' alternatives under different belief conditions. Either:

> K believes that others know *abc.* Therefore she does not believe that she can conceal it from them.

Or:

> K believes that others do not know *abc.* Therefore she believes that she can conceal it from them.

But not what in fact we have:

> K believes that others know *abc.* Therefore she believes that she can conceal it from them.

The effect of 'it was obvious' on 'pretending' is to shift the two statements out of the normal deviance class into a paradox which cannot be internally resolved.

It is here that the instructions given at the beginning of the interview become important because they tell us which term to select in order to resolve the paradox. Changing the second term might raise questions about the accuracy of the teller of the tale's description of what K was doing. This is ruled out by the authorization rules (see above). Changing the first term implies that what is obvious to others is not obvious to K. Then K believes that others do not know *abc* even though it is obvious. So K is not on the same wave-length as others; she is not seeing what is obvious to anyone else. That is the cutting out operation.

The same device is at work in the following c-structure:

(i) When something had gone radically wrong, obviously by her doing,

(ii) she would blandly deny all knowledge....   (98–100)

Contrast structure type two: standard pattern rule anomalies

Here is another kind of c-structure:

(i) she would bath religiously every night and pin up her hair,

(ii) but she would leave the bath dirty.   (89–91)

This kind of c-structure works differently from the foregoing. Part i gives a rule which is derived from routine features of K's behavior; part ii shows that she also routinely violates that rule. The procedure is something like this – from the occurrence of *a* and *b* expect *c*. But you do not get *c*, you get *x*.

Note that the ordinary sociological notions of expectation do not work here, as they probably never really do. For the following reason: that to get the expectation of *c* from the occurrence of *a* and *b* involves reference to a model or pattern in which these items occur regularly in that sequence. Seeing them as a series implies having grasped a model or pattern which is known in advance and on other grounds. One kind of rule here is what might be called a 'standard pattern rule', like the alphabet. For there is nothing that holds the alphabet together as an ordered series of letters except customary usage. There would be no way in which you could infer which letter must follow from any other without knowing already how it occurs.

Another type of rule is a formation rule which generates the series. The typical exercise which illustrates this type of rule is one in which a 'subject' is given a series of signs such as '1,2,3...' or '2,4,6...' and is asked to continue the series. She may be told what rule to follow in doing so, but it is a common intellectual game and one that IQ tests sometimes make use of, to ask the subject to derive the rule for continuing the series from the series as it has been presented to her. We have a procedure like that here. The reader/hearer is instructed, I think, in virtue of the contrast structure to find from the first part the rule for continuing the series. The rule which she will presumably find would be some kind of 'be clean' rule which can be rewritten as [bathe religiously every night, pin up your hair, leave the bath clean]. Part ii of the contrast structure would, however, read back to the simple deviance transformation of that rule. The two procedures can be stated as follows (the arrow means 'rewrite as'):

Be clean → [every night do the following: bathe, pin up your hair, leave the bath clean]

Do not be clean → [every night do not do the following: bathe, pin up your hair, or, if you bathe, do not leave the bath clean]

From the first part of the c-structure we get a formation rule which is antonymous to the formation rule derived from part ii. And vice versa. So we find that we cannot retrieve a rule that does for both. But this is weak as a construction of m.i. type behavior because it is fairly easy to find an alternative rule which provides for the coherence of the set. For although this assemblage does not work under formation rules derived from looking at the items as a series, it could work perfectly well under a standard pattern type of rule, e.g. I might say, 'Well, some people who take a lot of trouble with their personal appearance etc. are otherwise slobs' (or inconsiderate, or what have you). 'They just are that way,' I might say. Which I take to be an appeal to a standard pattern rule which would permit this series.

A similar construction can be found later in the same paragraph as follows:

(i)   She would wash the dishes,
(ii) and leave them dirty too.   (91)

Here the contrast structure is not built syntactically but is derived from the contradiction between the two parts. It could be, I suppose, a normal incompetence to find someone who washes dishes but does not wash them very well, so that bits of noodle, egg, etc., can still be found on fork and plate after the washing up is done. Leaving them dirty after washing them is more than incompetent. Indeed it is almost Dada and an achievement in itself. To leave dishes dirty after washing them is not just normal incompetence. In fact it is almost 'against nature' so that the straining to realize what K has made available as m.i. type behavior does here, I think, overstep the limits of credibility.

Another and somewhat more successful instance of this kind of c-structure is the following:

(i)   When you meet her, you are struck by a sweet girlish
      appearance. She will sit quietly in company smiling sweetly
      at all times, and seems disarmingly appealing.   (42–5)
(ii) But when there were young men in the company, she would
      find it harder than ever to carry on a conversation, and
      would excuse herself and leave very soon.   (46–8)

Contrast structure type three: normatively generated anomalies

Here is a contrast structure in three parts:

(i)   We would go to the beach or pool on a hot day,
(ii)   I would sort of dip in and just lie in the sun
(iii) while K insisted that she had to swim 30 lengths.   (24–6)

Part i identifies an occasion and part iii the behavior, but it is clear that parts i and iii alone are not sufficient to show how K's behavior is odd. The day is hot and K insists on swimming 30 lengths – so? The middle term (part ii), by giving an example of behavior which is properly instructed by that type of occasion, provides the norm that generates the behavioral anomaly. The first two parts combined set up a model of occasion and fitting behavior which is more restrictive than part i alone. I suspect that

38

quite a lot of work is done by the specification 'hot day' since that sets the instructions for the 'lazing' behavior which is confirmed as the rule by the description of Angela's behavior. Thus K's behavior is not instructed by the occasion as it is specified by both part i and part ii together. Part i by itself would permit the behavior described in part iii so that the model of the occasion must be elaborated to give the swimming thirty lengths as anomalous. More work is then done by giving K's behavior an obsessional cast. She 'insisted that she had to swim 30 lengths'. So it is displayed in an imperative form without being referred to a social structure which would warrant that imperative.

I think there is a definite imperfection in the account here because we are still close to the categorization of K as 'so very athletic' (line 7), which plugs into a social structure which would warrant this imperative. True this term is not 'active' at this point, i.e. it has not been brought forward by the teller of the tale to define the actors and their relationship. At this point the working category appears to be 'friend', and since Angela appears to establish a 'friends do the same things and have the same interests' model of friendship, that category probably also works to establish the relevance of what Angela does on a hot day at the pool as a model for what K should do.

More important is the operation of the authorization rules described above. These provide the instructions that have already established Angela's authoritative voice and, in this case, Angela's entitlement to treat her own behavior as a norm *vis-à-vis* which K's appears anomalous. The positioning of the reading subject has already been set up, and this c-structure relies on this in accomplishing K's actions as ill-fitting.

Other types of contrast structures

Here is a c-structure that recalls the 'obviously'/'blandly denied' contrast structure examined in type one. But there is something else involved here.

(i)   When something had gone radically wrong ... she would blandly deny all knowledge
(ii) but got very upset at little things, like a blown fuse. (98–101)

This c-structure can be expressed in the language of psychiatric symptomalogy as an instance of 'inappropriate affect' – the degree of feeling should be proportionate to the 'value' of the event. Correspondingly the proper value of an event is displayed by exhibiting the proper degree of feeling in the response. If something has gone *radically* wrong, the upset should be proportionate. In the above instance, it is not K's *denial* that something has gone radically wrong that is operative (i.e. this is not an example of c-structure type one) but that it is *blandly* denied. K's indifference to a serious problem is contrasted with getting very upset at little things in part ii.

The matter may be formally stated as follows. The rule that the degree of feeling should be proportionate to the seriousness of the events may be written as instructions on how much to care when things go wrong, as follows:

When something goes seriously wrong, be seriously upset.
When something goes mildly wrong, be mildly upset.

So from the 'something has gone radically wrong' given by part i of the c-structure, we get the instruction 'be very upset'. The negative transformation would read 'do not be very upset'. And that is what we have. I am not at this time sure whether that is properly provided for by the rule, because there are other instances which could be had by a straightforward transformation, for example:

Nearly every morning K would cry in the car, being upset about little things. (12–13)

It seems to me that this c-structure is one of those rules where the negative is not provided. Otherwise it would be hard to get the 'inappropriate affect' effect, and we do get it. But in any case the c-structure above is reinforced by showing that a possibly negative transformation, 'do not be upset' does not hold either since K does get very upset at little things. The c-structure here thus works rather like the ones in type two, because the rule you generate from either tail of the c-structure does not hold for the other. So K is shown not to discriminate properly between things that go radically wrong and little things that go wrong.

There is also a device which is not properly a contrast structure, except perhaps in reverse. I have suggested that the contrast structures are ways of supplying the contexts with reference to which K's behavior can be seen as m.i. type, and the implication is that, if it were described without those contexts, then the description of the behavior alone would not do the trick. There are, however, some types of non-routine behavior which normally require contextualization, or rather require to be shown as specially situationally instructed, in order to establish them as properly motivated. Some examples from the interview are tiptoeing (117) and whispering (119). These kinds of behavior are, I think, usually provided with a 'reason' since they are behaviors which do not occur routinely in our culture. Routine occurrences are those where either no explanation need be given because it is assumed that there is some routine explanation; or where the occurrence itself suggests its typical grounds for occurring. The strategy here is to exhibit these without supplying an adequate reason, as follows:

She'd tiptoe through the apartment, when there was no need to. (117–18)

She'd always speak in a whisper.... (118–19)

An analogous device is used in the instance discussed above ('She insisted that she had to swim 30 lengths.') where K's behavior is given an obsessional cast by depriving the imperative of proper warrant. I suspect that instances of this type will form a greater proportion in accounts of m.i. type behavior which are stranger than this.

Other constructions of 'anomalies'

This section examines some items that do not display a contrast structure. It will address those few items where K is shown to have a peculiar relation to material objects. These are:

She would buy the most impractical things, such as a broom, although they already had one.

(95–6)

She did not seem to absorb the simplest information regarding the working of the stove or other household implements.

(101–3)

She had definite food-fads, and would take condiments such as ketchup, pepper to excess. Also things like tinned fruit and honey, she would eat them by the jar, at one go.

(103–6)

K was unable to put on a teapot cover correctly, she would not reverse its position to make it fit, but would simply keep slamming it down on the pot.

(76–8)

G.H. Mea.¹ has described how ordinary material objects – tables, chairs, etc. – as well as more complex social forms, are constituted by socially organized responses which refine and elaborate their uses out of the possibilities given by their sheerly physical properties (Mead 1934: 75–82). The object itself, thus constituted in its social organization, may thus also be understood as yielding sets of instructions for how to act towards it, how it may be inserted into human programs of action. And as with occasions and situations, a failure to act within the terms provided by these instructions displays the actor as failing to recognize the object as it is for anyone else. In these examples we may notice a much stronger structure than that which arises when rules or definitions of situations are in question. The objects themselves are treated as sufficient. Their definition does not have to be further elaborated or worked up to show K's failure to enter into that intersubjective world which is 'ours'. Yet the constructions are implicitly more complex than they seem. I shall discuss the first of these in another and later context. Here I just want to draw the reader's attention to these instances of misusage – that, for example, tinned fruit and honey carry the 'instruction' 'use in bits at intervals'; that ketchup etc. carries the 'instruction' 'eat in small quantities'; that a teapot in relation to its lid is constructed so that the sticky-out bit on the top fits into a notch in the rim of the pot and hence the 'instruction' – 'if the top does not fit the first time around then rotate it until the sticky-out bit fits into the notch'. And beyond these, not just that K does not recognize these objects as they are constituted for anyone else, but that she is also apparently unable to 'absorb' the simplest information about such uses.

Similarly departures from household budgeting rules are presented not as 'extravagance' or normal incompetence, but as a failure to grasp the ordinary properties of things – a new broom when they already had one; six pounds of hamburger – and the social structures which define their uses. With respect to the broom, for example, it would have been odd on the part of the teller of the tale if she had said that K had 'bought a spoon, although they already had one'. The social structure of a household requires that its members eat simultaneously, but not that they sweep simultaneously; therefore a spoon for each is 'needed', but only one broom. This follows from the form and typical inventory of occasioned activities characteristic of household organization in our culture. It is enough, however, in the account merely to refer to the inappropriate uses of the objects. The rules do not have to be further elaborated presumably because they may be taken to be known at large. Unlike other features, they are 'obvious' without having to be declared as 'obvious'. The objects are treated as 'carrying' or simply implying the rules for using them. The latter do not need further explication or identification. These analyses by no means exhaust the types of behavioral descriptions included in the account. But they are sufficient to show the kinds of analyses that can be done and to subtend the notion of the cutting out operation introduced earlier.

'Cutting out' is done by constructing relationships between rules or definitions of situations and descriptions of K's behavior such that the former do not properly provide for the latter. The behavior is then exhibited as anomalous. Reading back from the anomaly gives the effect that the rule or situation which obtains is not recognized by K as it is. The specification of what it is is entrusted to the teller of the tale, whose status as definer and witness has been sanctioned by the authorization rules. K is thereby excluded from the circle of those who know. The circle of those who know includes now – in virtue of the bridging function of the teller of the tale – both Angela *et al.* and ourselves as reader/hearers. The transition between the different logical levels is made possible by their common term, namely Angela who is both a personage in the story and the teller of the tale.

THE COLLECTION AS A WHOLE

Turning from the individual items, I want to see now how the collection works as a whole. Rather than trying to identify a set of rules that are breached when people are recognized as mentally ill, or when behavior is recognized as m.i. type behavior, I suggest that this indeterminacy be placed at the heart of the problem. The institution of mental illness, its conceptual organization, forms of social action, authorized actors and sites, and so forth, are concerned precisely with creating an order, a coherence, at those points where members of a community have been unable or unwilling to find it in the behavior of a particular individual. This suggests a rule for assembling this collection which says that 'for this collection, find that there is no rule'. There is a visual analogy to the effect I am trying to specify. Paintings such as Ben Cunningham's combine different perspectival instructions. The looker in imagination must be continually shifting her position in relation to the events in the painting. She is never permitted to adopt a decisive relation resolving them into a single perspectival direction. I am looking for an analogue of that here.

There are indications from other descriptions of how people come to be categorized as mentally ill that this indeterminacy may be an essential preliminary phase to arriving at that label. The process described by the teller of the tale, when 'Trudi and I found ourselves discussing [K's] foibles in her absence. I still tried to find explanations and excuses...' (114–15) suggests that not being able to find them may be a regular feature of the process. Compare Yarrow, Schwartz, Murphy, and Deasy's account of wives' descriptions of the process by which they came to see their husbands as mentally ill:

> Initial interpretations, whatever their content, are seldom
> held with great confidence by the wives. Many recall their
> earlier reactions to their husbands' behavior as full of
> puzzling confusion and uncertainty. Something is wrong, they
> know, but, in general, they stop short of a firm explanation.
>
> (Yarrow *et al.* 1955:20)

Those wives who do not fairly early on arrive at the categorization 'mentally ill',

cast around for situationally and momentarily adequate
explanations. As the situation changes or as the husband's
behavior changes, these wives find reasons and excuses but
lack underlying or synthesizing theory. Successive
interpretations tend to bear little relation to one another.

(Yarrow *et al.* 1955:20)

This seems to be analogous to the process described above,
whereby alternative rules are sought and discarded or extenuations and excuses are sought and discarded. While an explanation may hold for one instance, it does not hold up for the next.
Treating the collection as a whole means that a rule or extenuation
found for any item must also hold for other items. A microcosm of
the process is exhibited in the passage describing K's behavior at
Angela's mother's (63–78) home. The incident of the wrong
breakfast is explained first of all by Angela's mother as a misunder-
standing (75). That is an extenuation rule which removes any
particular significance from the episode. But that principle cannot
be extended to the following episode of the teapot lid. One
cannot, so to speak, misunderstand a teapot. The previous extenuation is removed once it is held that the two episodes must be
treated as 'a collection' such that a rule that is found for one must
also hold for the other.

There are probably many instances of items in this collection
for which it would be easy to find extenuations or alternative rules.
It is the stipulation 'one rule for all' which inhibits this procedure
and serves to fix the weaker anomalies. Take for example the
household passage which runs from lines 87 through 109 of the
interview. If the instructions to read the following behavior as
'queer' are removed and if certain of the items are also removed,
the passage reads as incompetence rather than mental illness, as
follows:

She would wash dishes, but leave them dirty too. They would
try and live within a strict budget, and take turns in cooking
dinner and shopping for it, each for one week. K (frequently)
overshot the budget by several dollars. She would buy the
most impractical things.... She would burn practically
everything.... She did not seem to absorb the simplest

information regarding the working of the stove or other household implements.

(91–103)

This could add up to K just being a hopeless housekeeper. Adding the items which do not precisely fit that categorization, namely the bathing religiously item, the food-fads, the bland denial when things go radically wrong, makes it difficult to fix the explanation under the stipulation that any explanation you find must serve for all. Weaknesses in the construction at the level of individual items are worked up by setting them into multiple constructions, which just make it harder to find a simple rule which provides for the whole. For example, in the passage:

They would try and live within a strict budget, and take turns in cooking dinner and shopping for it, each for one week. K invariably overshot the budget by several dollars. She would buy the most impractical things, such as a broom, although they already had one, 6lbs of hamburger at one go, which they would have to eat the whole week.

(92–8)

This works, I think, by the cumulation of small things. Any one item could be discounted as accident (overshooting the weekly budget) or oversight (the surplus broom) or inexperience (six pounds of hamburger), but the sequence as a collection exhibits K's actions as instances of the underlying state. She 'invariably' overshot the budget, so it could not be accident or oversight; buying an extra broom or six pounds of hamburger are expressed as instances or examples of what ails her. The grammar is conditional; not she did, but she *would* do this or that. The onus shifts from each partic- ular as act or event to each particular as an expression or instance of K's state of being.

When we examine the workings of the collection as a whole, the active part the reader/hearer must play to find out how to read the narrative as an account of someone becoming mentally ill becomes more visible. The conceptual schema of mental illness operates, as I have suggested, like a set of instructions for how to go about dealing with doubtful instances or weaknesses in the story as a story of someone becoming mentally ill. Finding some items as anomalous depends on the reader/hearer bringing together one part of the account to interpret another. In an earlier example (of K's swimming thirty lengths of a pool on a hot day), I pointed out how generating the anomaly depended upon a privileging of Angela's standpoint already accomplished by the authorization rules; it depends also on inhibiting the bringing forward of an earlier reference to K as 'very athletic'. This is reader/hearer's work but it is work that is instructed by the mental illness schema.

The following example also depends on referencing an earlier segment of the interview to accomplish it as anomalous.

> It was very difficult to carry on an intelligent conversation with her, this became apparent when I wanted to discuss a particularly good movie, and she would make childish inane remarks, completely off the point.
>
> (26–30)

Here again we can see the operation of the authorization rules in establishing the normative standpoint from which the reader/hearer is to view K's behavior. But given this, the item still fails to meet the criteria for anomalous behavior. The deviant behavior is fully provided for by the rule; the inverse of intelligence is stupidity; *vis-à-vis* the norm of intelligent conversation, inane remarks are deviant. Reading this as anomalous calls for the reader/hearer to reference back to the characterization of K as a good student (7) that establishes the initial norm against which K's deterioration becomes apparent. The reader/hearer can then assemble a first-term–second-term problem like that described as type two, where each part of the c-structure yields a rule which does not provide for the behavior in the other. If K is intelligent, a good student, etc., then her conversation should be intelligent; if K's conversation is inane and off the point, then K is not able to participate intelligently in conversation, *ergo* she is not intelligent.

The local weaknesses that are presented in many items are obscured by the cumulation of items which give different sorts of renderings and by the way in which one part of the story can be brought to bear in interpreting another. The cumulation has a progressive effect. The reader/hearer looks for how each next item can be read as a further instance. Each further instance works retroactively on the previous one. It is this property of the collection as a whole, as well as the structure of particular items, which gives the effect I found in my first hearing of the interview material – namely of K becoming 'more and more disorganized'. The effect of disorganization attributed thus to K is produced by the reader being unable to come to rest on any principle of organization which would generate the whole collection.

CONCLUSION

This conclusion points to, although it does not fully design, a general procedure for the analysis of such accounts. It suggests to the reader/hearer that she might treat the foregoing analysis not just as saying something about mental illness but as having a more general sociological relevance.

The analysis of the account has dealt with two main aspects. First, its social organization. Under this term I include both the structure which relates the original events described in the text of the interview to the present of the reader/hearer and the authorization rules which instruct the reader/hearer on what criteria to use in determining the adequacy of the description and credibility of the account. Such a social organizational analysis could be made of any such text, including, of course, a clinical psychiatric history. Its specific features would be systematically different and would display typical features of the institutional structure which provide the general contexts of its production and uses. For example, clinical histories commonly include no authorization procedures and we may take it that these instructions are established externally to the text.

Second, the analysis of contrast structures and of the collection as a whole brings out a procedure for constructing an account of behavior so that it can be recognized by any member of the relevant cultural community as mentally ill type behavior. This procedure I have called the 'cutting out' procedure. Cutting out is done by constructing relationships between rules and definitions of situations on the one hand and descriptions of K's behavior on the other such that the former do not provide for the latter. The aim of such an analysis would be to spell out this procedure as instructions for generating such descriptions. Their adequacy could then be proved (in the pudding sense) by using them to write descriptions and seeing whether others could recognize them as accounts of someone who is mentally ill.

I do not think I have succeeded in explicating the procedure to this degree, but I think I have gone far enough to justify that as a direction. I have suggested that an alternative account of what happened is possible. In fact, theoretically a number of alternative accounts are possible since the problem is only to show how in K's behavior can be found rules and contexts which provide for them adequately. There is certainly more than one way in which this might be do ie. One important restriction on the reader/hearer's being able to work on the account in this way is stabilized by the authorization rules which give a 'witness' a privileged status versus the reader/hearer. Any alternative account must be speculative. This consequence is to be understood as a product of the social organization of the account which places the reader/hearer at a disadvantage with respect to those who were involved, even though the outsider was not herself present but makes up her own account from the accounts of those who were.

The effect of the authorization rules here bears on another aspect of the account relevant to the making of alternative interpretations, namely the lack of sufficient information. It is a normal feature of such accounts that they do not contain irrelevant material. Irrelevant material is material which neither (a) establishes the adequacy of the authorization procedures used nor (b) is appropriate to and can hence be appropriated interpretively by the conceptual framework. The reader/hearer cannot go back to the personages of the original to recover material which might be relevant to an alternative construction. As a feature of the social organization, this may be contrasted with situations such as a court of law in which witnesses may be questioned to recover material making possible alternative accounts. Thus the construction of an alternative account in which K is not mentally ill is not possible on the basis of what is available.

I can, however, briefly show for some parts how it might be done. It would involve finding rules or contexts for K's behavior which would properly provide for the behavior described or, alternatively, being able to re-describe the behavior to the same effect. If the enterprise were successful *it would result in a description which would lack any systematic procedure for bringing these items together.*

The pieces of behavior would simply be fitted back into various contexts. The present account would disintegrate. The reader/hearer would be unable to recover from them a rule under which she could see what the account 'was all about'.

Take, for example, K's insisting that she had to swim thirty lengths (25–6). Earlier I fitted that back to the description of her 'as very athletic'. This involves finding a context which motivates the act. It can be done in a rather more complex way with the following set of items. When it is done, as the reader/hearer will see, there is nothing that holds them together other than that both are about K.

Here then very sketchily: let us go back to the instance of the second broom (95–6). And add to it a later item as follows:

Or she would ask, when is dinner ready, and when told in about 10 minutes, she would go and prepare something quite different for herself.

(126–9)

This item, like the broom item, can be treated as showing that K does not share the ordinary practical knowledge of how a household is structured, i.e. that the rules are that members should eat simultaneously and that they should not or need not sweep simultaneously (it is not one of the inventory of concerted occasions that 'doing' a household requires). These instances can be fitted to a context if we write a version of the relations among Angela, Trudi, and K which contradicts that given in the account. It is maintained throughout that Angela and Trudi and K are friends. This is the basis on which they share an apartment. Trudi has some reservations about K but it is not suggested that these are serious; K's performance in the household does not meet Angela's and Trudi's standards. Ordinary experiences of such household arrangements suggest that difficulties often do arise. Sociological experiences of three-person groups suggest that these are particularly difficult to manage without trouble (Caplow 1968). Yet nowhere is any irritation, annoyance, or dislike recorded. The two items of behavior that I have introduced here could be warranted by recovering a social organization contradicting the united household presented in the text. Or put in another way, K's behavior can be read as 'recognizing' two households in one set of premises.

This preliminary reading can be tied into a more general reconstruction of what is reported from then on. There are indications of a ganging up process similar to that which Lemert (1962) has described in his paper on 'Paranoia and the dynamics of exclusion'. The last sequence when things came to a head can be interpreted in this frame: Angela *et al.* are together working up an account of K as mentally ill. K is excluded from this process, yet is the object of it. Angela *et al.* are involved with one another in the business of establishing that there is something wrong with K. Take K's reported utterance 'Oh yes, and the little black sheep and the lambs...' (123) as recognizing this and it makes perfectly good sense. Angela *et al.* are the lambs and K is the little black sheep, the outsider, the no-good, the marginal member who is never fully a member.

The credibility of the account and the reader/hearer's obedience to the restrictions on search procedures, as well as her authorization of the teller of the tale, depend upon accepting Angela *et al.* as K's friends. The contradictory interpretation provides a context for much of what is reported of K after Angela and Trudi had decided that 'she just could not cope' (107) and found themselves 'discussing her foibles in her absence' (114). The friendship version of their relationship depends upon successfully defining K as 'mentally ill'. Conversely, defining K as 'mentally ill' depends upon preserving that version. So I take it as crucial that it is K's statement about 'the little black sheep and the lambs' which receives the gloss from the teller of the tale. 'This was really completely out of touch' (143–4). The social organization of the account plays a crucial part in the construction of the fact that 'K is mentally ill'.

Chapter Three

THE SOCIAL ORGANIZATION OF SUBJECTIVITY: AN ANALYSIS OF THE MICRO-POLITICS OF A MEETING

EXPLORING THE SOCIAL ORGANIZATION OF SUBJECTIVITY

Social reality is not external to she who experiences, makes, or observes it. Conceive of it this way: people bring into being for one another a 'structure' (I use this term metaphorically here) which they inhabit temporarily and which drops away behind them; of course it is not made any way we want; what we put together in the past shapes the direction and framework of the future; what we build interlocks with what others build; we build what we know how to build with the materials that come to hand. None the less, we move into the future as into a building, the walls, floors, and roof of which we put together with one another as we go into it. It is an ongoing creation of and in *action*.

The sociologist investigating this process grasps it interpretively. She makes use of her member's knowledge of how to do it as a means of explicating how it is done: 'sociologists *must* (and do) employ their own expertise in employing and recognizing methodical procedures for accomplishing activities' (Turner 1974a); and further 'the task of the sociologist in analyzing naturally occurring scenes is not to deny his competence in making sense of activities but to *explicate* it' (Turner 1974a).

This chapter reports some preliminary work in explicating how, on a particular occasion, people put together for one another a local historical organization of intersubjectivity that passed beyond the immediate moment of their co-presence and thus beyond that immediate now in which every consciousness has its primary location. The occasion is a meeting at which a paper was read. The

53

analysis presented here explicates the local organization of subjectivity and the order of the text that is nested within it. It explores the social organization articulating a local site of reading (the meeting) to the order of the text (the paper presented at the meeting), the passage from the local into the textual, and with the interrelations of the two 'levels'. Analysis will disclose how the procedures positioning subjects in the meeting and in the text shift the operative social realities of the occasion from a mode in which local political continuities are active to a detached and objectified mode positioning subjects outside the present of the meeting.

The occasion was the last of a two-day series of four meetings of faculty and students at the University of British Columbia in 1969 when the state of the university was under discussion. The occasion was recorded and transcribed. The material used here was a transcription of the final session of the day. I was not present at it, though I had been at an earlier session of the same series.[1]

My analysis works on the transcribed document exclusively. What is included in the transcription was what was said in so far as the transcriber could make it out. Not all that was said is included, since recordings were made only of what was spoken into the microphones. But what is present to me and present to anyone else to whom the text becomes available is what was also there for them on that occasion in this aspect of their talk. And it was an occasion when most of what was done was done in talk.

Because I am working exclusively with transcribed data and hence with a text, I have made no attempt to explicate how the talk given on that occasion was actually received and made out by those present then. My analysis will make a sparer claim, which is to explicate the procedures constituting the social organization of subjectivity as that becomes available from what was said and is recorded.

THE SOCIAL ORGANIZATION OF CONSCIOUSNESS

Alfred Schutz, the great ethnographer of cognitive consciousness, draws a primary contrast between consciousness located in the paramount reality of a world of action and direct manipulation, and cognitive domains differentiated from and within it. He describes the cognitive mode of the subject within the paramount reality as follows:

> The wide-awake man within the natural attitude is primarily interested in that sector of the world of his everyday life which is within his scope and which is centered in space and time around himself. The place which my body occupies within the world, my actual Here, is the starting point from which I take my bearing in space. It is, so to speak, the center O of my system of coordinates. Relative to my body I group the elements of my surroundings under categories of right and left, before and behind, above and below, near and far, and so on. And in a similar way my actual Now is the origin of all time perspectives under which I organize the events within the world such as the categories of fore and after, past and future, simultaneity and succession, etc.
>
> (Schutz 1962b: 222–3)

This is the consciousness of an embodied subject whose knowing is organized from the bodily site of her experiencing. Yet in his description Schutz has already moved beyond the tight localization of experiencing from within a bodily organization; he has already moved to the level of the *categories* of right and left and so forth; he has already moved to the level of language and hence to the level of a social organization of the subject that is displaced from a tight interpretation of the bodily site of the knower. The individual's experiencing from within the here/now moment of her own consciousness constrains the knowing expressed and displaced in the deictic categories that have already construed the subject within the social. Through such categories the subject's bodily site is entered into the social as a social organization of subjectivity.

Schutz's account gives primacy to a social organization of consciousness for which the subject's bodily location is determinant. If people who are co-present are to enter the same temporal and spatial coordinates, locate themselves in the same way, and arrive at the same particulars in referencing one another's talk and gestures, their coordinates must be intersubjectively organized in language.

The procedures by which the center O, or, as Schutz calls it elsewhere, the null point, is locked into a definite position in a social structure so that the individual's coordinates are socially rather than individually structured, I call deictic locking procedures or devices. They are identified as procedures to bring into focus some of the practices that organize consciousness socially and coordinate the orientation of subjects. John Lyons gives this account of deixis:

> The notion of deixis (which is merely the Greek word for 'pointing' or 'indicating' – it has become a technical term of grammatical theory) is introduced to handle the 'orientati·nal' features of language which are relative to the time and place of utterance.
>
> (Lyons 1963: 275)

'Now', 'here', 'there', 'then' as well as the pronominals, 'we', 'I', 'they', 'you', and so forth are deictic terms. They organize socially, as what is present for both speaker and hearer (and writer and reader), time and distance, and the positions and arrangements of persons with reference to the 'position' of the speaker. What they refer to can be identified only when the position of the speaker and the context in which they are used is known. Lyons addresses the problem of the 'null point' coordinates as follows:

> The typical situation of utterance is egocentric: the role of speaker is transferred from one participant to another in a conversation, so that the 'centre' of the deictic system switches (I being used by each speaker to refer to himself, you being used to refer to the hearer).
>
> (Lyons 1963: 275)

But Lyons here confounds the null point as center of consciousness with socially structured deictic procedures. The null point is always center of its own 'system of coordinates' and no other can occupy anyone else's position. But the system of coordinates referenced by deictic terms may be, indeed perhaps always is, socially structured. The 'same' position may be occupied by more than one subject as for example when the speaker makes statements using the pronomial 'we'. The deictic terms 'now' and 'then' do not necessarily switch with the position of the speaker for we may have a now of a particular occasion which we participate in together and recognize as *our* now.

It may seem that the spatial coordinates referenced by orientational terms such as 'here' and 'there' are primary since they can be ostensively identified. But in fact what is 'here' may be a common location occupied by more than one. We three sitting here under the tree looking at the cow on the other side of the river. We sitting here in our garden watching the neighbors barbecue steaks next door. The spatial referencing of 'nows', 'theres', and 'heres' used in such contexts depends upon a social structuring of space (and time) which takes its primary determination from, but cannot be reduced to, coordinates radiating from a center of bodily location. Even less can the referencing of pronominals be established by simple ostensive procedures. Pointing alone does not do to identify who is assembled under a given 'we' unless you already know whom to point to, i.e. you already know the instructions upon which referencing depends. There are socially organized 'systems of coordinates' upon which deictic uses depend for their proper referencing on given occasions. I shall use the term 'deictic order' for these. The term will identify the procedures operative in a given setting or text for locating subjects *vis-à-vis* one another, ordering temporal properties, subject–object relations, and so forth – all those procedures, in fact, providing for participants a shared set of referencing procedures coordinating for them their referencing of deictic terms.

As features of a deictic order, deictic locking devices can be identified that serve to insert the null point of the individual's consciousness into a social relation so that her working system of coordinates is socially organized. In primitive paintings for example the scene is spread out before the gaze without the perspective that positions the latter in relation to it. Contrast that with Brueghel's device in his painting of the village fair. A scene which apparently does not locate the viewer turns out on closer examination to do so with some cunning. The only position from which she could survey the scene in its many parts is a site in a tree some way up a slope on this side of the picture and looking down on it all. The instruction to lock in at this position is given by the way in which it is all spread out before us. A specific cue is added by a tree in the foreground of the painting, directly below our position, in the crotch of which a man is sitting looking out over the same scene that we look out on. Alternatives are those such as Robbe-Grillet's novel *The Voyeur* which places the reader in the null point of the protagonist and teller of the tale, or she may occupy the unstated position of a 'we' in relation to the 'them' of Joyce Carol Oates's novel *Them*. The procedures by which subjectivities are thus placed are the deictic locking procedures.

Texts create their own internal ordering of subjectivity independent of the local setting in which the embodied subject reads, hears, or looks yet no deictic order or locking procedure is completed in the text or document. It remains to be completed in the relation between that and where the reader or hearer stands already. For example, in this book I have made use of the pronomial 'she' instead of using 'he' as the singular universal pronoun. Women who have been educated by the women's movement are not able to treat that 'he' as applicable to them any more. Any use of 'he' identifies someone of the male sex. To use 'she' therefore permits women to lock in at the 'she' or 'her' of any sentence referring to women as a class rather than a specific woman. They can 'test' that statement as to how it sounds as something said from or about themselves. It is presumably a political act for men to lock into it in that way. They will have presumably the same kind of problem with 'she' as I now have with 'he' in similar contexts.

Schutz's emphasis on the primacy of a cognitive organization grounded in the embodied subject problematizes the subject's participation in those cognitive domains detached from particular local sites, such as the domain of scientific theorizing. Here an analogous transition is explored. The subjects participating in the meeting share a socially structured and localized deictic order based on their bodily sites and presence for one another. The reading of the paper enters them into a deictic order displacing the localizing deictic order of the meeting. Yet, as we shall see, these two orders do not exist side by side as alternatives. The text marks and establishes a transition within the local order and from the local order into a theoretical province of meaning displacing a locally embodied experience. Entry to the 'theoretical province' is made from within the localized social organization. This will become visible as we examine a contradiction that emerged between the local order and the textual order for at least one sub-set of members of the occasion.

NESTED SOCIAL RELATIONS

In any given encounter between persons, more than one social relation, each with its distinctive deictic order and level of generality, may intersect. People are apparently able to move between such differing levels without difficulty. They can readily find how to index on one and the same occasion such statements as:

There are mikes distributed around the place. $(h-i)^2$

as well as statements such as:

The Columbia University episode commenced with a rally much like many other ones.[3]

Both statements are from the transcript of the meeting. They operate quite different coordinates. Referencing the first presupposes the spatial arrangements differentiating chair and audience and establishing for the latter a communal co-ordering of located subjects. 'We' look around; 'we' can see the mikes. The temporal positioning of the 'we' interpellated by the chair is the now of the meeting, its 'theres' and 'heres'. The second fails to set up coordinates positioning the subject and instructing her how to reference deictic terms. The subject's now is defined only by its relation to the past of the event of which the speaker speaks, but that is insufficiently determinate to establish coordinates of reference for the hearer. Columbia is elsewhere but not located so as to define the subject's here; the Columbia University episode happened in the past, but is not located so as to define the subject's now. People at the meeting where the paper is read are shifted as subjects from a locally organized world to the world of theoretical thought (based in texts), a shift from a cognitive domain in which the coordinates organized by the null point prevail and a domain in which the personal subject and her site of consciousness are suppressed entering the subject to a specifically impersonal domain of knowing.

In Schutz's account, these are shifts in consciousness and the different worlds are states of consciousness. Here, however, we attend to the different cognitive domains as socially organized practices. We are interested in how such modes of consciousness and such differences in cognitive orientation are socially organized and sustained as actual practices. In exploring the transcript of a meeting at which a paper is read, we can see transitions perhaps more ordinarily made in the privacy of a home or the quiet of a library, from local to textual, from 'working world' to 'theoretical province of meaning', as they are publicly ordered in the deictic orders of occasion and paper.

Though Schutz describes the different organization of the subject in the different cognitive domains,he calls multiple realities (Schutz 1962b). He neglects in his analysis the essential dependence of all finite provinces of meaning upon the paramount reality. The paramount reality does not lapse as it fades out of attentional focus. The tension of consciousness specific to the theoretical province of meaning must be provided for continuously within the paramount reality. Furthermore the constitution of a finite province of meaning as an intersubjective order on a definite occasion must involve procedures for shifting 'the center O' into the social organization of the occasion as well as shifting – and suppressing – it beyond that into the theoretical province. Each finite province of meaning must have, therefore, its distinctive deictic order.

The transcription makes available to analysis the chair's instructions, the paper-as-read, and the discussion. The occasion transcribed has a distinctive deictic organization that establishes first the coordination of subjectivities in the paramount reality and, as a feature of that reality, projects its members beyond it into a textually grounded theoretical order. A paper is read at a meeting. The paper, the reading, sets up its own deictic order, the order of the meeting itself. An organization providing for an intersubjective participation in a theoretical province of meaning is brought into being. This is done on the occasion itself as part of the events of the occasion. The two levels noted above are part of what happens and how it happens. The level of the occasion itself belongs in the finite province of the paramount reality. The theoretical province, the textually grounded order, is nested within the paramount reality, produced and constituted within it.

Each level has its own deictic order. The deictic organization of the occasion includes a sequence which passes the members of the occasion from one level to the other, from one finite province of meaning to the other. It is like a science fiction story in which a box turns out to have a wall which opens up into a different kind of world where the relations between past and future, now and then, before and after, have a different scale and different sets of referents from that in which the box itself exists. You have to go into the box to enter the other kind of world. The box, of course, is the meeting; the wall is (the text of) the paper that is read.

THE SOCIAL ORGANIZATION OF THE OCCASION

Here is how the meeting opens for readers of the transcribed text. The chair speaks:

a OK. Well, the aim of this little session was to be fairly
b informal. Just to crystallize some issues though I asked
c Mr. Robinson whether he'd present a paper on 'Student Movements,'
d then after that we can discuss not only the contents of his
e paper but also things which we raised in the debate today and
f anything else that is of interest to people generally.
g I would ask for people not necessarily to have to confine
h themselves to the content of Mr. Robinson's paper. There are
i mikes distributed around the place. These aren't live to a
j public address system. They are only to record any questions
k that people ask and any debate that takes place across the
l floor between different individuals. So, if you find yourself
m wanting to spiel about something at some length get hold of a
n mike and we'll get it recorded and this will then be available
o for transcribing afterwards.

(111:1–14)[4]

To find the referents of the chair's pronomial use, or perhaps better, to find how his use of pronouns orders the relations of the occasion, we make use of 'anyone's' knowledge of the organization of meetings. This enables us to determine the set and sub-sets to which the chair's pronomials are referenced. The set and sub-sets of the occasion are:

1   we = the members of the occasion. Ordinarily this would include everyone present. (Under some rules menials

present as servers would be excluded from membership. They would then not enter the deictic system at this pronomial.)

2   I = the chair.

3   Mr Robinson/his = the speaker.

4   people/you = the audience. The audience under the special instructions to be found in lines k–1 above may be resolved into different individuals under the conditions stated by the chair for the conduct of the debate.

The set of members includes the others, that is (1) includes (2), (3), and (4). It is not altogether clear from the chair's remarks that the speaker is included in the 'we' of the occasion. But at least he is not excluded.

The set of members, subdivided into chair, speaker, and audience I shall call the base organization of the occasion. The base organization of meetings is (typically) mapped into a spatial ordering of those present. The deictic order depends for its referencing procedures on articulating the coordinates of the null point centered by the subject's body to the social relations of the meeting. Speaker and chair are ordinarily spatially opposed to the audience. Such a spatial ordering can be inferred in back of lines h–o. There are mikes for 'people' to ask questions into. They are also for debate across the floor between different individuals. The pronomial sequence of lines b–1 which goes I, he, we, people, dichotomizes the I and he from the people. The floor is where the people are. Not where the chair and speaker are. The spatial ordering of members of the occasion is of great importance in complementing the uses of pronomials in deictic locking. It coordinates the deictic procedures of the natural attitude which are organized around the location of the body with the social organization to be entered at a given position. The social organizational referents can be ostensively made. If I am positioned on the floor with others and the chair says:

There are mikes distributed around the place.... So, if you find yourself wanting to spiel about something at some length get hold of a mike.

(h–n)

62

I know that you means me. I look around for the mikes and I know that these are the conditions that apply to my use of them.

The members of the occasion adopt the history of the series of which it is a part as theirs. The past of this occasion is taken as the past of the 'we' who are members of the occasion:

things which *we raised* in the debate today. (My emphasis)   (e)

The 'we' which was actively present at the earlier session is the same as the 'we' present as members on this occasion. Thus suppose someone to be present on this occasion who had not been present at the earlier session, this procedure would make references to what she was doing that afternoon inadmissible as part of the history of the present. Members cannot substitute 'biographical' alternatives for the socially organized past. What has happened on that earlier occasion becomes the past of members of the present. The same procedure is apparent in how a university teacher may assume that instructions given out in class on one occasion have been communicated to every member regardless of whether they were actually present on that occasion or not. She does not treat it as an excuse that a student was not a member of that particular occasion (was not present). The history, the memory, the knowledge, established as the history, memory, knowledge of members of the series of occasions obtains for all its members on each occasion.

Following the same procedure, the chair projects events for the future of this occasion. These events are projected as features of the occasion. These are the events of the meeting into which 'we', the members of the occasion, are entered:

1   after that *we can discuss* not only the contents of his paper but also things which we raised in the debate today. (My emphasis)

(d–e)

2   I don't know whether people would like to break now and get some beer and *then we can take up* questions again after people have. . . . (From original transcript = my emphasis)

Both in constituting the past and in proposing a future, the chair treats what in fact has been, or will be, done by only a few of those present – discussing, debating, taking up questions – as what 'we' did or will do. The 'we' of the occasion appropriates the events of the meeting (those planned at least) as *its* acts.

A lot will happen at such a meeting which will not be treated as part of the events of the occasion. The chair's preliminary instructions identify, as a program for the meeting, two activities – the presentation of a paper and a discussion. These categories name the constitutive events of the meeting. The occasion as it unfolds can be understood as continuously organized (or disorganized) with reference to this plan. Moreover the program or plan for the occasion, by naming types of events in advance of their occurrence, appropriates those events to the meeting as its events. Events not so named and not part of the ordinarily recognizable organizational features of meetings will not be recognized as meeting events. Thus a statement like 'The meeting broke up in disorder' expresses the cessation of events and acts which can be appropriated as components of the meeting. This is also how the 'we' of the occasion appropriates the meeting events as what 'we' have done.

Procedures such as these (not wholly reducible to verbal instructions in the form of a plan or the like) for determining what is an event of the occasion and what is not, are consequential for the editorial practice which produces the transcript. Thus clearly the 'break' which intervenes between the presentation of the paper and the discussion is not treated as an event of the occasion. The deictic order of the meeting lapses at such moments. The beginnings and ends of meetings are distinctly marked; meetings are called to order, adjourned, or otherwise segregated from what thereby become their contexts. I talked once to a patient in a mental hospital about the group meetings on her ward. I asked her, 'What happens at the meetings?' She responded by telling me how she felt at meetings, the thoughts that went through her mind, and the like. She did not give me this response as a reason for not knowing what happened at meetings. She gave it to me as a proper answer to my question (asked in fact more than once and in different forms). I did not recognize it as a proper answer. The deictic order of a meeting, at least as I am accustomed to practicing it, does not include what was going on in some individual's head while 'the meeting was going on'. I note this not as an insight into mental illness, but to point out the effect I am trying to characterize in another way. I had asked 'what happens'. Failing to recognize what she said as a proper answer depends upon a deictic order for 'meetings' that excludes referencing private feelings and thoughts and the biographical continuities of individuals. The deictic order of a meeting is characteristically public, the assigned topics rule (typically formalized as the agenda), and subjects enter an order of relevance established by such topics. Alternative referencing procedures are suspended.

Such practices constitute an intersubjective organization for the occasion. The subjectivities of participants are entered into a social organization coordinating the referencing procedures needed to interpret the chair's projection of past and future for the 'we' of the occasion. With respect to the events of the occasion and to its past, the members of the occasion are related to it from within and not as something external to them. Their here/now is mapped into a temporal sequence which is the sequence of the meeting or the series. Its temporal structuring becomes theirs. Or vice versa.

THE OCCASION AS MEMBER OF A SERIES

The series of which this occasion is a part consisted of a sequence of four meetings. They varied in content and form. Such a bounded series of occasions organized as the development of a single theme is a common academic temporal organization. A course is a longer string of similarly bounded occasions, plotted discontinuously into the repeating framework of the week to achieve a progression through a term. The intervals between the occasions are not part of what happens in the series. The one-after-anotherness of the series of occasions produces as a common slip of the tongue among university teachers, a reference to the previous class occasion as 'yesterday' when it was two days before or the previous week.

The movement from unit to unit of the series is scheduled. There is no internally generated movement such as comes about when there is a focus on getting something done. Accordingly each unit is scheduled by placing it in a definite temporal slot, time of day, day of the week, month, session, year, etc. The scheduling provides for the sequence, or rather for the movement of the sequence by a process of 'latering'. That is, the recurrence of identical temporal units produces a movement forward as the past stacks up in back of the present (students sometimes arrive at the end of the series unexpectedly (all of a sudden the exams are here)). The following types of statement presuppose a working knowledge of these kinds of temporal structures:

Mr Robinson[5] (during the reading of his paper: Now, we've had some reference to these notions of direct action of participatory democracy *today; this afternoon* such notions of political confrontation as against ideas of the regular formal democratic procedures in the Senate.... [6] (My emphasis)

Mr Jones (discussing): And then *today* I asked, did you make the public statement? what kind of public statement? He explained why he couldn't make a public statement.... (My emphasis)

Mr Robinson speaks from a positioning in the present that is differentiated from a 'not-now' already in the past. The positioning of the 'we' in the now of a present occasion nested in a series orders the temporal referents of 'today' and 'this afternoon' in the above passages. The now of the present is differentiated from the then of 'today'; 'today' is differentiated from yesterday, the first day of the series of meetings. Participants must know how to lodge the deixes in the social organization of the series. Mr Jones relies on the same temporal procedure to anchor the referents of the deixes. And once the earlier site is located, the pronomials following 'I', 'he', 'you' are also anchored in that site. Knowing how to reference the site in the series means knowing where to find the referent of the pronomials; they are also indexed to that occasion.

The present occasion, the last of the series, is given a program which closes it off against the future (what will happen next). The chair announces a format beginning with the reading of a paper followed by discussion. The discussion will point back to the paper or to 'things which we raised in the debate today'(e). This can be illustrated as in Figure 3.1. The boxes represent sessions; the

Figure 3.1 The enfolded temporal organization of the occasion

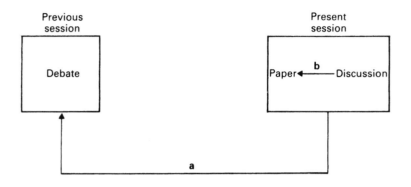

arrows motivational links. Where action is based upon, directed towards, grounded in, arising out of, etc., something that has happened in the past, a past state of affairs, or the like, it has the structure of a 'because of' motivational statement. When the statement presents the action as directed towards something that will happen, a future state of affairs, etc., then it has the structure of an 'in order to' motivational statement.[7] 'Because of' motives are represented thus ←; 'in order to' motives are represented thus →. Arrow 'a' represents 'things which we raised in the debate today' (e); arrow 'b' represents 'we can discuss ... the contents of his paper'(d–e). Both are 'because of' motives. The order established by the chair of the meeting and represented in Figure 3.1 turns in on itself and on its past and closes off the future beyond the conclusion of the meeting, containing the complete cycle of action within it or the series of which it is the terminal session.

There is an alternative temporal ordering that is present in, though not articulated in, the 'official' (and recorded and transcribed) order of the occasion, i.e. that order enunciated by the chair as the procedure for the meeting. One of those discussing the paper read at the session represents a view of the series as actively oriented towards a future beyond the series itself. He refers to:

the tenor of the discussion that's been going on the last two days, where the argument was essentially contentious in some sense as to the presentation of views, a counter-presentation of views, workings out or people demanding that other people work out strategies and implementations....

$$(vi-x)[8]$$

This proposes a different kind of temporal order. The series and its constituent sessions are directed towards bringing about action beyond them. The present is open towards a future that is not closed off by the termination of the series. Illustrated according to the same procedures it might look as in Figure 3.2.

Figure 3.2 An open-ended temporal ordering of the occasion

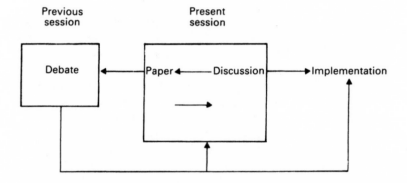

The debates of the previous sessions were, for some sub-set of members of the occasion, a process leading somewhere; the paper was to formulate the issues of the previous debate as a basis for a discussion of strategies and implementation. The present session was to take up and explore the issues further; discussion was to be oriented towards some form of action in the future. Such a series is not organized as a 'latering' order, rather the sequence of sessions is a course of action consisting of presentations of views, contentions, workings out oriented towards strategies for future action and implementations.

68

The closed temporal order of the occasion figured in Figure 3.1 is that of a typical academic organization. It disconnects the occasion and series of occasions from the surrounding texture of events, biographies, pragmatic relevances, facilitating its inter-section with an extra-local discursive order, an order mediated by the text. Such a local organization is at least *congruent* with the constitution of the theoretical finite province of meaning with its divorce of subjects from the pragmatic organization of the world of working and from their personal and local biographically given interests.

THE SUBJECT–OBJECT ORDER OF THE TEXT

The paper presented is part of the occasion. But it establishes a distinctive deictic order within it. It lays out for members of the occasion a finite province of meaning differentiated from the local order of the meeting. The local order of the meeting is thereby aligned with the extra-local relations of a textually mediated discourse.

The properties of this province of meaning are closely analo-gous to those of what Schutz calls 'the province of theoretical thought' (Schutz 1962b: 248). Schutz says that there is a

> peculiarity of theoretical thought of being in a certain sense independent of that segment of the world which is within the reach of the thinker.... In turning to the sphere of theoretical thinking, however, the human being 'puts in brackets' his physical existence and therewith also his body and the system of orientation of which his body is the center and origin. Consequently, unlike man in daily life, he does not look for solutions fitting his pragmatic personal and private problems which arise from his psycho-physical existence within this peculiar segment of the world which he calls his environ-ment.... The 'leap' into the province of theoretical thought involves the resolution of the individual to suspend his subjective point of view.
>
> (Schutz 1962b: 248)

Schutz's description remains at the conceptual level. His thinker leaps into the theoretical by a resolution. For Schutz it appears that as it may be said, so it may be considered to be done. Possibilities of relating the conceptual properties of the various finite provinces of meaning to their actual 'real-life' practice (Smith 1990) are cut off. The subject has to have the equivalent of a *Star Trek* matter transporter capable of transporting him instantly from one province of meaning to another. How does his thinker make and sustain the theoretical epoch? Is it really just something in his head or is there some social connection here, some materiality that is its condition, some local organization enabling him to neglect the ordinarily imperious paramount reality? It is our interest here to explore the actual socially organized practices of the flight from paramount to theoretical cognitive domains. Since we seek to describe how the epoch of the theoretical province of meaning was socially constructed on an actual occasion we depart as follows from Schutz's formulation.

1   The constitution of the theoretical province of thought is treated as a practice. We are concerned, then, with discovering how it was done on this particular occasion.

2   The materiality of the theoretical province is grounded in texts as embodied and indefinitely replicable sets of meaning. The reading of a paper in a given setting locates the occasion in relation to the text-based relations of a discourse or discourses beyond it.

3   Entry to and participation in the theoretical province of meaning appears for Schutz as a solitary activity. Of course it is also always social since the theoretical province of meaning participates in a discourse (scientific, philosophic, or the like). But here entry and participation are intersubjectively structured. The discard of body and the system of coordinates of which body is center and origin is socially organized. The 'leap' into the theoretical province is a coordinated 'leap' socially organized on the particular occasion. We look to the text, therefore, for what it provides in the way of 'instructions' coordinating the 'leap' for members of the occasion.

'The subjectivity of the thinker as a man among fellow-men [*sic*]' (Schutz 1962b) must be suspended for members of the occasion. Their physical existences and the systems of orientation with the body as center must be bracketed. Members must disengage from biographical systems of relevance which organize memory, information, interests, etc., around the individual subjectivity as central point of reference. They must detach themselves from personal and pragmatic problems and from the environment in which those arise and which they make relevant. This must be accomplished within the framework of the occasion; the social organization of the occasion must provide for its being done as a concerted social act.

Some of the work has already been done in the organization of the occasion on which the paper is to be read. We have seen already how the deictic locking procedures of the occasion enter subjects to an order supplanting the biographically organized system of coordinates. The system of coordinates and of relevances organized around personal subjectivity is already socially bracketed. The occasion does indeed constitute the science fiction box which must be entered to be transcended. The organization of the setting and the type of involvement rules (Goffman 1963) applying to the occasion will typically serve to suspend focus upon the body and its coordinates. We do not have access to these from the text of the transcribed meeting, but can rely on an ordinary knowledge of how such meetings are put together in our society. Typically such occasions are arranged spatially so as to minimize focus upon the bodily presence and to maximize focus upon the talk and the distribution of talk characteristic of the occasion (audience vs. speaker etc.). Bodily movements are ordered so as to display the appropriate involvement and to disattend each other's physical presence as focus. The equipment – mikes etc. – provides for the accentuation of talk as focus as well as for its eventual perpetuation in readable form. All these serve to abstract the talk as focus from other aspects of possibilities of presence and activity. This is an important part of how the bracketing of physical existence is brought about as an actual social practice.

The presentation of the paper is integral to the activity constituting the occasion. It is an event of the occasion. But the paper itself does not fully belong to the occasion. It exists somehow apart from the occasion and is presented in it. Imagine as contrast a speech or address directed wholly to the occasion and those present in it. A paper is made for more than one occasion of its being read or heard. This occasion is only one such instance. Though the transcribed text does not have specific references, the text bears traces of its intertextuality.

This situating of the read paper both in the occasion and in social relations beyond the occasion, instructs a reading of the 'we' of the paper so that it does not coincide with the 'we' of the occasion. The 'we' of the paper subsumes the latter, but extends also to those anonymous others who remain in the wings waiting for the moment to enter and continue the textual act. The 'we' of the paper is thus a 'we +' relative to the members of the occasion. It is possible for we who are not members of the occasion even at this distance to read the paper and to lock into its 'we'. This effect attenuates the lock between the 'we' of the occasion and the 'we' of the paper.

The paper is not structured so as to enter into the occasion as a pragmatically motivated act directed towards what 'we' might do next. The subject matter of the paper is student movements of the period. The conventions of the theoretical province of meaning are observed, bracketing biography and the pragmatic relevances of the local setting of its reading. Thus, somehow the 'we' of the occasion must be disengaged from 'the action' which is the topic. We may view the attenuated relation between the 'we' of the occasion and the 'we +' of the meeting both as facilitating this and as an effect thereof.

Though the text and its reading signals a transition from a local to a non-local order, the reading of a paper as such does not precipitate disengagement. Disengagement is brought about by using what I shall call a subject/mediation/object procedure. This is a procedure interposing between the textual subject and object a mediating term which is an act done by the subject to or towards the object. The object is thereby constituted as such for the 'we' who enter as subjects. The objects are events of the student movement of the period; many of the audience are students, some activists; the subject–object disjuncture is a specifically textual construct.

Table 3.1 is a list of the subject/mediation/object procedures found in the paper in which 'we' or 'our' positions the subject.

Table 3.1 Subject/mediation/object constructions

Subject	Mediation	Object
Our sitting here	to talk about	student activism and student movements
We	have had some reference to	these notions this afternoon
if we	step back and attempt to get a general view of	how this activism
if we	admit	there are no hierarchies
we	should stop and take note of	something quite interesting in the process
we	find	the primacy of morality in the tactics
we	can find	that students of both Left and Right
we	also find	this in the fact that there is a constant succession
we	note	that during the Columbia University demonstration
we	can also find	this tendency
we	've touched on	the nature of relations among members of student groups
Now we	should briefly take a look at	the way in which ideologies have been constructed
And so we	find	that the student movement changes
And now we	find	that there are demands for active participation

The mediations into which 'we' is entered in relation to the topic of the paper are those of looking at, noting, finding, and talking. The student movement, its various features, occasions, and characteristics are set before us (note again the openness of the pronominal allowing writer and any reader to enter the text on the same basis as those present at the reading) as objects to be examined. As the speaker guides us through the course of the paper, we are shown different aspects of the matter. The subject/ mediation/object procedure constitutes *a series of statements about* student movements as objects 'we look at'. In this way, students and the student movement are externalized so that the topic of the occasion is placed outside it. Students and student activists are 'them' in the context of the paper, and hence in the context of the occasion.

Some of those discussing the paper find this ordering of relations difficult. One of them, a student, expresses his difficulty in terms which recognize a contradiction between the order of the text and the order of the meeting and series of meetings. He puts forward in fact a version of the series of meetings that accords with the alternative temporal order represented in Figure 3.2 (p.68).

i I find myself puzzled by lots of things in ... and again I find it difficult to put my
ii finger on exactly what's going on, outside of the fact of recognizing that we've got
iii a description here and then I notice there are a lot of – like my colleagues here – who
iv are involved in political action, and so, like we've got the description, and we say,
v well, it more or less did or didn't happen that way, and we're sort of stuck with
vi them. I think there's probably a very difficult shift to make between the tenor of
vii the discussion that's been going on the last two days, where the argument was essen-
viii tially contentious in some sense as to the presentation of views, a counter-
ix presentation of views, workings out or people demanding that other people work out
x strategies and implementations, and here we've got description and I think that that
xi perhaps causes some sense of confusion that I feel myself, and I noticed that other
xii people seemed to feel that in the talk in between [the presentation of the paper and
xiii the discussion].[9]

The student, whom we will call Mr Jones, contrasts the descriptive mode of the paper presented with the ordering of the series of meetings, at least for student participants, and finds them in some puzzling way in contradiction. The substance of the paper is not at odds with the topic of the series of meetings and the discussions that had been going on; nor is it 'politically' objectionable. But something about how the paper puts things together is at odds with

the tenor of the discussion that's been going on the last two days, where the argument was essentially contentious in some sense as to the presentation of views, a counter-presentation of views, workings out or people demanding that other people work out strategies and implementations.

(vi–x)

The paper in some way blocks the forward movement of the discussion by throwing the order of the occasion into a 'descriptive' (and characteristically academic) mode.

This disjuncture can be examined as a contradiction between the deictic locking procedures of the occasion or series, as student participants had been active in them, and the order of relations introduced by the text presented. According to the discussant,

74

what was happening (at least for the 'we' of the student activists, a sub-set of the members of the occasion) in these two days including 'this afternoon' was a pragmatic political work in itself. The contradiction between the deictic locking procedures of the occasion and the series and those of the subject/mediation/ object order of the text creates a problem for students, particularly student activists in the audience. If they are entered as subjects in the pragmatic political process of debate and struggle towards change beyond the confines of the series of meetings, the positioning of the subject in the text displaces them as subjects in that relation. They are called on in two contradictory sites in the order of the text: as members of the occasion at large, they are called on to participate in the generalized 'we' of the paper to whom student movements are objects; as students and activists, they are also the objects of that look. (See Figure 3.3.)

According to Mr Jones, student activists experienced the 'tenor' of the paper as confusing. Our analysis suggests the contradictory organization of their positioning as subjects as source of that confusion. As members of the occasion they lock into the text as observers; as activists, they are also positioned as objects of that observation. Though the object of observation is the same as the theme of the series of meetings, activists as members of the occasion positioned in the text at its 'wes' and 'ours' find themselves disengaged from the ongoing pragmatic relevances of the struggle that had been their enterprise during the series of meetings. The reading of the text as part of the meeting displaces the activist program for the series. Its deictic order disengages the series from a course of action consisting of debate, strategizing and, down the road, implementation. This effect is explored further in the next section.

THE TEMPORAL ORDER OF THE TEXT

The type of subject/mediation/object procedure chosen by the speaker places us in a special kind of relation to the events he describes. The relation of the 'now' of the meeting to the movement of debate, struggle, implementation that Mr Jones expressed is quite different from the relation of that 'now' to the student

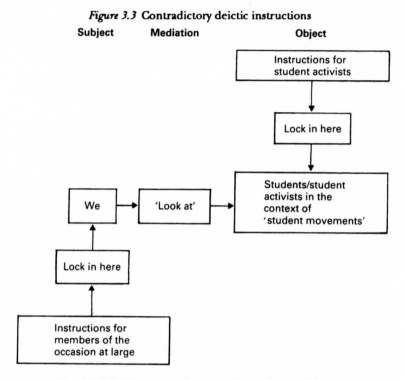

Figure 3.3 Contradictory deictic instructions

movement established by the text. Apart from the 'we' that positions the hearing or reading subject in the text, the referencing of deixes is internal to the object world constituted by the text. A peculiar temporal order is created, external to the order of the occasion, yet embedded in it.

The speaker talks about three instances of student uprisings, those at Berkeley, at Columbia, and in Paris. We are related to them as if they were specimens arrayed before us, which can be examined this way or that depending upon which aspect becomes theoretically relevant at different moments. This has two effects here: the absence of temporal movement in the object also suspends the 'now' of the reader/hearer. It is positioned not so much outside, as without, time; each instance is constituted as an episode.

Although each episode is described in the past tense, it is brought before us in an atemporal mode. The use of the past tense accords with the completed character of the event. To be an event, whatever happened is no longer happening, it is over. The events are mapped into a theoretical rather than a historical temporal order. Berkeley and Columbia are dated on their first mention, but subsequently no dates are given. References to the three do not conform to the historical sequence among them, and indeed they may appear in any order without apparent conformity to any rule other than, presumably, that of relevance to the speaker's immediate expository purpose. Here is a list of the order in which they appear on all occasions on which they are named in the text of the paper:

1 Berkeley, Columbia
2 Columbia, Paris
3 Columbia, Berkeley
4 Columbia, Berkeley, Paris
5 Berkeley, Columbia
6 Columbia, Berkeley
7 Paris
8 Columbia
9 Paris, Berkeley, Columbia

Each episode stands in a temporally undetermined relation to the present of position of the reader/hearer. The temporal order of the text is shown in Figure 3.4.

The order of the spoken text is 'objective'; the deictic procedures position the subject outside 'the action'. It is the intersubjective practice of a province of meaning corresponding to Schutz's theoretical province (Schutz 1962b); constituting the topic of the occasion as object suspends the presence and time of members of the occasion. By contrast, the now of the activists as expressed in Mr Jones's standpoint is from within the action; from that standpoint the occasion itself is included in the same ongoing historical struggle as the student 'uprisings' at Berkeley, Paris, and Columbia. It might be diagramed as in Figure 3.5.

The 'we, here/now' is not separable from the 'we' of the movement. The 'we' would be the 'we' of the student movement and would not be equivalent to the 'we' of the occasion. Thus the 'we' of the activists intersects with, but is not reducible to, the 'we' of the occasion. It therefore does not terminate when the events of the occasion (or of the series) are concluded.

77

Figure 3.4 The 'now' of the text

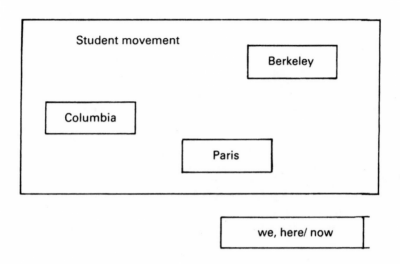

Figure 3.5 The 'now' of the activists

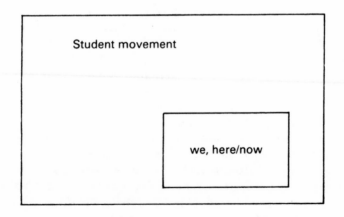

The episodic structure of the constituents of the movement, Berkeley, Paris, Columbia, also serves to detach the deictic order of the text from the deictic order of the meeting. Each of the episodes is constituted as complete in itself by a characteristic cycle of events which do not as such pass beyond the boundaries of the episode. Indeed the boundaries of the episode are the completed cycle. Hence the use of the past tense for the events internal to them. The text speaks of mass protest arising from a 'sense of moral outrage' in response to 'a concrete event, an existing political arrangement or an immediate state of affairs'. The internal sequence conforms to the 'because of' motivational linkages that were explicated in Figure 3.1 (p. 67). The cycle constituting each episode can be represented as in Figure 3.6.

Figure 3.6 The internal order of each episode

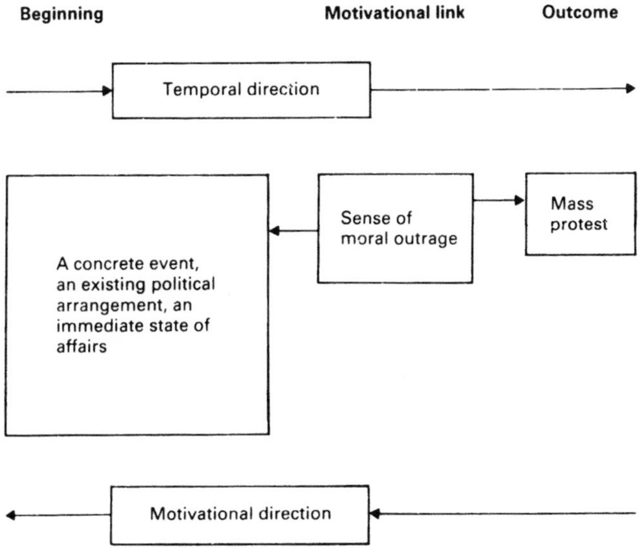

The internal order of each episode is closed off *vis-à-vis* the future. The movement is from 'concrete event' or state of affairs to 'mass protest'. But mass protest is not represented as oriented towards some state of affairs in the future. The motivational direction ties the internal movement of each episode back to its *point d'appui.* Each episode thus displays an internal temporal order which is self-contained and the same for all episodes of that class.[10] Thus the episodes themselves are not represented as having a direction beyond themselves.

Towards the end of his account the speaker draws a second kind of relation between the movement and the present of the occasion by subsuming both in a more inclusive structure.

> Now, I've taken us past the student movement purposely, for I want to drive home the point that this wave of change is part of a general current in American society.

But this siting of the 'movements' in a broader 'current' of change does not change the relation of the here/now of the occasion to the textually accomplished temporal order. Though the statement presents a broad inclusion capable of *subsuming* the here/now of the occasion (apart from the doubtful applicability of 'American' to a Canadian setting), the logic of the procedure implies taking up the standpoint provided by the text regarding the activist program for the series of meetings. The present as a site of struggle focused programmatically on future implementation is to be seen now at one remove as a closed-off episode in a general flow of change. The standpoint shifts to the textual discourse; the here-and-now is subsumed as an instance of its schema. The site of consciousness and activity is displaced from the locally organized politics of the university then and there to the theoretical province of meaning sustained by the text.

CONCLUSION

This chapter explores the social practices co-ordering the sites, relations, and referencing procedures of subjects on the occasion of a late 1960s meeting among students and faculty about the state of the university. The transcription of what was said at the meeting makes available two modes in which subjects are entered and participate, one that of the meeting itself and the other that of a paper read at the meeting. The meeting is a particular local historical organization of intersubjectivity that its participants are assembling as they go along. Within the meeting, a textual space is created setting up, within the now of the meeting that establishes the primary location of the embodied subject, an order beyond it.

In exploring the social organization of subjectivity we began with Alfred Schutz's investigation of multiple realities. This takes as its base what he calls the 'null point' of consciousness, that point that is no point where the coordinates of time and space centered in the body intersect. The orientation of a subject in the paramount reality is organized in relation to the null point. Yet his analysis presupposes the use of language, particularly of what John Lyons calls 'deixes', namely pronouns of person, time, and distance. The anchoring of the subject in the body and the ordering of deictic referencing in relation to the body are surely primary, but they are also socially mediated. Though no one consciousness can occupy the same location and experience the world as another, socially organized deictic procedures set up common sites and coordinated deictic referencing practices among participants.

Schutz contrasts the paramount reality, where consciousness is organized in relation to the null point, with the domain of scientific theorizing in which the 'personal' relevances of the paramount reality are suspended. In Schutz's narrative the transition between the two is merely a passage without interval from one cognitive state to another. Here, however, such transitions are seen as socially organized. The materiality of the text (the printed paper, the TV screen, the computer monitor) is key to the socially organized transition from paramount reality to the domain of scientific theorizing or other textually grounded domains. The text, the paper read at the meeting, marks and establishes a transition within and from the local order of the meeting into an extra-locally organized province of meaning overriding it.

The deictic order of the meeting mediates between the null point organization of subjectivity and the deictic order of the text. The temporal ordering practices of the meeting bracket local and biographical continuities of memory and relevance. However, they coordinate socially rather than suppress an orientation of subjectivity from a 'collective' null point, establishing among participants common referencing procedures for their 'heres', 'theres', 'nows', and 'thens'.

The deictic order of the meeting and the series of which it is part constitute a public order, the temporal schema of which anchors the referencing procedures of those speaking at the meeting. A 'collective' site is constituted, allocated to topics and tasks tied into social relations beyond the series, in this case issues of university function and organization brought forward by the North American student movement. Within this social relation, different temporal sequences are projected. One is that of a self-contained sequence, the temporal movement of which is one of 'latering', a pushing forward of the present of consciousness as units of the series stack up in back of it. The series as such does not have an objective, does not articulate to a project beyond the present. Its site in extended social relations is as it is occasioned by and provides interpretations for its individual members. They as individuals may carry these interpretations away as future readers of the texts of a student movement, or of the university, or the like.

Some of those present interpolate an extension or modification of the one-follows-the-other temporal order of the series. They take up the meeting as orienting to *collective* objectives beyond the series, projecting the work of the meeting towards bringing about some state of affairs beyond its temporal boundaries. Here are the first indications of a political contradiction between the essentially 'academic' parameters of the temporal order of the meeting and series as these are referenced by participants (chair and audience), and the temporal order of the political project sustained by the student activists. It could have gone either way.

The public order of the meeting, its referencing procedures and its topics, organize the presence and activity of subjects within that order. In entering its deictic order, the subject is engaged, geared in, to use Schutz's phrase. The deictic order becomes the operating procedure of her reality. The dissenting Mr Jones is fully *within* (and relies on) the deictic order of the meeting as he refers to the 'the discussion that's been going on today', to the 'lots of things' he is puzzled by, to the fact 'that we've got a description here', and as he assembles a 'we' who have heard the reading of the paper and can discuss whether 'it more or less did happen that way'. The contradiction develops because student activists have entered the deictic order of the meeting and as a result are in place to be caught up as subjects of the text of a paper that positions them *qua activists* as objects, not as subjects. The 'we' of the paper is open to those assembled at the meeting. As participants they are geared in to the subject–object relations of the text; they become, so to speak, members of the text. It is as subjects already entered into the deictic order of the meeting that student activists, too, are assembled in the 'we' of the paper. They are cast thus into a contradictory relation with themselves; assembled as subjects within the text, they and their enterprise become objects under scrutiny.

The social organization of subjectivity at the conjunction of meeting and text has been explored in detail. Entering a deictic order sets up the referencing procedures through which subjects experience and accomplish for one another a social reality. The operative deictic order of the meeting positions subjects in differentiated collective categories – audience, speaker, chair; it sets up coordinated referencing procedures, recovering from deictic terms the same referents – 'today' references a unit of a two-day series, identifying an earlier meeting on the same and second day.

The micro-politics of the meeting works off the deictic order of the meeting. The paper presented is not critical of student movements nor of the enterprise student activists have brought to the meeting. Yet the paper stalls or deflects the political enterprise. The meeting establishes the common deictic ground on which participants build their unfolding social reality. The text inserts its own deictic order intersecting with that of the meeting, thereby capturing as subjects participants whose project calls for very different collective deictic coordinates. The type of subject/mediation/object procedure chosen by the speaker places us in an external relation to 'episodes' constituted as objects of description. The paper positions those at a 'we' coordinated by the textual accomplishment of objects observed, looked at. Its positioning claims any member of the audience, excludes no one, and provides no alternative place to stand. It is, as Mr Jones says, a 'description'. There is one place from which to look and no alternatives. The paper suspends and supplants the multiple positions *vis-à-vis* the topics under discussion that Mr Jones refers to:

there's probably a very difficult shift to make between the
tenor of the discussion that's been going on the last two days,
where the argument was essentially contentious in some sense

as to the presentation of views, a counter-presentation of views, workings out or people demanding that other people work out strategies and implementations, and here we've got description....

(vii–x)

The paper does not take one side or the other; nor does it provide a synthesis. It shifts into a different gear in which there is only one position. It introduces a temporal organization external to the local historical continuities of personal and communal action. Along with anyone else, activist subjects are positioned by the paper outside and looking at the course of action they had earlier been part of. The interpolation of the text disrupts an ongoing process of political contention by substituting as the operative procedures for the meeting an incompatible and over-riding deictic order. A self-contained object world named in the same way as the topic of the meeting is introduced as the operative focus of the meeting. Subjects are shifted into a supervening 'level' of organization transcending the local setting. In a sense the paper substitutes a simulacrum for the topic under discussion.

The analysis of the transcription has enabled us to explore the positioning of the subject in the text as it operated in a particular actual site of hearing it read. The reader or hearer of this paper is no abstract reader posited by the text or derived from it. The deictic order of the text of the paper as it is read enters into and organizes the local setting of its reading. It interpolates its distinct-ive subject–object relations, its temporal order, and the position-ing of the subject it sets up.

This is not exceptional. Though texts only occasionally enter into public occasions, establishing their deictic order for all those present, the effect I have been analyzing works for the reader in the library, at home, on the subway, or as she watches television in the evening. The local continuities of her setting, and the deictic practices that constitute its effective reality for her, are reordered as she enters the text as subject. She is caught up into a deictic order that sets new coordinates and points of reference. Just what are the relations between the text on the one hand and the deictic order of the setting and of the local continuities of action and enterprise on the other is a matter for research not for theorizing.

They too have their micro-politics and, as we have seen in this instance, the micro-politics of the social organization of deixes are articulated to a macro-social and political process.

Chapter Four

ON SOCIOLOGICAL DESCRIPTION: A METHOD FROM MARX[1]

MAKING ACCOUNTS OF MAKING ACCOUNTS

This chapter addresses problems arising out of a research project in the social organization of knowledge. The project was concerned with the social and technical processes interposing between actual happenings and factual accounts of those happenings vested in texts. It was a study of the social organization of news in a newspaper. The research approach was ethnographic. The research was modest in scope. I was assisted in it by Nancy Jackson who was largely responsible for the observational work.[2] We shared the interviewing. In the course of our inquiry, the problematic *of* our research also became a problem *for* our research. If the facticity, content, and structure of news was to be seen as an organizational accomplishment and as standing in a far from simple relation to events it claimed to represent, did not this same problem apply to our own work? What was the status of *our* description? This chapter investigates that problem, beginning with the dilemma posed for description by ethnomethodology. An alternative strategy is extrapolated from Marx whose method presupposes a determinate relation between the language of political economy and the language of everyday life. This notion is developed here as a relation between different 'language-games' (Wittgenstein 1953). The problem of sociological description is elucidated by examining the relation between different types of language-games as these are embedded in social relations. It will be argued that our problem in part arises out of a confounding of the practices of one language-game with those of another, and that as we understand how they are related, so too we can begin to see, first how we have attributed to the actuality intended by the description properties of the relation in which the description arises, and second, how we might proceed with an alternative descriptive strategy making use of the language of everyday life as its *point d'appui.*

THE PROBLEM OF SOCIOLOGICAL DESCRIPTION: THE ETHNOMETHODOLOGICAL CRITIQUE

Sociological description is to represent what actually happened, what was there, or some describable state of affairs. An actuality capable of direct observation and report is to be rendered into text and thus made accessible to other sociologists in a manner which enables them to treat that report as datum. The aim is not just any old description but a description which is both relevant sociologically (whatever that may be) and one which can be used and relied on for use by others. It has to be a description, then, which is not only accurate, but can 'stand in' for the original for those who cannot make the observations themselves. It must, in short, be an objective description. What is meant by an objective account is not one which says everything that could be said (impossible) but one which says what needs to be said for the sociologist who must rely on such a description for her knowledge of the original. It is therefore a description which must describe the observed rather than the observer, and which does not distort the original in ways which are products of the observer's particular perspective or interest. It must be constituted methodologically so that it is a description of what it claims to be, of the original as it is – street corner society, for example, and not of street corner society as it becomes when W. F. Whyte is around observing it (Whyte 1955).

The ethnomethodological critique has proposed that there is a radical indeterminacy in this enterprise. These are the main problems:

1   Social phenomena arise for the sociological observer only in an interpretive act. What is there for her is constituted by her observational work. Hence, it arises in an active relation between herself and what she observes. There is no such thing as non-participant observation. The problem is not how her presence may or may not influence the events she

is concerned to observe. It is more fundamental, lying in the social character of the events themselves and how it is that they arise for us as they are. The detached observer is also at work in making what she observes. Her detachment is a specific constituent of its ongoing social organization. She stands in a determinate active relation to what goes on and that structures her interpretive work.

2 The sociologist uses background understandings, expectancies, and knowledge to make sense of 'appearances', or the actual sequences she observes. They enter in as an unexplicated resource. Not everything upon which the source of the description depends can be explicit in it. The reader herself fills out the text by reading in background knowledge to accomplish its meaningful character. As the describer has taken advantage of what she knows but does not tell in the making of the description, so also the reader must read in what is not actually present in the text in order to know what it says and hence to know what it describes. The problem cannot be solved by more exhaustive description. Each next description merely repeats the same problem (Garfinkel 1967a; Sacks 1963).

3 The descriptive work is done in definite settings governed by their particular relevances, methods of accomplishing the sense and rationality of the work that is done, the practical exigencies of doing the work, and so forth. Hence, the descriptive enterprise is determined by the setting in which the description does or will make sense and the socially organized enterprise at which it aims. Its full subordination to the representational work it claims to do is again drawn into question.

4 Finally, there is the problem of the relation of the descriptive language to the original it intends. This in its simplest form is the problem of what enters into the work of coding or categorizing other than the properties of the event and is either a property of the observational process itself or the conditions of the setting in which the description is done. At a more complex level, acts or behavior identified at one point as potential members of a class in the settings in which they occur may be re-identified as they are reinterpreted at a later point in the development of that

context. The last problem voids for the sociologist the possibility of the literal description upon which a systematically deductive science depends. If a member of a class cannot be identified independent of its context, and further, if its identification depends on its context in such a way that located otherwise it cannot even be determinately treated as the same, then literal description is an impossibility (Sacks 1963; Wilson 1970). There is also the more extreme view involving a shift to a meta-level of inquiry which forgoes the very possibility of description. In this view, a social process takes on a determinate character only in the descriptive practice itself. Hence, interest shifts from what is described to the practices of inquiry and discourse accomplishing the determinate character of events.

The paradox of description, as ethnomethodology has explored it, is formulated thus by Silverman:

Now, if you want to deny this, to say that events might stand outside of our descriptions, you are faced with certain dilemmas. First, the character of the world is not self-defined. Events do not speak for themselves. Second (and this is equally true for my assertion), to characterize the world in a particular way (in your case, as 'outside' descriptions), can itself be viewed as a persuasive account; in either case, the world 'itself' remains to be addressed. Even where we should happen to agree about the 'real' character of the world, that very agreement can be viewed as an outcome of the practices through which we come to generate and recognize 'agreement'; and, yet again, we would have said nothing about the world.

(Silverman 1972: 22)

HOW THERE IS A WORLD TO BE DESCRIBED

Although we take these issues seriously, we begin from a different position, are oriented towards a different enterprise, and make use of somewhat different procedures:

1 First and in particular in relation to the last, we do suppose
   that there is a world that can be described; that this world
   has determinate socially constituted features which are the
   stable production of members, and that it is organized in
   such a way that language and meaning are integral to its
   production. We suppose that this is a world that is brought
   into being essentially in the practical activities of women
   and men (actual individuals) and that interpretation is also
   an activity, a practice isolating and differentiating meaning.
   Murders, tables, and houses arise as such in social practices,
   which reconstitute them as such – that is, as the same event,
   thing – on each occasion of their appearance. The
   categories we use to describe these as 'classes' of events etc.
   are integral to the socially constituted identity of the
   particulars. We suppose that the problem is not whether
   this world can be investigated and described but how.

2 The enterprise we are concerned with is different and
   perhaps more modest. Some of the implications of the
   ethnomethodological critique, notably the issue of literal
   description, lack interest and force for us, since we are
   concerned with a science locating our work and its object in
   a particular historical form. We are not aiming at the
   construction of a domain of social facts as the grounding of
   a generalizing social science, whether its aim is law or
   invariant features. We are concerned rather to explicate
   how our everyday experience and everyday practices are
   articulated to social relations characteristic of this stage of
   capitalism. If there is to be a science which goes beyond
   systematic description and analysis, it must lie in the
   dynamism of the historical development of these relations.
   The fact that the analysis of social relations in this sense has
   not done much at the micro-level should not deter us.

3 At every point we attempt to view our topic or subject
   matter, the object of our inquiry, as practices, methods,
   procedures – as activity, rather than as an entity. This harks
   back to the ancient ethnomethodological interest in
   accomplishments and practice. But as we shall see, it is a
   little different. In following this procedure and in attending
   to the ethnomethodological critique, we do not attempt to
   do away with the critique-in-particular since it is grounded

in a careful observation and analysis of how sociological work is done in a variety of settings. The critique is thus taken up as saying something about the actual processes involved in the doing of sociological description. How things actually get done cannot, by some methodological convention or device, be disattended. A descriptive methodology in sociology must not be obviously at war with how descriptive work is actually done. Rather, it must build upon and build in the actual practices explicitly.

4   Finally, in how we have proceeded, we have removed the ethnomethodological safeguard – the device of 'member's practices' – which serves to objectify what we know and can know only as insiders. In doing a social science we must engage with the problems which arise because our work begins and ends in language. Hence, when we address the actual practices involved in the doing of sociological description, we address these as our own practices – as what we know as a matter of our methods of proceeding and know as doing and in the doing. We cannot step outside. We enter ourselves into the relations we are concerned to explicate as methods or practices.

This does not imply beginning by examining our own subjective states or with a personally biographical account of our relation to the ethnographic situation. These have their place, but it is not here. The issue is to transform 'members' practices' into our practices as members, or rather to discover how to take up methods of inquiry in which the method itself is explicated as an integral aspect of the inquiry. The remainder of this chapter explores critically the descriptive practices which we ordinarily use as sociologists, and know how to accomplish as both she who does the description and she who accomplishes it as such in her reading.

Here critique is itself an inquiry. It involves explicating our practices of doing, hearing, and reading descriptions to identify how these practices interpose between us and that of which we speak. It identifies a problem in how these practices structure our relation to what is described. Working on in the same way indicates a method of describing or explicating which depends directly and explicitly on how the ethnographer learns the uses of the language of the setting, and learns how to mean properly in those settings.

Ethnomethodology and some cognate enterprises have sought a solution to these dilemmas in a new solipsism whereby members' methods of accomplishing sense, order, rationality, and facticity become the only incorruptible object and ground of inquiry. In contrast, we say 'there is a world'. It is a world which defines itself independently of our inquiry. It is a world which remains to be discovered by methods aiming at recovering how it actually is put together and to be described by methods – old and boring as it may seem – where the validation of the account resides in the faithfulness of what it says to that of which it claims to speak. We shall see what that faith might mean.

The method then is one that attempts to take up the very ways in which we are and can become members as a resource for methodical description. The learning of a setting as socially organized courses of action, and as social relations, is the ethnographer's work formally prior to any description she may make. We aim at a method of describing which explicates these practical and tacit prerequisites to any ordinary descriptive work which we might do.

A METHOD FROM MARX

The method we followed is derived from Marx. The account I shall give of this cannot be treated, and is not intended, as an exposition. Marx originated a method which was the basis for how he went about a critique of political economy. Here we are doing a sociology and furthermore adopting a method intended for the analysis of a mode of production for analysis at the micro-sociological level. Thus, no claims are made to an interpretation of Marxist texts. We have simply seen that we had something to learn from how Marx proceeded, which is relevant to the problems with which we are concerned; and further, that these methods serve to articulate the work we do at the micro-sociological level to the social relations of the larger social and economic organization of capitalism. It makes sense to us to be able to do this. Marx's method in the critique of political economy presupposes a definite relation between the categories of political economy and actual social relations. As I.I.Rubin has stated this: 'the basic notions or categories of political economy express the basic social–economic forms which characterize various types of production relation among people' (Rubin 1973: 31).

Terms such as wages, commodities, capital, profits, etc., are not in their origin the technical vocabulary of political economists. They are the terms that are used in and are *of* the original social process. Political economy takes up these terms and incorporates them into its theoretical system. For example, 'Classical Political Economy borrowed the category "price of labour" from everyday life without further criticism, and then simply asked the question, how is this price determined?' (Marx 1977: 677–8).

The categories are indeed, to use Marx's term, the categories of real life. By importing them uncritically into the scientific discourse, the actual social relations expressed in them become invisible. The theoretical constructions are divorced from the constraints of actuality. But the categories are still anchored there. They 'arise ... from the relations of production themselves. They are categories for the forms of appearance of essential relations' (Marx 1977: 677). As they lose sight of the actual social relations in which the categories arise and which they express, political economists come to treat the categories of capitalist social relations as the permanent features of economic processes (Marx 1977: 678). They come to practice ideology rather than science.

Marx proceeded in the 'opposite' direction.

At first glance all the basic concepts of Political Economy (value, money, capital, profit, rent, wages, etc.) have a material character. Marx showed that under each of them is hidden a definite social production relation which in the commodity economy is realized only through things, a determined, objectively-social character, a 'determination of form' (more precisely, a social form), as Marx often put it. Analyzing any economic category, we must first of all point to the social production relation expressed by it.

(Rubin 1973: 45)

Such procedures can be generalized by a method which might be described as substructing. Beginning from the terms, from the categories of a political economy if you like, the social scientist proceeds to an examination of the social relations which they express. These social relations arise in the actual practices of actual living individuals.

When we talk of social relations in the context of Marx's thinking, we are not talking of social relations as sociologists are accustomed to do. Social relations for the sociologist refer to the abstracted forms of normative structures held to link positions or roles, the relation between husband and wife, between positions in an authority structure, the interpersonal relations of group members, and the like. For Marx, by contrast, social relations are the actual coordinated activities of actual people in which the phenomena of political economy arise. Relations are not norms, concepts, or structures apart from activities, determining and being expressed through activities. They are coordinated or articulated processes of action among persons taking place in time and having determinate form. Social relations are thus sequences which no one individual completes. The construction of a social object such as a commodity is completed over the course of exchange on a market. Any particular thing becomes a commodity only by being entered into relations of exchange and is only fully realized – made real – *as a commodity* as it is subject to the social courses of action that conclude in its final use, its consumption. The basis of analysis is not the act, the action, or the actor. It is the social relation coordinating individual activity and giving people's activities form and determination. What an act is may be grasped in any way we can, but it takes on determinate social form as it is entered into a social relation.

Let me give an example from my own experience. Once, I had a paper on ideology that raised theoretical and political issues for how Marxists go about theorizing. I wanted an opportunity to discuss these issues with the Marxists I knew on the west coast of the United States. I had something to say. I wanted to meet with them to say it. I was invited to be part of a session on Marxism at a sociology conference taking place in San José, California. Here was my opportunity. At that time I lived in Vancouver, British Columbia, so I got on a bus and went. When I arrived, I found my paper was part of a session in which five other lengthy papers were to be presented. The time, as usual in such situations, was inadequate. We had ten minutes each in which to present our papers. The crowd was huge. I had come for dialogue. What could get done in that situation was only a performance. My act, my intention, was entered into the social relations organizing and accomplishing the professional discourse of sociologists. My dialogic intention disappeared. A political process was suppressed in the ordering of the occasion. The latter reproduced the speakers' texts as instances of sociological discourse. They were entered into the relations of the discourse. My intentions were a matter of indifference; they were not consequential for the social organization of the act of presentation. Whatever I meant to do, the speaking of my text in that setting lifted it out of the context of the political relations I had wanted for it and entered it into the social relations of academic sociological discourse. It was heard and responded to in that mode.

I emphasize that the local organization of that moment is not in itself final, for that local organization (as Marx shows us in his analysis of the relation of productive organization to the relations of capital)[3] is coordinated with and given shape by the extended social relations to which it is articulated.

From the outset of our research, Jackson and I had intended to make use of what we then understood as this method in its application to sociology. We intended to begin with the categories of the everyday world of the newspaper office as a point of entry into the descriptive process. Originally, we worked with the notion that phenomena were constituted in correspondence with the categories referencing them. We therefore started by taking up categories used in, and to describe features of, the setting and tried to substruct them by locating, in the actual practices of the newsroom, how the phenomena they seemed to name were constituted. We tried to find how the phenomenon the term seemed to identify was accomplished in the practices of members of the setting. This was a mistake, though not so far a mistake that we could not find out that we were mistaken.

One term on which we focused in this manner was 'assignment'. In the organization of the newsroom, the city editor or city desk assigns stories to reporters as their task for the shift that they are working. In the course of an attempt to do an ethnography which would examine the actual practices constituting assignments, we began by constituting assignments as if our object was to describe them. Our observational procedures were useful, though our objectives were problematic. We kept a record of the ways in which reporters talked about assignments, or used the associated verb 'assign' etc. We found that we had a collection of overheards which were not readily intelligible as such. These would be phrases such as, 'so and so has been assigned to this story', 'this story has been assigned to so and so', 'I had too many assignments', and when the ethnographer asked, 'What is an assignment?', she might well be shown a piece of paper with a typewritten passage on it and some scribbles, and told 'this is an assignment'. These were ordinary uses of the terms 'assignment' or 'assign' which could not readily be made sense of without a knowledge of the actual working practices of the newsroom.

With our collection of phrases and on the basis of further investigation, we began to construct a 'something' that we could describe as an assignment. We said (it is now embarrassing to confess) that assignments were authorizations to use and deploy the resources of the organization in the collection of news. It was at this point that we suddenly realized that we had fallen into error. What we had done was to go from the various kinds of usage of 'assignment' which we had found in an actual working setting, to set out a general descriptive procedure – at the next level up – which would provide for all those types of uses. We found a definition which would reference all these instances and allow us to talk again.

We had thus constituted assigning and assignments as a socio-logical category. We could now enter the sociological discourse and talk as sociologists about assignments as an organizational feature. We had developed out of observation and interviews with informants a conceptual organization that would organize and assemble out of actual courses of action and actual social relations an open-ended set of *instances* of the category. We would now know how to read from observed or described actualities into our socio-logical analysis and how to read what we observed as expressions of our analytic category.

Arriving at this step, we considered what we had done. We saw indeed that we had landed ourselves in precisely that situation from which we had tried to move in our method of doing sociology – that our practice was ideological rather than scientific. We were in business making up our own ideological forms as methods for detaching the concept from the actual social relations it expresses (Smith 1974a; Smith 1990). The problem arose in part from how we had conceived the method of substructing. We had proceeded

96

in the ethnographic work as if there were indeed a category of 'assignment', and our aim was to locate and describe the practices which accomplish assignments as phenomena. It was only in giving this a summary form in this way that our attention was drawn to our method of work. We had in fact invented a categorization which would retroactively treat our overheards, answers to questions, and observations, as instances.

Though we were dissatisfied with the ideological outcome, we could not initially see that the problem went beyond that difficulty, so we went forward by trying to improve our descriptions of 'assignments'. At first, we retained the categorization procedure as our instructions for how to look at and describe what was there. It provided the frame to which our findings should conform. By proceeding in these ways, we were using methods of doing descriptions in this setting which negated the enterprise of recovering the actual social relations and organization we had been concerned to describe. It took time to get beyond this.

THE LANGUAGE-GAME OF SOCIOLOGICAL DESCRIPTION

We have a problem at this point of a term 'assignment' with two contexts of use and two methods of reading it – those of the sociological discourse and of the original setting. Our aim is to describe the social organization of an original setting. Somehow, the process of a sociological description of itself appears to interpose a barrier, or a distorting process. The term (or set of terms: 'assign', 'assignment', etc.) used in one mode in its original setting comes to mean differently in the context of sociological discourse. Here we can follow directly a recommendation that Wittgenstein made for philosophers:

> When philosophers use a word – 'knowledge,' 'being,'
> 'object,' 'I,' 'proposition,' 'name' – and try to grasp the
> essence of the thing, one must always ask oneself: is the word
> ever actually used in this way in the language-game which is its
> original home? What we do is to bring words back from their
> metaphysical to their everyday use.
>
> (Wittgenstein 1953: 48)

Though we cannot substitute the everyday uses of the original, our enterprise is analogous. It is to bring back words from their descriptive to their everyday use. The language-game of socio-logical description involves a distinctive method of meaning. Terms used in doing sociological description are taken up from the language-game or games of their original setting. The terms are preserved. Their 'referents' are not changed. But their uses, how they mean, in the language-game of sociological description, differ from the original. We cannot simply bring words back from their sociological to their everyday use.

We take for granted that we know what it is to do descriptions. Where we must now begin is by bracketing that assumption. To make descriptions available to us as a practice, we will make use of that method of work which explicates 'our practices as mem-bers'(see above in section on 'how there is a world' p. 89) as contrasted with the objectified 'members' practices'. We ourselves are active in the constitution of a given text as description. Its character as description arises for us in our reading. In our writing, we intend our work to be read as description. When we locate ourselves as readers at the beginning of the act through which the description arises as such on every occasion of its being read as such, we make available the resources of our knowledge – a tacit knowledge (Polyani 1967) – of our method of meaning, and of how to read a text as a description. Hence, by 'entering' ourselves as subjects in this process, we can become aware of how our methods of accomplishing sociological description confound properties of the descriptive procedure with properties or features of the 'original'. The shift is analogous to the shift from a geocen-tric to a heliocentric cosmology. The geocentric view establishes the observer in a fixed position at the center of the solar system. Her position is unvarying. The observed movements of the planets are their movements. Once the heliocentric view prevails, the observer is found to be herself moving in relation to what she observes as moving. Previously, the moving relation of her site of observation to the moving planets had been confounded with the planetary movements. Once her own position is seen as a moving relation to what moves, it is possible to grasp her observations as a relation rather than as objectified. Only then can an accurate conception of the solar system emerge. Similarly here, conven-tional methods of sociological description record as observations properties of the descriptive method. Once, however, we locate the description as an active relation between the reader and the text and through the text to an object, the character of that relation can be made explicit.

THE DOUBLE RELATION

When we embed the language-game of sociological description and the language-game of its original in the everyday world, a double relation comes into view. The categories of political economy or of the conceptual frameworks and categories of sociology are embedded in the social relations of the relevant discourse – political economy in the nineteenth century, the sociology of today. The terms are integral to the original social relations, capital, commodity, and assignment; they are inserted into the practices of a discourse that makes those original social relations the object of its inquiry. Thus, the same set of terms may be located in two intersecting social relations; terms such as wages or profit arise on the one hand as part of the original working relations of a political economy where the naming is a part of how those relations are practiced. On the other hand, they are also caught up into political–economic or sociological discourse. It is precisely this double character of the relations in which the terms are situated that is concealed and mystified by the normal positivism[4] of social scientific discourse. The language, which is part of the object of study and how that object becomes known within a discourse, is incorporated into the discourse and organized by its social and technical relations.[5]

The double relation appears to be the implicit paradigm of ethnomethodology, comparable in its organizing effect to Goffman's (1959) dramaturgical model but explicit only in the kinds of instances that ethnomethodology has made the focus of its work. Most of these involve the imposition of categories or coding procedures originating outside the actual settings to which they are applied and which they should record (cf. Garfinkel 1967a; Cicourel 1969; Atkinson 1978). It is a relation at the intersection of a professional discourse or bureaucracy (or similar organizational form), and a lived world which the coding or descriptive procedure must make objectively available to the discourse or administrative process. The double relation is characteristic of our work as sociologists.

When we bring this double relation into view, we can see more clearly the problems that arise in doing descriptions where the descriptive language is organized by the sense-making practices of the discourse. In that context, they 'work' quite differently from how they operate in the original setting they now describe. Further, the language uses of the discourse are not constrained by the practical contexts of use characterizing the original. A system of categories may be formed from the original working terms and the categories may then be used to conceptualize relations having little to do with the social relations of the setting in which the terms originated (Smith 1974a). The categories of the discourse appear to reference the actuality they have been taken up from. In fact, the categories and the system of categories organize what they seem to name in ways that do not conform to the social organization of the everyday setting in which they originate.

In back of the two disjoined language-games is a particular form of class relation, where a formalized professional discourse or bureaucratic process on the one hand confronts the lived world it seeks to name, manage, control, and organize within its conceptual and practical jurisdiction. The disjoining is examined in the work of labeling theorists. It is clearly available in Melvin Pollner's critique of labeling theory (Pollner 1974). It is essentially present in the problem of the relation between the methods sociologists use to mean as they seek to describe and 'take home' to the discourse selectively treated processes of the everyday lived relations they observe.

In the course of our research, and when we were examining our own practices in making 'sociological' descriptions, three different kinds of talk or writing could be observed in the course of Jackson's ethnographic work. First, there was the kind of talk that she heard in the course of her observations, or the talk done by people in the newsroom in doing their work or in talking with others around and about their work. Our ethnographic focus was chiefly on the work of the city editor, the city desk, and the reporters who were on assignment. This was a fairly circumscribed mode of work exchanges, much done in talk, whether on the telephone or among the individuals concerned, or on the typewriter. The talk and the writing were important aspects of the work process. I shall call this 'Level One' talk.

The second level of talk Jackson observed was characteristically done when she was talking to an 'informant' and a description was being given to her. This type of talk was done as a routine part of the ethnographic procedure of learning from someone who is a competent member of the setting. Such descriptive talk made use of the same terms as could be heard or overheard in Level One talk, but it produced a different usage of these terms. Further, the sense that descriptions at this level could make to the ethnographer very often depended upon her having learned how the talk worked at the first level and how to do first-level kind of talk. These differences in level, and the dependence of Level Two on Level One talk, became visible when Jackson shared such descriptions with me, and I, who did not share Jackson's prior knowledge, had to get her to fill out what had been said to make it intelligible. This is that process which Garfinkel has described:

> ...suppose I furnish you an account of the organization of a hospital. The question may then be asked in return: Did you take into account the ways in which you were knowledgeable about those arrangements, and did you use as a resource your own grasp of those arrangements so that what you did was to engage in an explicating procedure in which something otherwise familiar was made invisible once more?
>
> (Garfinkel 1968: 112)

Level Two talk for the informant depended upon her prior familiarity with the work processes and courses of action which were both context and substance of Level One talk. Descriptions, guidance, and information which informants were giving the sociologist at Level Two referenced, explicated, and glossed the work process at Level One. At Level Two, terms used in Level One talk were used outside the practices in which they were 'naturally' embedded and in which their everyday use arose. The sociologist's work was to learn how to see what she would go on to observe or perhaps had already observed as that of which the informant spoke and as 'explained by' or 'made intelligible by' the informant's description. In this retrospective/prospective fashion, the sense that the ethnographer could make of Level Two talk depended upon how talk was done at Level One. The level of talk or writing was that which was part of the sociological discourse, and which Jackson and I did as part of how we were participating in the discourse and having that in mind.

Level Two talk involved modes of categorization and sense-making practices conforming to those of the discourse as we made them accountable. It was, incidentally, in a less specialized and less 'technical' form, a mode of categorization which reporters and editors would also do at times when they were reflecting on their work to the sociologist, formulating general statements about news or the like very much as sociologists do. The latter contrasted with the Level Two talk they did when they were trying to tell the sociologist about their work and how newsmaking was organized in the settings of their experience of it. I am calling this level of categorization or description, practiced by both sociologists and our informants, Level Three language-games. Reporters made use of an array of categories defining a less technical shared discourse of intelligentsia – our *lingua franca* so to speak. A distinctive property or effect of the language-games of this level (Level Three) is that they subsume and organize the kinds of talk and sense done at Levels One and Two.

The concept of 'assignment' that Jackson and I had worked up was passed up these different levels of language-games. It would operate for us at Level Three where the sociological discourse came into play; it would have this happy appearance of being grounded in informants' accounts of the settings of their work; we could treat it as a 'feature' of the original setting. Its arrival at Level Three in the type of language-game that would do this specialized work was mediated by the interviewing procedure at Level Two. But, of course, at Level Three, it no longer meant as it did in the talk of reporters and editors in the settings of their work.

These three levels represent two sets of social relations mediated by the interrogatory and descriptive process at Level Two. When again we locate these levels in social relations, we can also see how we ourselves were located in the work. Level One is quite simply where the routine production of news in a newspaper in Vancouver, British Columbia, was getting done. As they were getting their work done they talked to others in the setting and on the telephone, wrote messages, read, as well as writing news stories or the like. Level Two talk arises only on the way to the sociological text. Here both informant and sociologist entered as active and knowledgeable practitioners of doing and hearing descriptive talk. Further, as a result of the time Jackson had spent in the newsroom making observations she knew pretty well how to take informants' descriptions of the setting she observed, how to hear the talk as description of that setting, and how to use what came thus to be her knowledge of the setting as the basis for her field notes and primary descriptive writing. The second level mediates; it is transitional between an ongoing work process itself producing accounts; it creates the first set of texts, either primary ethnographic material or the transcribed texts of interviews; it is an integral moment to the next stage or level when the product is entered into sociological discourse.

Thus as we usually practice sociological description, it is a compound and confounded product of the double relation: on the one hand, the actual organization of practices in the setting that become a resource for, and provide the underlying determinations of, description and, on the other, a sociological enterprise using sociological conceptual practices to structure the ethnography. The final sociological description is a product of this compound. Practices integral to accomplishing the description as a description are transposed in this process, so that they appear as properties of the original. A kind of textual narcissism is set up whereby the view from the sociological discourse is of its own reflection.

Here is where the issues of the ethnomethodological critique are located. They are, I shall suggest, problems arising and continuing to arise, so long as we remain rooted in a 'geocentric' sociology.

DESCRIPTION AS A SPECIALIZED LANGUAGE-GAME

When we see these practices as embedded in social relations and ourselves as organizing our practices in these relations, we can explore our own knowledge of how those practices structure what becomes (for us) the original of the description; we can explore description as a language-game. In doing so, I shall focus only on those aspects of our practices in accomplishing descriptions relevant to the relation between the language of the setting and the language of the description[6] that has been problematized here.

103

Descriptions are one of a family of practices identified here as factual accounts. In general, factual methods of reading have this special character that in our reading we 'pass through' the text to an actuality 'on the other side' (Smith 1990). This distinguishes the reading of factual from the reading of fictional accounts (Holland 1975). In reading fiction, Holland suggests, the text is fused with the self of the reader, but in reading as fact a world to be questioned beyond the text arises for the reader. Factual methods of reading constitute an actuality for the reader to which existence is attributed in its fullness; there is always more that could be known about it than has been or can be written or said. That imputed 'actuality' is normative *vis-à-vis* any account which may be given. Hence, the factual description may be corrected, impugned, criticized, seen as inadequate, insufficiently detailed, etc., in terms of the actuality arising for the reader as she accomplishes a text as factual.

Referencing as a practice or method of meaning is key to the language-game of description. Reading a descriptive account, we make use of a referencing method of meaning, taking the terms to intend something out there, object or action, beyond the text. Reference is not essential to meaning as such; it is not the only way in which words can mean; reference is a definite practice of making sense. The understanding that 'this is a description' instructs the sociologist to hear her informant as speaking of what is out there. She takes what is referred to in the description as just that. Referencing constitutes the relation between the descriptive discourse and what it intends. Our methods of reading descriptions constitute the text as derived from an original actual state of affairs; its terms are taken as referencing something out there.

The prior existence of the original is the reader's accomplishment even as she relies on it. When you listen to an informant giving a description, she is telling you about something and you hear her for the 'something' referenced in her description. The questions you ask point behind or beyond her talk to what is spoken of – 'Can you tell me some more about that?' As she describes, you take it that you can somehow or other reference the actuality intended by her description. That is what you are talking about.

The language-game of description, as sociologists presently know how to do it, distorts that procedure in a funny way. We take a term out of the actual settings in which it is used and enter it into a description of that setting. In so doing, the ways in which it means, or the method of interpretation used, may be changed. In description, whether the informant's or the sociologist's, terms are wrenched out of the setting. The social relations of which they are part and which control how they mean in the setting itself (where control is a social not an individual process) are suppressed. The terms are entered into a form of social relation of which the descriptive process is a practice. They enter trailing a debris of meaning behind them which we may describe as 'connotation' when we attempt to analyze the present intimations of its uses in an original and absent setting. That debris of meaning originates in the social organization and relations of the setting to be described; it bleeds properties of that organization and those relations into the descriptive text. In a sense the social organization or relations of that setting determines any description that can be written of it.

But the uses or meaning of a term thus wrenched, extracted, and relocated in the descriptive game are changed. The descriptive method of reading references an object or discrete entity of some kind, corresponding to the term. This was the method I used when, following Marx, I first began to look at terms as expressing social relations. I thought of them as 'naming' the social relations which constituted the phenomena so named (Searle 1969). The language-game of description uses terms to do referencing, to locate and organize an object, and to do categorizing. Thus, that organization of meaning is 'inserted' into the textual represent-ation of the setting as if it were a feature of its organization. The reader using the interpretive practices of descriptive reading reads that organization back into the represented original.

An example which recurs in the context of studying the making of news is the question 'What is news?' When reporters talk to sociologists about news, it is this question that they find most difficult. It is one they often anticipate in advance of anything the sociologist has said. They expect (in Level Three talk) to be able to find a referencing procedure for the term. Sometimes, this is presented to the sociologist as a puzzle she might be able to solve. Sometimes, reporters brood on their inability to find an answer to this question of all questions which would seem to be the one they could most readily and expertly answer. Newspeople find it difficult to provide any kind of criteria which would enable one to go out into the world, so to speak, and identify news. Newspeople here are talking about news in the context of a descriptive game. The method of reading in this game takes the term and goes from that to look for what it is they are talking of. We use a referencing procedure when hearing them. Anticipating that method of interpretation, the newspeople we talk to search for a method of making that referencing successful.

We see that newspeople have a problem deciding what it is for the purposes of description, but only for the purposes of description. They do not have any problem in using the term in the actual contexts of their work. So here is a notorious example of just exactly the type of problem which arises when a term which means such and such (however it does mean) in the working contexts of its use will not perform a referencing work of meaning when that is required of it in the context of description. News as a working term can be defined only as an actual organization of relations between the work of the reporter and of the editor, the production process, circulation, etc., of the newspaper. It is a term that is part of the work and does the work in talking about the work. In those contexts, it is used in special ways but it is not used at all to describe as when a description is being done. In the descriptive context, quite different things are done with that term. It is treated as if it named something that we could find very much as we might walk through the fields looking for a certain named species of butterfly, or carrying our copy of Smith's *Field Guide to Western Fewmets,* looking for a certain named type of dropping. When we take the descriptive method of reading and apply it to a term taken up out of its original context and entered into the descriptive game, we reconstitute the relation between that term and the original. The term names something, perhaps even a social relation, and the sociologist's procedure might then seem to be to look for that of which the description has spoken for, or is to be found back there in the original setting described.

This is how Jackson and I went to work. We started out, as I have described above, with a bunch of terms we did not understand or know how to use which were used familiarly, casually, and competently by members of the setting. We tried to discover how the phenomena we took them to name were constituted in the actual practices of the newsroom. We tried to make the newsroom describable in accordance with this method of reading. When that could not simply and directly be done, then we resorted to the procedure we have described above. We took advantage of our knowledge of sociological conceptual practices to construct a concept 'assignment' which would constitute the contexted uses of assign/assignment etc. as an object. Then, what we had observed or overheard and had been described became the object required by the language-game of description. But once we saw that we should attend to our experience with this term and with terms like 'news' as aspects of 'how it worked', we could begin to discover a different method of work. An alternative strategy is suggested by the suppressed but implicit presence in the description of the social organization and relations in which the ordinary use of terms participated and which the terms have trailed after them into the description.

EXPLICATING SOCIAL ORGANIZATION AND RELATIONS AS AN ALTERNATIVE STRATEGY

In doing the descriptive work, the method used by the describer is controlled by her knowledge of the socially organized processes in which categories are used to name objects, events, etc., arising in that social process. She takes her knowledge of the original for granted as a competent member. She knows it as one who can explore it further and can say more about what it is than that which is contained in any one descriptive sequence. Her knowledge of the socially organized processes which constitute the features of the setting, and the relations which they articulate and are articulated to, is the background knowledge upon which she draws in making her description. But she does not draw on it as a matter which is already objectified for her in the form in which it will be described. She draws on it as already known and taken for granted, and already organized. That organization 'enters into' the description as a constraint. It is normative with respect to how it makes sense to her to speak, or to use terms (the relations which can be intelligibly asserted). It often appears most markedly on those occasions when the description makes sense to the describer, does not make sense to the hearer, and the describer cannot see what is missing in her description. It appears also in how the describer can hear the hearer's questions as 'wrong'.

There is no way in which a description of a particular setting can be written or spoken without that being in fundamental and essential ways determined by the social organization of the setting. The social organization may not be described as such. Whatever it is that is being described may not be adequately described. But the social organization of the setting is necessarily present in the description in what the describer knows how to describe. That social organization is not externalized or observable to her as such. She knows it as member and practitioner – however imperfectly – as it arises in working relations. What is observable is embedded in and arises in those relations, but the relations themselves are not observable. Her relation to the setting, how it becomes observable to her, the sense it makes, the ways in which terms mean and may be used are organized prior to her descriptive work. They enter into any description that she can make, for any description she can make presupposes her tacit knowledge as practitioner of the relations in which the sense of the setting arises for her.

Ethnomethodology has addressed this as the problem of the unexplicated background knowledge of social structures on which the sense of an account depends. As ethnomethodology has formulated the problem, the sense of the text is necessarily dependent upon what cannot be fully explicated in it. Hence, the claim of a description to describe is always a qualified claim. As we have examined the relation between description and original here, a rather different conclusion and different possibility follow. If the description is determined by the sense-making practices of the original, such that the uses of terms brought forward from the setting to be described are controlled, perhaps even determined by the social organization of that setting and the part played by those terms in its processes, then that organization is implicitly present in the text (Jules-Rosette 1978; Smith 1979). The description has not addressed this and does not describe it, but whatever it does describe (given that the describer is at some level a member of the setting she describes) is determined by the social organization of the setting. That social organization is an implicit presence in the description. It must be so. That any social setting is describable presupposes interpretation on the part of she who describes. The very feature which appeared to give us problems at the outset of the inquiry we have been engaged in here, now appears as guarantee to what must be presupposed if we are to find an alternative method of work.

The proposal for an alternative is simple to state, and difficult to do. It is to proceed by explicating the implicit social organization. In approaching an alternative, we began with the transposition of the language of the original to the descriptive game. Rather than terms identifying phenomena constituted in a social process, they can be thought of as 'aspects' of organized practices, and their methods of meaning as integrated in and articulated to such practices. How they mean in the original setting is to be learned as part of the process of learning its organization. It is a familiar experience – the sense of not knowing quite how to speak, quite how to use terms correctly, at the stage when we are only beginners in a setting. The words used are essentially part of the activity which forms a phase of the social relations. The social relations are not a context for the use of the term but the use of the term, how it means there, is part of the activity forming the relation. Thus, learning how to 'mean' with words correctly in that setting is learning how it is socially organized.

It is that social organization which we can aim to explicate. We can begin its explication, at least in the context of a newsroom where so much is done in words, with the terms which are used there, the terms which give us trouble and the terms which appear as keys in the linking processes between the world out there which newspeople seek to report and the reports they produce. In developing our knowledge, one method is to examine a close alternative to unpick its difference and attempt to display the explicative method in the process. Since I have learned a lot from Gaye Tuchman's work, I am going to draw on her work for such an examination. In a paper 'Making news by doing work', Tuchman discusses news and different kinds of news (Tuchman 1973). I want to suggest how a particular interpretation can been seen as a construct of the descriptive procedure whereby 'setting' terms have been transposed into descriptions and are read as referencing entities in the original setting. Tuchman's procedure is essentially the same as that which Jackson and I had begun to follow in developing the concept of 'assignment'. She leads up to a general statement of the relation between happenings in the everyday world and the making of news by describing the differences between spot news, developing news, continuing news, and the like. Here is her description of developing news:

> Developing news concerns 'emergent situations' ... as indicated by the following prototypical example. A plane crashes. Although this event is unexpected, there are, nonetheless, limitations upon the 'facts' it can possibly contain. The newsmen would not expect to run a story stating that those reported dead have come to life. Nor would they expect to run a report of an official denial that a crash had occurred. The 'facts' of the news story are: a plane crashed at 2:00 p.m. in Ellen Park, when an engine caught fire and another went dead, damaging two houses, killing eight people and injuring an additional 15 persons. All else is amplification. Since the plane crash was specifically unexpected, reporters were not present to record 'facts' accurately. 'Facts' must be reconstructed and as more information becomes known the 'facts' will be more 'accurate.' Although the actual event remains the same, the account of the event changes, or as the newsmen put it, 'the story develops.' Ongoing changes of this sort are called 'developing news.'
>
> (Tuchman 1973)

The descriptive procedure in this passage is organized by the notion of events typified as news. The typification mediates between happenings in the everyday world and the organizational course of action. 'Developing news' is a type of news in which the ongoing course of action is modified by new information. 'Developing news' is a variant of the more general procedure of passing from event through typification to 'the story'. Tuchman summarizes this procedure in a general statement: 'The discussion insistently suggests that newsmen typify events-as-news to transform the problematic events of the everyday world into raw material which can be subjected to routine processing and dissemination' (Tuchman 1973: 125). The articulation of the 'problematic events of the everyday world' to their routine processing is the work of newspeople typifying events-as-news. The sequence goes from the 'events' through 'typification' (events-as-news) to the organizational course of action. The relations set up can be diagramed thus:

110

events → typification as news → organizational course of action

The schema at which Tuchman arrives can be seen as generated by the sociologist's work of inquiry, involving precisely that shift in meaning from Level One to Level Three described earlier. I suggest that the event-typification schema arises in something like the following fashion. Newspeople talk about their work and they talk about different types of news – spot news, developing news (as above), and continuing news. They talk to Gaye Tuchman, the ethnographer, about their work. In making descriptions of the work process, they transpose terms used in the ordinary course of their work to the language-game of description in which they are engaged with Tuchman. Their terms are then made use of referentially; that is, a descriptive game instructs the use of words, substantive nouns particularly, to reference objects taken to be identifiable independently of the game of description and existing as the ground of the description. Tuchman (who did much observational work in the newspaper setting) did this kind of work herself. Thus the terms as used in the descriptive game, as they mean in a descriptive setting, become the sociologist's model for the organization of the phenomena in the original. Terms used descriptively are read to reference phenomena in the original setting. The descriptive method thus becomes treated as if it were the members' method of analyzing and recognizing their world for the purpose of acting in it. The entities constituted as there by the descriptive procedure are taken to be there in the same kind of way for newspeople at work.

Tuchman's formulation suggests that newspeople must first determine the character of events-as-news prior to subjecting them to routine processing and dissemination. Typification mediates events in the world and socially organized responses to them. I suggest that here she is working ideologically just as Jackson and I were when we had found a general way of talking about assigning and assignments. Typification as a sociological device ascribes the descriptive practices of the sociological reading to the social practices of members in the original. In the descriptive context, news appears to reference an object. Typification constitutes that object out of the whole cloth of the original observations and inquiry. However, if we begin with the original setting and the original organization of practices which put together what is sometimes spoken of as these different types of news, we would not find organized sequences of action corresponding to the model diagramed above. For example, developing news is organized by the timing of the events in relation to the process of getting the newspaper out as well as by the organization of the information process. Developing news is that information which is sufficient to make a news story but is incomplete, arrives just in time to be covered in a preliminary way, and gets into the paper that day. Its developing character then arises out of the organized practices which identify the story as incomplete.

Typically, the work of government and similar agencies in producing information or response to events which have been registered as news are called 'developments'. 'Developments' as a work process in the organization arise as, say, the city desk assigns a reporter to follow up the story. She telephones the government agency concerned for further information on a news story that has already been started. That further information to be sought, that further information when acquired, is a 'development'. The status of the event itself may not have changed at all. The relevant agency may have now decided to release information it had not released earlier. Developing news is not a type of news existing 'out there'. It *is* a particular conjunction of an organizational and inter-organizational course of action (including the timing of release of information by agencies who are sources) with the production schedule of the newspaper.

Spot news is a further example. It too is a particular course of action. In the organizational processes, as Jackson and I observed in the newsroom setting of our study, 'spot news' arose in a sequence beginning with monitoring the police radio, radio network broadcasts, and other reports. This is a continuous process of routine attention done in the newspaper we observed at the city desk. Every now and again, an event is identified calling for the immediate and rapid mobilization of a reporter and possibly a photographer to go to the actual location. In this process, there is no moment at which a categorization procedure intervenes. The event does not have to be first identified as spot news. (It is hard to get beyond descriptions of this type.) If you examine this further, you find that spot news is and can only be defined in relation to the pace and timing of the newspaper itself. It is news which requires a reporter to be on the spot to observe and report events. It would seem then to have that as its determinate character. But its character of immediacy is by no means a simple property of the event. As a type of news, it arises in social relations among newspapers and other news sources. These are competitive. Newspapers and other news sources compete with one another directly when they publish on the same time band – that is, they are appearing to the public at about the same time. Events which are developing rapidly and are publicly available are fed very rapidly into the news system. A key thing in the formation of an event as spot news is the character of the news in relation to newspapers and news sources in competition with one another and the timing of the news process. The timing of the event coming over the monitor in relation to the production process of the newspaper and the time band of the competing news sources which may also pick up the event as news are also constitutive of spot news. If the event comes over the monitoring process early in the day in a daily newspaper going to press in the afternoon, it can be covered in a more routine way than if it comes in late in the day when it requires mobilization to draw reporters off other stories, possibly a reorganization of planned layout, and so forth, in order to get the news into the newspaper before the deadline.

Behind the term 'spot news' in Tuchman's account are yet more extended relations. Newspapers are tied into international networks of news sources. The timing of news of a particular event makes it a different type of news in different time zones. 'The New York Times London Bureau processes and relays international stories from far-flung regions of the world because the London time zone enables bureau members to get a jump on the schedules of people working in the New York time zone' (Tuchman 1973: 120).

It is in the context of such competitive relations that spot news arises and may be spoken of as spot news. It is a term which is not likely to be used to identify a class of events; it will be used rather in talking to the next shift about what happened, when the city editor reports to the managing editor, or the like. Spot news arises in this way in the work processes and relations of a particular newspaper and in the relation of that newspaper to others and other organizations. It becomes observable in the relations in which those particularly organized phases of activity are reported.

The term itself as a working term appears primarily in how it names and provides for the accountability of a type of work process, or a course of action.

Tuchman seeks to locate news as a socially constructed phenomenon. Therefore, she does not work by trying to establish criteria for the category in order to identify a determinate class of phenomena in the setting. This, of course, is the procedure which yields the 'literal description' problem referred to above (Sacks 1963; Wilson 1970). Nevertheless, her method conforms to the requirements of the descriptive language-game. She makes use of the device of 'typification' as a method of constructing the 'entity' corresponding to the category. Her description of 'developing news' formulates it as a type. 'Developing news' is news which concerns 'emergent situations', where information is incomplete and the account of the event is changing over the course of reporting it. In this way, she constructs a type as contrasted with a class of objects.

Tuchman's method also carefully grounds the typifications in the members' own knowledge of the world which is their practice and arises in their practice. Her informants' knowledge of how they do their work is a basic resource and also her methodological ground. Hence, the typification procedure may be and is attributed to the organization of the setting as the practices of members of the setting. The methodological sophistication of her work has its own traps. They are just those in which Jackson and I first walked into when elaborating the concept of 'assignment'.

These are some of the procedures by which the interpretive practices of the descriptive language-game become an organization attributed to the setting itself. As terms are given a referential usage in the descriptive language-game, the device of typification constitutes the phenomena corresponding to them. In Tuchman's account of news, the organization is represented as:

event → typification → course of action

Such procedures are an ordinary feature of the syntactic forms summoned by the language-game of description. A virtually identical structure can be found above in my critique of Tuchman's method. It is used in the following statement: 'Events which are developing rapidly and are publicly available are fed very rapidly into the news system.'

In generating the order of terms in this fashion, an event is constituted as something already there prior to the process and independent of it. Events have definite properties and are capable of being the objects of action. The structure generating relations between the terms represents the sequence of a social course of action when it is treated descriptively. It is only on further investigation that the *essentially* 'colloquial' character of the statement becomes apparent.

For Marx, the categories of a given social formation express its social relations. True, there is ambiguity in Marx's account of the relation between the language of the social relations (or of the setting in the context of our work) and the language of the discourse. This can be seen in how he speaks interchangeably, though in different contexts, of social relations as *reflected* in the mind and the categories (of political economy) and as *expressing* the social relations of capitalism. This, I think, represents the presence of the double relation which has not yet developed as a distinctive aperture in the social consciousness. Thus, it is present but as yet not expressed in the categories distinctly. On the one hand, we have the categories of the discourse and their relation to the setting expressed in the relation of 'reflection' in the mind, and on the other, the social relations of the setting 'expressed' in its categories. None the less, it is clear that in neither case does his method permit categories to float free from the constraints of the social relations they express. The conceptual procedures must make explicit in thought the social relations of the original. The ordering of categories must be generated by conceptual procedures isomorphic with an actual organization.

In search of a method from Marx for sociological description, we can seek a similar grounding for the terms of the setting in its social relations. Though they may perhaps reflect the social relations of the setting, they do not name them. We have to take them up rather differently. They are working terms. And we must in the course of our investigation at some point depend upon the informants' description of their setting. If for example we treat news as naming something, we will locate ourselves on this side of the language which describes and from which we must learn the setting. Here it becomes a veil. Our problem begins with the social relations which make it possible to speak of news as 'out there'. It is also possible to speak of it as routinely processed and produced in a course of action, and possible to speak of it as it is taken up by those who read what appears in newspapers as news. Similarly, of course, the solution to how it is possible to speak of 'assigning' and 'assignments' and to point to pieces of paper, to describe courses of action, and perform 'assigning', is not to be found by assembling these moments as a type, but by an explication of the social relations in the context of which these usages make their current sense. If we see that the terms of the setting must be taken up as expressing its social relations rather than as categorization procedures, and hence that a work of inquiry must investigate the social relations in which such usages as these and others are both possible and sensible in that context, we will be able to move to a non-ideological method of sociological description.

CONCLUSION

The problem this chapter has addressed is that of the indeterminacy of the relation between the descriptive language and the actuality it intends. This is the problem raised for us by ethnomethodology. It is clearly central in the position put forward by Silverman, which denies the very possibility of the descriptive claim (Silverman 1972). It is clearly present in the questions raised by Cicourel (1969) and by Zimmerman and Pollner (1971) of the relation between social categories or descriptive categories and the phenomena they name. It is raised by Wilson (1970) and Sacks (1963) in their discussions of the problem of literal description. It is also present in a less explicitly analyzable form in the problem presented by Garfinkel of background knowledge as an essential and implicit resource in sociological accounts of settings (Garfinkel 1968).

This indeterminacy has been the topic of the chapter. The method we have undertaken is derived from Marx. It readdresses the problem by locating the categories of description in the first place in the setting they describe and viewing them at the primary level; that is, at the level of their usage in the original as expressing the social relations of that setting. In that setting, they are not indeterminate. In that setting, their uses are (generally) not descriptive. It is only in the specialized relation between ethnographer and informant or between ethnographer as informant and the professional discourse which her work mediates that the indeterminacy arises.

Descriptions, we suggested, are a particular type of language-game. The indeterminacy problem arises in part as terms are transported from the original setting to the language-game of descriptions in which the governing interpretive procedure is no longer that of their everyday use (Wittgenstein 1953). Referencing and coding are not the only mode in which substantive terms can mean. The method of using words in the original setting is modified in the setting of descriptions.

The radical indeterminacy of the ethnomethodological critique can be seen to arise in a special relation of the sociological discourse to its setting. It is one occurring at the conjuncture of bureaucratic/professional forms of discourse and the lived world which the sociologist addresses and investigates. This double relation is unavoidable. The special problems located by ethno-methodology can be seen as distinctive to categories of description (or more generally, categories of factual accounts) devised by the discourse and imposed upon the lived world. The 'deep' problem is one which comes about because the categories used in doing factual accounts do not arise in the setting itself, and do not conform in any way to its social relations, but are pieces of the bureaucratic/professional apparatus, parts of its enterprise, and do its work and mean as they mean in that context. The sociologist's ordinary work goes from what she learns in any way she learns it in the setting she will describe, to factual accounts subjected to this further wrenching of the sense she has learnt how to make. The mediating process is descriptive.

Even when the sociologist works with a commitment to the members' own method of constructing their world, with members' own knowledge of the setting and with the members' practices as the phenomena of her investigation, the mediating descriptive work transforms imperceptibly the ways the terms of the setting mean. The referencing practices of the language-game of des-cription intend objects and entities. She looks for objects and entities in members' practices. In looking for them, she finds them. She constructs them using devices such as typification. The ordering of the descriptive procedure thus becomes the ordering attributed to courses of action and to the social relations of the setting itself.

I have suggested that the indeterminacy problem as posed by ethnomethodology has its particular place in a particular form of 'the double relation'. The direction of our discussion points to the possibility that matters which are essential problems in this relation can in fact provide the necessary basis for a different grounding of sociological description. Such a grounding begins from the essential presence of background expectations or background knowledge of social structures as an unexplicated resource in standard sociological accounts. It begins from the essential dependence of the observer's knowledge of a setting upon interpretation and her participation as a member in the constitution of the setting. With respect to the latter, it only assumes that part of the sociologist's work is or should be how she learns the setting as a set of social relations, or as a social form. Thus, a method inquiring into the social relations of the setting to make these explicit in description must begin with the language uses of the setting, and with the speech of those who are members of the setting to the sociologist. As they tell her what is going on, and as they explain, name, and explicate ostensively, their teaching is continually informed by their implicit knowledge of the organization of the setting and the sense of what they say expresses that and depends on that. They can hear how the sociologist's questions do not quite make sense. Their own knowledge of the social relations of the setting enters into how their description makes sense to them.

Thus, we can begin with the notion that there is already an intimate linkage between the terms members use to describe settings to newcomers and the social organization of the setting described. The social organization is always necessarily 'present' in the description, and the description depends upon it though it does not explicate it. It depends upon it in a manner analogous to how phenomenology sees the relation between the pre-predicative level of knowing and the predicative. What is said necessarily depends upon a knowing which is prior to speaking and provides for it. Similarly, the doing of a setting's description depends upon a knowledge of the organization of that setting prior to des-cription, and prior to the interpretive work involved in going from that to the forms of knowledge of the discourse. This organization is already 'in' the description.

How the describer who is a member of the setting does her

description is controlled by her knowledge of the socially organized processes in which the terms and how they mean are embedded. The sense that they do and can make in the descriptive context is 'controlled' by her knowledge of the social organization of the setting. There is the possibility, then, of tracking back through a description – as I began to do with Tuchman's work – and of doing a sociological description differently. It must be emphasized that *this is necessarily an inquiry*. It is not done just by reading the descriptive work and thinking back through (though perhaps more could be done in this way than we might think). If we track back through the description to that 'background knowledge of social structures' on which it depends, we can take that up as analogous to a grammar.

There is a constraint on how many terms may be used and seen as properly used, which the describers' knowledge of their setting imposes on the uses of terms and the relations they may enter into. The organization of the setting is, I suggest, present in those constraints. There is an interrelation of the speech of a setting and description based on the speech of the setting to the social relations organizing the setting. We can recognize it in the 'normative' moment of hearing how we do not know how to speak in settings to which we are newcomers. This experience points to what is known but not available. The preliminary analysis of the social relations of news, developed in the critique made of Tuchman's work above, suggests what such a description might look like. Another example can be found in Jackson's work where she contrasts the conventional sociological mode of description with an explicative description of the same social process in a newsroom (Jackson 1974). But, at this time, only the elementary claim is made that members' background knowledge of social organization and relations is buried in how they can speak of what they do and know and is transmitted to any description that is built on that, whether it is systematically explicated or no. It is this hidden presence that we are trying to find out how to describe.

THE ACTIVE TEXT: A TEXTUAL ANALYSIS OF THE SOCIAL RELATIONS OF PUBLIC TEXTUAL DISCOURSE[1]

TEXTS AS CONSTITUENTS OF SOCIAL RELATIONS

Textual materials have generally presented themselves to the sociologist as sources of information about something else, rather than as phenomena in their own right. This is, however, beginning to change. A body of work is beginning to emerge, at present very eclectic in its strategies and thematic foci, but having in common the text as a distinct phenomenon for sociological investigation. A partial list of work of this kind would include William Darrough (1978), Beng-Huat Chua (1979), Peter Eglin (1979), Alasdair McHoul (1981), Ken Morrison (1981), Bryan Green (1983), as well as my own studies appearing in Chapters 2 and 3 of this volume; there are no doubt others. Though there is a common source for some of these in ethnomethodology, the approaches are very various. Darrough (the original investigator of the texts that Eglin used and I am exploring here) exhibits the dialectical process at work in the contradictions between two versions of reality as an aspect of a social process; Eglin uses these two contradictory versions of the same event to elicit readers' methods of handling reality disjunctures; Morrison explicates structural properties accomplishing the specific character of the text as such; and Chua focuses on texts as aspects of a political process. In spite of their variety, the approaches share a presupposition from which this chapter attempts systematically to depart. I shall call it the assumption of the inertia of the text. All the analytic strategies presuppose the text as something that appears before the sociologist already in its character as a specimen, inert, dead, and out of context. Even when analysis focuses upon the reader's interaction with the text, as does McHoul's, the text itself appears as inoperative, uncontexted. Even when it is contexted and represented as part of an active process of dialogue, as it is in Darrough's work, the analysis itself still works from the presupposition of the inertia of the text, the dead text which the sociologist has read for its content, finding in that the dialectic of social conflict. The active text, by contrast, might be thought of as more like a crystal which bends the light as it passes through. The text itself is to be seen as organizing a course of concerted social action. As an operative part of a social relation it is activated, of course, by the reader but its structuring effect is its own.

That it is activated by the reader means that the activity or operation of the text is dependent upon the reader's interpretive practices. These too are constituents of social relations rather than merely the idiosyncrasies of individuals. They are social in origin and built into social relations. Analysis, therefore, depends upon the analyst-as-member's knowledge of the interpretive practices and schemata relevant to the reading of a particular text.

This must be made a self-conscious matter, for our analysis of texts finds in them only what we know how to read from them. Analysis therefore draws on our competences as members. The interpretive practices deployed in analyzing the text must be those which the text intends. The assumption here is that the text intends methods and schemata of interpretation and that these can be recovered through analysis. If the reader's interpretive practices conform to those intended by the text, analysis will display *how* the text makes sense (in those respects on which the research is focused). The capacity of analysis to disclose the accomplishment of the text's coherence is the proof (in the pudding sense) that the analyst has brought to the text an interpretive schema it intends. The enterprise depends upon the possibility of being wrong. It depends upon the possibility that the analyst may lack competence and the text, therefore, be impenetrable to her inquiry. From time to time, of course, genuinely incoherent texts are produced, but great care must be taken in assigning texts to this class since text for which the reader does not command the interpretive key will be incoherent for that reader.[2]

The investigation of texts as constituents of social relations offers access to the ontological ground of institutional processes which organize, govern, and regulate the kind of society in which we live, for these are to a significant degree forms of social action mediated by texts. Bureaucracy, professional and scientific discourse, objective forms of management, are in various ways dependent upon textual communications, increasingly, of course, in the form of computer print-outs or video displays, but textual none the less. If we have not seen the text as an active constituent of organizational process, it is, I think, because we are ourselves so habituated to its use, to its appearance before us in that simple moment of engagement in which we seek to find out what it says and take what we have learned from it as our resource, rather than addressing that process as a topic. The text comes before us without any apparent attachments. It seems to stand on its own, to be inert, without impetus or power. But in the situations of our everyday life as contrasted with our scholarly activities, we find texts operative in many ways. We fill in forms to register for conferences; we receive brochures informing us about the prices and appurtenances of hotels; we write cheques and show our driver's licenses; we make use of credit cards. We are constantly engaged in textually mediated forms of action which are somehow efficacious. We engage with textual materials daily as we read the newspaper, or, if I extend the notion of text, as we watch television. Perhaps, as I am, we might be trying to replace a kitchen appliance and have been studying the advertisements in *Buy and Sell*. In our work situations, the textual flow and our part in it is virtually a continuous part of our daily routine. The level of textual flow of information in the organizations we work for is an aspect of our working lives we complain about but endure. We are continually writing memos; we receive salary statements itemizing deductions; we go to the dentist and make a claim (if you have a dental plan) for reimbursement; we prepare a curriculum vitae when an application for a travel grant is made and fill in the relevant forms; we write course descriptions, prepare bibliographies, etc. The textual event is pervasive yet almost entirely unnoticed. Face-to-face communication has been the archetypical sociological phenomenon and with its fascinating equivocalities has upstaged the mundane and often tiresomely impenetrable universe of textual communication and textually mediated action.

This chapter investigates texts as active constituents of the social relations of public textual discourse. It is concerned with the *active* ways in which texts organize relations within textual discourse, both with respect to how local happenings are entered into its interpretive practices and to how its social relations are organized. By 'public textual discourse' I refer to that order of social relations mediated by texts which is otherwise identified by such terms as 'public opinion', 'mass communications', and the like. These are social relations which arise on the basis of mass media of communication but their social character cannot be reduced to their material organization. They constitute a discrete order of social relations characterized by the detachment of discourse from the locally situated speaker and her particular biography, the substitution of categorical forms for actual members and of accounts for actual events, the anonymity of readers (or watchers) and the one-way movement of messages. It is a medium in which the world exists for the participant as a textual construct, and in which belief is a commitment to one construct rather than another, and arises quite differently from the immediacies of our experienced reality. The textual analysis presented here will focus upon social construction of such commitment.

The analysis and discussion presented here is concerned with two texts.[3] One is a letter with editorial comments published in an underground newspaper in Berkeley, California, in the 1960s. It describes a confrontation between police and people on the street, written by a professor who observed it. The letter charges the police with attempting to provoke the crowd and with an excessive and arbitrary use of force. The second text is a response from the Mayor of Berkeley claiming, on the basis of an internal investigation, that the police acted entirely properly. The Mayor's response was distributed in stores and banks, etc., throughout the community.[4] It presents an alternative account of the events, redescribing them as proper police procedure. It also asks the public to become more sophisticated as readers of the news by learning how easy it is for the naïve to misinterpret what may be seen on the streets, read about in the news, or seen on television.

The two texts have been the topic of two previous papers (Darrough 1978; and Eglin 1979). When I first encountered them I addressed the texts as both Darrough and Eglin do, by focusing upon the problem of two versions of the same event. In addressing the problem of how they were actively at work in the context of the social relations in which they arose I found that this approach would not answer as a means of making their activity observable. Indeed it became apparent that the equivocality of the two versions of the same event arose not from how the texts worked in the local historical context in which they originated, but in the context of the academic setting and the academic relation in which they were researched.

It is only in the latter setting that the texts are both available to us together at one moment in time, allowing us to move back and forth between them, comparing the two accounts, and so confronting the intrinsic insolubility of the issue of which is true. But in the original setting, the texts do not appear like that. They appear, indeed, one after the other, first the appearance in the *Berkeley Barb* of the Professor's letter and then the Mayor's response. For a local reader, encountering both, there would be a course of reading, a definite sequence, and hence the experience in reading of going from one to the other in which her commitment undergoes the active work of each. It is the sequence of the reading, the relations into which that is inserted, and the relations organized in that active and interactive sequencing of texts which is our concern here. The first text poses a problem or a 'challenge'; the second operates on the first to structure for the reader a definite reflection working retroactively upon the experience of that reading.

Let me reintroduce briefly the notion of social relation. In the previous chapter (Chapter 4) I developed the term not to identify a particular class of social events, but to identify how individuals' actual practices are articulated to and coordinated in social courses of action. As a concept it enables us to locate particular analytic sites, particular experiences, or 'evidences' (such as these texts) of a social process, as constituents of sequences of action in which many individuals and many individual courses of action play a part. Actual sites, experiences, or evidenced events are located in temporally ordered sequences of social action. Social relations appear as patterned and recurrent in the methodical accomplishment of the orderly social character of events, things, persons, objects, etc., but are not to be sought as the recurrence of patterned sequences of action.

The notion of social relation thus introduces the idea of actions concerted in time as well as the more familiar concept of the methodical character of their concerting. In taking up a text as a constituent of a social relation, we are constrained not only to understand it as a moment in a sequence, but also to recognize that the interpretive practices which activate it are embedded in a relational process. Textual practices are operative in the work of accomplishing the social relations in which texts occur.

The two texts are operative in the social relations of the public textual discourse. They originate in a specific local context to which it is articulated. Though clearly the membrane between discourse and 'everyday life' is permeable, the interpretive schemata used in these texts to evaluate the propriety of police procedure are properties of discourse and do not refer to the legal and administrative definitions and everyday working rules actually governing the activities of the Berkeley police force. Of course people make use of schemata of discourse to interpret everyday experience, though perhaps most compellingly when it is to be made accountable, when it is to be reported, for example. Darrough (1978) is no doubt perfectly correct in arguing that the citizen generally misconceives the nature of police practice, but in terms of our interests here, what he describes as their misconceptions locate social relations organizing the translation of actual police practices into the public textual discourse through which they become known and interpreted to 'citizens'.

TWO TEXTS: TWO VERSIONS

The two texts (presented virtually complete below) entered the public textual discourse at a particular moment in local political history. They articulate the local political struggle between the 'movement' (linking anti-Vietnam war organization with countercultural values and way of life) and the local representatives of law enforcement to the wider national public textual discourse. Their immediate context was a local history of confrontations between 'movement' people and the police. Shortly before the publication of the Professor's letter in the *Berkeley Barb* a rally had been held without permit and the police had been ordered by City Council to disband it. The resulting resistance led to the imposition (requested by the police) of a curfew on the city. Enforcing it produced many complaints of harassment and the excessive use of force. When this problem was raised in City

125

Council, a majority voted to condemn police behavior. The Mayor was strongly opposed to the motion. Thus there was already polarization on the issue and the response of the public at large as voters was clearly of importance to the Mayor and Chief of Police.[5]

Both texts in different ways also make connections with the larger, wider set of relations of the public textual discourse. The first text, the Professor's letter (A), was published as a letter with editorial comment in an underground newspaper with a wide circulation beyond as well as in the Bay area. The second text had a narrower circulation. It was put out in mimeographed form by the Mayor's office and distributed to the public through stores, banks, etc.[6] Both documents contain internal references to the wider context of the public textual discourse. Text A, the Professor's, explicitly construes what he saw as a local expression of 'law and order' Wallace or Chicago style. Text B, the Mayor's, is concerned not only with the incident reported by the Professor, but with a second case (not discussed here) of a newspaper picture of police struggling with a young woman which had been circulated nationally. As a result, the Mayor had received critical letters from other parts of the country. Each text ties its references to a wider public discourse. Each is an operative constituent of the social relations of public textual discourse, and was 'actively at work' in their organization.

We have no means of telling how these texts were actually taken up and how therefore their activity was accomplished in that taking up by unknown readers. We can only address the operating properties of the texts in tying a local political context with the wider public textual discourses. We can recognize two sides. We can also recognize that there is a third party, not active in the confrontations between the two sides, but whose relation to such events is constituted by the social relations of the public textual discourse; whose interrelations are one-sided as readers, watchers, and hearers (not as speakers), who are unknown other than as, like the Professor, they write a letter to a newspaper; who are also voters. This is the public whose interconnections are created by newspaper and magazine subscriptions, by newsstands, bookstores, television sets, radios, etc., whose responses are constituted as 'opinion' by pollsters.

As I have said, occasionally they/we write letters to newspapers. And here is one of them, the Professor. Not a hippie, not a beatnik as he takes care to point out (76).[7] He is a 'law-abiding, tax-paying, property-owning citizen' (78–9). He witnessed a series of events on Telegraph Avenue on the evening of 9 September 1968, which led him to write a letter to the Chief of Police in Berkeley and to send a copy of that letter to an underground newspaper. The letter thus represents an individual member of the public who has openly on this issue aligned himself with the 'movement'.

The Mayor's response conforms to this convention. His letter is addressed to the Professor. It contains an abridged version of the Professor's letter and the substance of a report from the Police Chief. But it is also a public document. The interchange between Professor and Mayor is enacted in public. The frame established for the public reading of this exchange in the Mayor's letter is announced in the heading as 'The difficulties of law enforcement on Telegraph Avenue'. The exchange of letters between Professor and Mayor, contained in the Mayor's response, illustrates the difficulties. As I mentioned earlier, the exchange of letters was followed by an account of an article which had appeared in the 'regular press' with a photograph of 'two Berkeley policemen holding a blonde young woman who had just been arrested'. The widespread publication of this picture resulted in critical response, one of which from a minister in Flint, Michigan, is included. The whole concludes with a paragraph urging the public to become more sophisticated.

> It is obvious that in an era of instant, capsule news there is an urgency that the public becomes more sophisticated in its viewpoint toward the news, an urgency that the young be educated to get the full story before reaching conclusions, an urgency that the difficulties of law enforcement in a permissive society be recognized.

Here then are the texts.[8]

Part A: the Professor's letter

Bravo! Prof. Challenges Chief

Chief of Police
Berkeley Police Department
Berkeley, California

127

Sir:

001 Yesterday (Monday), September 9, between 6:15 and 6:30 pm, I was
002 personally witness to what must have been a classical exercise in the
003 performance of 'law and order' Wallace or Chicago style, only it was in
004 Berkeley. As a naturalized, non-native American citizen who has seen
005 first-hand experience with Nazi and 'SS' tactics, I find it most difficult to
006 believe what I saw.
007   I was walking toward my car parked off Telegraph Avenue. On Haste
008 and Telegraph I saw several (three, I believe) police cars with four men
009 each. In front of Cody's two men, for whatever reason, were being dragged
010 to one of the patrol cars. Many people were standing round, watching
011 quietly.
012   I was standing just below the corner of Haste and Telegraph opposite
013 Cody's and I saw a boy, 16 or 17 years old, walking up Haste and past two
014 policemen.
015   Suddenly a young policeman in his early twenties, with a cigar he had
016 just lit in his mouth, grabbed this young man, rudely spun him around,
017 pinned him against his patrol car, tore at his clothes and pockets as though
018 searching for something, without so much as saying one word of explanation.
019 Then he pushed him roughly up the street yelling at him to get
020 moving.

'Never forget'

021   I shall never forget the face of that policemen, his eyes bulging out, his face
022 distorted by a vile sneer, his whole countenance exuding hatred, his cigar
023 arrogantly sticking out of that obscene mouth. It was a frightening sight,
024 especially to someone uninitiated to police tactics such as I was.
025   Then several things happened: in a doorway a few yards away a young
026 woman of 18–19 years was standing holding a baby in her arms.
027 Suddenly two policemen, no, two uniformed thugs, were upon her,
028 seemingly trying to pull her into a car but at the same time trying to tear
029 the baby from her, tearing, pulling, pushing, quite oblivious to the tragedy
030 which might have ensued had the baby been dropped and likely trampled
031 upon in the melee.
032   Nearby another equally young girl was on the pavement and I saw a
033 cop's club repeatedly descending on her with all might!
034 What a sickening sight! A huge, strong man having the audacity to beat
035 up a young girl in open view of a hundred people!
036   I had moved out of the way in the meantime, across the street. Several
037 people were yelling at the uniformed hoods to lay off the girls and the baby.
038 Some people yelled 'pigs'. I would have joined them but I was unable
039 to say anything. Besides, such an epithet, I am now convinced, was much
040 too mild for the perpetrators of such bestiality.
041   Of course, I am only speaking of the 4–5 individuals actually involved
042 in those acts of violence, not the many policemen who were standing around
043 with their clubs ready, though these, because they failed to restrain their
044 comrades were no less guilty.

Hate

045 Then an empty beer can flew across the street hitting the pavement harm-
046 lessly. Immediately, the young, cigar-smoking cop sprinted across the
047 street charging like a vicious bull, the most vicious and horrifying look of
048 hatred and contempt on his contorted face, his club raised, shouting. If hate
049 could kill, that savage's look would have killed everyone in sight.
050 How can a man be entrusted with safeguarding the law and protecting
051 the citizens, all citizens, if he becomes so easily the victim of such neurotic
052 behavior that blinds him to all reason?
053 In a split second this savage and another cop were upon a young man,
054 clubbing him to the ground, twisting his arm on his back, then literally
055 sitting on the man's head.
056 Why? I presume that they thought that he had thrown that harmless
057 empty beer can, but I am ready to state under oath – and I will – that
058 that young man did in fact not throw the can. As all others around him he
059 was merely an aroused, ired, angered bystander.
060 But what's the difference? All the uniformed thugs wanted was some-
061 one to vent their spleen on.

Charges

062 I herewith state and charge that from all evident appearances the entire
063 fracas had been staged and organized by the police in an obvious attempt to
064 provoke the people there into a confrontation with the heavily armed cops.
065 Witness the presence of several squad cars with four men in each at the
066 scene already, or within minutes of the beginning.
067 I further charge that the policemen used force which was totally out of
068 keeping with the reality of the situation, and blatantly directed at a few,
069 selected victims.
070 I accuse the involved savage cops with actions and behavior totally
071 unbecoming civilized human beings, actions which degraded the concept of
072 justice and of true law and order.
073 The fact that only relatively few of the police were involved in the
074 actual perpetration of the crimes against the people, as described above, is
075 in no way a mitigating circumstance.

Not hippie

076 I am neither a hippie nor a beatnik. For the past four years I have been a
077 member of the faculty of the University of Santa Clara. I am what is
078 commonly referred to as a law-abiding, tax-paying, property-owning
079 citizen. As such, but not only as such, as a human being, I have the right to
080 demand an explanation for the events as outlined above.
081 I further demand a full investigation without delay in the events of
082 yesterday, with particular attention directed at the savage actions of the
083 cigar-smoking policeman, those who so violently and viciously struggled
084 with the woman and the baby, and those who clubbed a defenseless girl on
085 the pavement.

Determined

086   I am prepared, willing and able to identify the thugs involved and to testify
087   under oath before a court or grand jury on the events in the late afternoon
088   of Monday, September 9, 1968 at Telegraph and Haste.
089   I am determined to see the matter through and I will not allow myself
090   to be put off by a few meaningless words of reply from you.

> Ernesto G. Auerbach
> Santa Clara, California

cc. Mayor Wallace Johnson

Afterthought

Sept. 11, 1968

Editor:
091   As an afterthought I am sending you the enclosed copy of a letter to the
092   Berkeley Chief of Police. It is self-explanatory. Please read it. The incident
093   described in it is only a 'minor' one, perhaps, but to me it exemplifies what
094   is becoming more and more the standard operating procedure of the police
095   in this country.

> Sincerely yours,
> Ernesto G. Auerbach
> (*Berkeley Barb*, 12–19 September 1968, no. 161, p.3)

Part B: The Mayor's response

September 26, 1968

Wallace Johnson
Mayor of Berkeley

The difficulties of law enforcement on Telegraph Avenue

096   The difficulty of law enforcement on Telegraph Avenue (the 2400 block) is
097   illustrated by a recent letter to the Mayor and the Police Chief. Pertinent
098   excerpts from this letter:

September 10, 1968

Sir:
099   Yesterday, September 9, between 6:15 and 6:30pm ... I was walking
100   toward my car parked off Telegraph Avenue. On Haste and Telegraph I
101   saw several (three, I believe) police cars with four men each. In front of
102   Cody's two men, for whatever reason, were being dragged to one of the
103   patrol cars ... and I saw a boy, 16 or 17 years old, walking up Haste and
104   past two policemen.
105   Suddenly a young policeman ... grabbed this young man, rudely spun

106 him around, pinned him against his patrol car, tore at his clothes and
107 pockets as though searching for something, without so much as saying one
108 word of explanation....
109   Then several things happened: in a doorway a few yards away a young
110 woman of 18–19 years was standing holding a baby in her arms. Suddenly
111 two policemen ... were upon her, seemingly trying to pull her into a car but
112 at the same time trying to tear the baby from her, tearing, pulling, pushing.
113 ... Nearby another equally young girl was on the pavement and I saw a
114 cop's club repeatedly descending on her with all might.... I had moved out
115 of the way in the meantime, across the street.... Then an empty beer can
116 flew across the street hitting the pavement harmlessly. Immediately, the
117 young cop sprinted across the street ... his club raised, shouting.... In a
118 split second this savage and another cop were upon a young man, clubbing
119 him into the ground, twisting his arm on his back, then literally sitting on
120 the man's head. Why? ... I am ready to state under oath – and I will –
121 that that young man did in fact not throw the can....
122   I herewith state and charge that from all evident appearances the
123 entire fracas had been staged and organized by the police in an obvious
124 attempt to provoke the people there into a confrontation with the heavily
125 armed cops. Witness the presence of several squad cars with four men in
126 each at the scene already, or within minutes of the beginning....

127   Before the Police Chief or I received the letter quoted, it had been
128 published in toto as a feature article in the local underground press.
129   Promptly upon the receipt of this letter I telephoned the man and suggested
130 he come to see me. He did. I listened to the full story of the incidents he
131 observed and assured him that I would investigate the incidents and advise
132 him of what I could determine. I did:

September 19, 1968

Dear

133   In accordance with our conversations on the subject of the incidents at
134 Telegraph and Haste on September 9, I have checked into the matter and
135 advise you as follows:
136   You referred to four incidents which you were able to at least partially
137 observe. The first concerned a young man who was frisked and who
138 appeared to be then released. In fact this man was a juvenile who
139 was arrested and charged with being a minor in possession of alcoholic
140 beverages. He pleaded guilty and the court suspended judgement. This
141 young man was one of three involved in the event which precipitated the
142 subsequent events to which you refer.
143   The second incident you referred to involved a young woman with a
144 child. Investigation revealed that this young woman was screaming vile
145 profanity at the police and was agitating the crowd. Two officers
146 approached her in front of 2441 Haste Street, informing her that she was
147 under arrest. The woman and an unidentified man standing next to her
148 were holding a baby. The man stated that the police officers were not going
149 to take her away and the couple locked arms. The officers attempted
150 to talk to the woman, but she continued screaming and swearing. At one
151 point another of the officers reached for the baby, intending to give it to the

152 man, who appeared to be her husband. One of the officers talked to the
153 woman and endeavored to start her toward the patrol car. It became
154 apparent to the officers that arresting her would be an extremely difficult
155 task, because of her attitude and because of the baby, and the officers
156 retired without arresting her. To the best of my ability to investigate this
157 matter, I do not find that there was any pulling, tearing, or shoving of the
158 woman in this incident.
159   The third incident to which you referred involved another woman. To
160 the best of my knowledge, you are referring to a young woman who was
161 attempting to interfere with the arrest of a man who had attacked a police
162 officer, punching him and ripping the officer's holster in a strenuous effort
163 to seize his gun. Throughout the struggle involving this man and the police
164 officer, this woman kept screaming and attempting to grab the man away
165 from the officers. She was on the ground next to him when he was subdued
166 but she was, to the best of my investigation, never struck with a baton or hit
167 with a fist....
168   The fourth incident you related involved the beer can and the man who
169 was arrested at the time the beer can was thrown. You are quite correct,
170 the man arrested was not the man who threw the beer can. The man who
171 threw the can was initially pursued by the officer but as he started this
172 pursuit he was body-blocked by the man who was arrested. This man was
173 caught and arrested after a brief struggle. He was charged with resisting
174 arrest. He pleaded guilty and was given a suspended judgement on penalty
175 of five days in the County Jail.
176   Regarding the last paragraph on the second page of your letter, there
177 is no evidence that the 'entire fracas had been staged and organized'. You
178 must keep in mind ... that these incidents you observed, however exciting
179 and unusual to you, represent a typical problem at the present time on
180 Telegraph Avenue. A simple arrest is likely to escalate to a major happen-
181 ing because so frequently a crowd of people gathers and tries to interfere
182 with the making of an arrest. In this case the arrest of three people
183 for drinking in public resulted in the several incidents you mentioned.
184 Because of the difficulty of making arrests in this area without interference
185 from the people in the vicinity, the Berkeley Police have found it necessary
186 to use more than one man at a time.... Therefore it is not at all surprising
187 that when the crowd gathered because of the original arrest, additional
188 police officers were promptly summoned to handle the situation....
189   Thank you for relating to me your civic concern. I am sure we both
190 share a common desire to cultivate respect for law and law enforcement
191 officers, and at the same time to insure that professional conduct is
192 observed at all times.

THE DIRECTLY VERSUS THE ORGANIZATIONALLY KNOWN

Both texts in different ways provide an account lifting a particular
local event into public textual discourse. Though we cannot trace
the social production of these accounts independently of what
they themselves have to tell us about it, each displays the social
organization of its grounding in an actuality. Again I would remind

the reader that what we are addressing is the events as worked up in accounts of them and never the events themselves.

The version in the Professor's letter is that of a witness to the events (002). He is careful to detail his location in relation to the events and to indicate his moves from one to another.

> I was walking toward my car parked off Telegraph Avenue. On Haste and Telegraph I saw....
>
> (007–8)

> I was standing just below the corner of Haste and Telegraph opposite Cody's and I saw....
>
> (012–13)

> ...in a doorway a few yards away....
>
> (025)

> Nearby another equally young girl....
>
> (032)

> I had moved out of the way in the meantime, across the street.
>
> (036)

The organization of observation is from where he is located. His account is carefully restricted to the temporal and spatial boundaries of his witnessing of the events. If he spoke to anyone also present to ask about what had gone on before he arrived or what was happening as supplement to his own observation, that is not recorded. Everything that is presented here is presented as what he saw. He arrives in the middle of police action. Two men were 'being dragged to one of the patrol cars' (009–10). The boundaries of his witnessing are marked by the phrase 'for whatever reason' (009). He makes no attempt to extrapolate to what happened before his arrival on the scene.

Descriptions of police behavior provide primary detail of a kind determined by an actual seeing. For example:

> ...a young policeman in his early twenties, with a cigar he had just lit in his mouth, grabbed this young man, rudely spun

him around, pinned him against his patrol car, tore at his
clothes and pockets as though searching for something without so much as saying one word of explanation.

(015–18)

Vivid detailing of police appearance and actions is central to
each episode. It marks the description as an observed description,
and one to which the observer responds with feeling:

I shall never forget the face of that policeman, his eyes bulging out, his face distorted by a vile sneer, his whole countenance exuding hatred, his cigar arrogantly sticking out of
that obscene mouth. It was a frightening sight....

(021–3)

The writing communicates a vivid present to the reader.
Witnessing implies the presence of the witness at the events of
which he writes. He plays this role *vis-à-vis* his reader, he is witness;
in the original events, he is participant.

The personages of the event constructed as text are the police
(and their permutations, 'thugs' etc.), the crowd, men and women
who are the object of police action, and the witness. The character
of the witness is not submerged in any other category in the
account. He is there watching. He does not become involved. His
relation to events is distanced by his seeing.

I saw several ... police cars.   (008)

I saw a boy....   (013)

I saw a cop's club repeatedly descending on her....   (032–3)

When the action gets close, he moves out of the way (036). He
describes no impetus to intervene. When the crowd responds, he
is tempted to join them but does not.

Some people yelled 'pigs'. I would have joined them but I was
unable to say anything.

(038–9)

The separation between himself and 'crowd' is clearly maintained, even when he responds to what he observes with an inclination to react as they do.

The police as a group are differentiated. A distinction is made between 'the 4–5 individuals actually involved in those acts of violence' and 'the many policemen who were standing around with their clubs ready' (041–3). More central, however, is the identification of one particular policeman, who is preserved as a character throughout and who plays a major role in initiating random violence in two of the episodes. Eight lines in all (015–16, 021–3, 046–8) are given to descriptions of his appearance. One such description has been cited above (021–3).

These are not the categories of the original event, they express the active relation between the original event and its determinate social properties and how it is made accountable with the production of the text. For example, the logic of description located in the null point (Schutz 1962b) of an observer and witness excludes the subject from the crowd, just as to the writer of a letter home from Hawaii, the place is full of tourists. To an actor in the events themselves, playing a differentiated role, a member of the police for example, the witness would have been one of the crowd. This witness sets himself off from the crowd in a way which distinctly represents his character as witness of, rather than participant in, the events, a stance consistent with his identification as 'citizen' and not 'hippie or beatnik'.

By contrast, the Mayor's version in document B has been assembled quite differently. It too has the character of being overheard in that it contains both an abridged version of the Professor's letter and a letter in reply from the Mayor in a frame which generalizes the significance of this exchange for more general problems in 'law enforcement'. The Mayor's reply to the Professor's letter is presented as the product of internal investigation. This is made visible in the account at a number of points:

I have checked into the matter and advise you as follows:

(134–5)

Investigation revealed....   (144)

To the best of my ability to investigate this matter....   (156-7)

...to the best of my investigation....   (166)

The knowledge therefore does not arise as a continuity of observation by one individual and is not situated in relation to his context of observation. It arises presumably from a number of individuals, namely the police, who were present themselves, on that occasion, who will presumably have already filed a report and to whom further questions could have been addressed. The basis of the account is itself organizational.

The account appears to us a report without a reporter, hence having the character of a presentation of the events without an intermediary. This gives us that effect of objectivity which results from the structural erasure of the witnesses to the original events as tellers of the tale. Here again we can mark a contrast with the Professor's account where the witness was present at the events and also speaks as himself directly in making his account. In the Mayor's account, the Mayor and his office, the Chief of the Berkeley Police and his organizational process, mediate invisibly between us and those who witnessed from the other side. The presence of this organizational erasure is implicit in the appearance the account has of not being constructed from the experience and accounts of the police.

The categories of persons present in the Mayor's version are not the same as those present in the Professor's version. The Professor himself is not, of course, observable. The crowd has almost disappeared, appearing only in the reasons given for the police attempt to arrest the woman holding the baby (she was 'agitating the crowd' (145)). It includes the set of persons against whom police action is taken, adding to them two additional people. The character of the account as organizational is further exhibited in the lack of differentiation between police who were active in the events and those standing around. All police in the account are interchangeable.

The knowledge embodied in the account has also a distinctly organizational character. Take, for example, the identification of the young man in the first incident as a 'juvenile' (138). The term and its application are essentially organizational functions. Identifying an individual as a member of this category is an essentially organizational accomplishment. The record constituting the permanent organizational relation between that individual and the organizational course of action defining him as a juvenile is also an organizational product and is stored in the organization's files. This organizational form of memory is complemented by the continuity of police work on a particular beat and hence by police knowledge of a particular area and its habitués. The category thus presupposes a complex institutional division of labor and processes of concerted action. Its use in a particular local context draws in relations which extend beyond it. Further, the Mayor's versions of the incidents refer in other ways to extended organizational courses of action involving events before and after those observed by the Professor: arrests which were not observed by the Professor, charges, court proceedings and sentences. In at least two incidents, and somewhat ambiguously in a third, these extended organizational courses of action provide for a further event not necessarily described in its place in the sequence. Three of those involved are described as pleading guilty to an offense. Hence the offense too may be supposed to have occurred.

The organizational language of the Mayor's version situates the events in what we shall call a 'mandated course of action'. Its organizational properties are built into linguistic practices (of which 'juvenile' is only one instance) which depend as a condition of their meaning on organizational process. It is, I shall go on to suggest, the mandated course of action which is at issue between the two accounts. The organizational language which is its necessary form of expression is, as we shall see, of considerable significance in the way in which the Mayor's version operates on the Professor's to subsume it as a local observation of an extended organizational sequence of action.

THE MANDATED COURSE OF ACTION AS A TEXTUAL OPERATION

The Mayor's version revises and corrects the Professor's version. In it the behavior of the police is represented as in conformity with a model of proper police behavior. With variations, the narration of the happenings in each incident conforms to a rather simple narrative formula: there has been the commission of an offense, or there is suspicion of an offense; the police take action against the individual involved; if successful, this leads to an arrest, to the individual being charged and court proceedings; a verdict is arrived at (in these incidents, by the individual concerned pleading guilty) and a sentence meted out. Each episode recounts events as instances of proper police procedure. Propriety is constituted by producing a correspondence between the actual events and what we are calling a 'mandated course of action'. This is an instance of a general and important social process by which organizations appropriate as theirs, that is, as an organizational action, the actions of individuals who 'perform' the organization. By acting on behalf of the organization in ways which can be subsumed by the mandated course of action, the actions of individuals are appropriated as acts of the organization or of individuals as representatives of the organization, rather than of individuals acting for themselves. The mandated course of action applying to these incidents can be represented as composed of a set of steps or stages as follows:

offense → arrest → charge → court proceedings

Police action can be seen as arising out of a previous stage and having as its objective the succeeding. Hence connecting each stage are a number of sub-sequences: e.g. searching a suspect (137); informing an individual that she is under arrest (146–7). Any of these may involve the police in the use of force. The use of force is mandated so long as it has an instrumental relation to the mandated course of action. The mandated course of action which applies to the events as told in both the Professor's and the Mayor's version has specific reference to the use of force. Hence for our purposes here we will schematize the mandated course of action in this way:

offense → [use of force] → arrest → charge → court proceedings

The use of force appears in square brackets to denote its instrumental character. It may also of course come into play at other points in the course of events, but we are concerned only with its use prior to the making of an arrest.

This mandated course of action, as a mode in which local actions are construed as representative of proper organizational behavior, is what is at stake in the operation of the two texts. Posed at the level of textual discourse, the question is of the application of the mandated course of action to the events at issue. The operative force of the texts is not strictly, therefore, an issue of what happened, but of its interpretation. Essentially, then, what we are investigating is the documentary method of interpretation as a textual operation.

The documentary method of interpretation as Garfinkel expounds it is summarized thus:

> The method consists of treating an actual appearance as 'the document of,' as 'pointing to,' as 'standing on behalf of' a presupposed underlying pattern. Not only is the underlying pattern derived from its individual documentary evidences, but the individual documentary evidences, in their turn, are interpreted on the basis of 'what is known' about the underlying pattern. Each is used to elaborate the other.
>
> (Garfinkel 1967a: 78)

As Mannheim discusses the documentary method and as Garfinkel represents it in this paragraph, the underlying pattern is held to derive from the assemblage of 'documents' and is not independent of them. However, a sub-type referred to by Garfinkel suggests an interpretive procedure conforming to this generally circular form arising as events are treated as documents of an 'underlying' schema originating in a textual discourse. Goffman's strategies for the management of impressions, or Parsons's value system are examples he gives. This sub-type I have described as an ideological circle (likening it to analyses made by Marx of this procedure) (Smith 1990): an interpretive schema is used to assemble and provide coherence for an array of particulars as an account of what actually happened; the particulars, thus selected and assembled, will intend, and will be interpretable by, the schema used to assemble them. The effect is peculiarly circular, for although questions of truth and falsity, accuracy and inaccuracy about the particulars may certainly be raised, the schema in itself is not called into question as a method of providing for the coherence of the collection of particulars as a whole.

139

This ideological procedure provides for the 'insertion' of connections – causal, motivational, etc. – which are derived from the textual discourse or the textually embodied order of an organizational process into the account of actual happenings. In this way happenings-as-described are represented as expressions of conceptual relations evolved in textual discourse. Actual local connectives are suppressed (Smith 1990) and happenings-as-described take on the character of instances of formulations embedded in textual discourse.

The particulars may or may not appear in any given account precisely in visible form as particulars. They do so appear (hence the term) in the account of the basis of a criminal charge. They can be present in other instances, e.g. in a psychiatric case history (Smith 1990). In many instances, however, the notion of 'particulars' serves to draw attention to a work going on in the construction of an account rather than to distinct properties of the account or accounts themselves. The final version may be such that particulars are not separate from interpretation.

What is of interest here, then, is a relation between the two versions or texts viewed in temporal sequence, beginning with an attempt to exhibit the failure of the mandated course of action as an interpretive schema making sense of what the Professor saw on Telegraph Avenue on the evening of 9 September 1968; and followed by its reinstatement which is coupled with a general method of handling similar types of 'assaults' on the ideological organization claiming the loyalty of the public to the ruling apparatus.

If we treat the reader in the course of reading as wholly claimed by the text she reads, we find an active process transforming relations between particulars and the underlying schemata they intend, an active process, therefore, within the documentary method of interpretation. We begin, reading the Professor's letter with 'particulars' drawn in such a way as to prevent the application of the mandated course of action as the interpretive schema providing for them. The next reading (the Mayor's response) restores to the Professor's observations the retroactive status of particulars to the mandated course of action by redescribing *the same events* so as to conform to it.

In the construction of both accounts, the mandated course of action provides a kind of narrative formula. It establishes something like an ordered series of slots into which actual sequences can be collected, controlling the permissible relations between actions and events. Thus it is the commission of an offense that entitles the use of force. It may be used in making a search or in the course of making an arrest, for example. The mandated course of action thus sets up particular motivational sequences and entitlements, operating in the interpretive context. It selects 'because of' and 'in order to' motives (Schutz 1962a) – the reasons the police were acting in this way or what they were attempting to do. These are available to the reader whether or not they are actually present in the text, and are resources on which she can draw in eking out what is available in the text to make up the coherence of the account. The narration of an actual event presenting it as a properly mandated course of action is one which *can be told* in terms of the formula. The 'formula' does not prescribe, but operates more like a grammar determining the proper descriptive and narrative forms for actions, connections between actions, and their occasions and outcomes. It provides thus for the mandating of an indefinite variety of actual sequences of action. It provides also, in this case, for the 'logic' of the telling of observations as particulars which break out of the mandated course of action as their schema of interpretation. The Professor's letter is in this sense as much governed by the narrative formula of the mandated course as is the Mayor's version.

In the relations between these two texts, the documentary method of interpretation appears as an active process not just in the reader's head but as a social course of action (within the public textual discourse). In her course of reading, the reader becomes committed to the ideological practices situating her on one or other side of the conflict between the 'movement' and the ruling apparatus. To take up the Professor's instructions to read his account of what happened as an instance of '"law and order" Wallace or Chicago style' is to do more than follow a method of reading. The reader becomes committed to a reading on the side of the 'movement'. Sustaining that commitment throughout the reading and hence discounting the Mayor's version expresses a longer-term commitment to the ideological practices of the 'movement'. Similarly, to have discounted the Professor's account at the outset expresses a commitment to the ideological practices of the ruling apparatus. The 'third party' – the member of the public, the citizen – is presupposed by both texts to be available to be claimed by her reading. Yet she can be supposed to be committed at the outset to the mandated course of action in the interpretation of police behavior. The force of the Professor's letter is to break *these events* out of the mandated course of action as their interpreter and, if the reader is claimed by this reading, to replace the ideological practices of the ruling apparatus with those of the 'movement'. In the Mayor's response the reader then discovers that the Professor's observations can be seen as imperfect representations of a properly mandated sequence of action. In the course of such a reading the authority of the ruling apparatus as an ideological resource for the reader is restored.

This course of reading is the basis of the analysis which follows.

THE TWO TEXTS AS A COURSE OF READING

As I have noted, the social relational processes which we are examining are already textual. Hence the 'appearances' which document or point to an underlying pattern are already worked up into textual form and have the character of particulars. The particulars have been selected, ordered, worked up, to articulate an underlying pattern. Thus though the Professor's account is a directly observational account, it is, as Darrough (1978) says, 'artful'. The reports of what he saw have been worked up as particulars which have two effects: (1) they preclude the use of the mandated course of action as an interpretive procedure; the construction of the particulars must thus *inhibit* the application of the mandated course of action as an interpretive schema to be used in assembling the sense and order of each episode and the episodes as a series; and (2) viewed as a sequence, they intend an alternative interpretive schema. This is presented to the reader as a guide to her reading in the opening lines of the letter. Note also that this introduction immediately connects the letter directly with the radical side of the struggle between police and students' movement. It enters the letter into that relation.

Yesterday ... I was personally witness to what must have been a
classical exercise in the performance of 'law and order'
Wallace or Chicago style, only it was in Berkeley. As a
naturalized, non-native American citizen who has seen
first-hand experience with Nazi and 'SS' tactics, I find it most
difficult to believe what I saw.

(001–6)

This illustrates for the reader the schema of interpretation that
will provide for the sense and coherence of the subsequent
account. Following this introduction the Professor tells of four
episodes he witnessed. Each of these involves the use of force in an
arbitrary or excessive way. They are told not only as distinct
episodes, but also as a series leading up to the general charge that

the entire fracas had been staged and organized by the police
in an obvious attempt to provoke the people there into a
confrontation with the heavily armed cops.

(062–4)

The methods involved in reading this account are, however,
more complex than those of the ideological circle going from
particulars to the schema intended and back. The claim of the
alternative schema, the '"law and order" Wallace or Chicago style',
depends upon demonstration of police action on that occasion as
antithetical to properly mandated forms of action. Hence the
narrative structure of the incidents is organized by the mandated
course of action as antithesis. The reader must know how to apply
it in order to read the episodes as instances of Wallace and
Chicago style 'law and order'. Each incident is constructed so as to
exhibit specific failures on the part of the police to conform to the
mandated course of action. The narrative structure must establish
the inapplicability of the mandated course of action as a method
of interpretation.

The 'stripping' process can be explicated by returning to the
notion of the 'mandated course of action' as a series of slots into
which actual happenings-as-described can be slotted. The collection of particulars is required to occur in a definite sequence

such that a must precede b, and b, c, and so forth. Filling the slots in the proper temporal sequence mandates any given actual course of action as organizationally warranted. The use of force *after* an offense has been committed and in order to secure the arrest of a suspect is then properly connected and hence properly motivated. The occurrence of an event categorizable as an offense is a proper occasion for an attempt to secure the arrest of the person who committed the offense. The use of force instrumentally in its place as a subsequence in the actual course of action is then, with reference to the mandated course of action, warranted both by its occasion and by its aim.

The main device used by the Professor in separating the happenings-as-described from the mandated course of action as their interpretive schema is to omit particulars which would fill the first slot in the sequence and hence 'occasion' the whole. In no instance does a described sequence of police action open with the commission of an offense or the suspicion of an offense. In one instance the absence of a particular which would fill the first slot is specifically marked by the phrase 'without so much as saying one word of explanation' (018).[9] Furthermore, in no instance does the sequence conclude with an arrest. Failure to fill these two slots removes the entitlement to use force. It removes the motivational connections linking police action to the mandated occasion and objective and leaves the use of force in each episode to stand unmotivated. Police action is already under way when the Professor arrives on the scene. Its occasion is left ambiguous.

> In front of Cody's two men, for whatever reason, were being
> dragged to one of the patrol cars.
>
> (009–10)

The three episodes which follow are initiated by the police without indication of a mandated occasion (offense or suspicion of offense) motivating the use of force.

In the first, a boy is seen walking up the street:

> Suddenly a young policeman ... grabbed this young man,
> rudely spun him around, pinned him against his patrol car,
> tore at his clothes and pockets as though searching for

something, without so much as saying one word of explanation.

(015–18)

In the second, a bystander, a woman holding a baby, is attacked:

Suddenly two policemen ... were upon her, seemingly trying to pull her into a car but at the same time trying to tear the baby from her, tearing, pulling, pushing, quite oblivious to the tragedy which might have ensued had the baby been dropped and likely trampled upon in the melee.

(027–31)

In the third:

Nearby an equally young girl was on the pavement and I saw a cop's club repeatedly descending on her with all might!

(032–3)

The fourth episode is initiated by the throwing of a beer can. The Professor removes the character of this as an occasion for police violence first by describing the can as empty and as hitting the pavement harmlessly (045–6). Second, the police use of force was applied to a person other than the one who had thrown the can.

Thus each episode with the doubtful exception of what was happening when the Professor came on the scene is an instance of the use of force by the police without mandated occasion. The missing occasion is located by the reader's use of the mandated course of action as a method of 'appraising' the narrative of each episode. The absence of an offense or suspected offense as an entitlement for the use of force by the police deprives it of organizational mandate. Its 'because of' or 'in order to' motives cannot be situated in relation to the mandated course proceeding from an offense to an arrest. Hence the police use of force devolves upon them as individuals and is represented by the Professor as arising from personal rather than organizational motives.

These are mainly ascribed to the one individual.

I shall never forget the face of that policeman, his eyes

bulging out, his face distorted by a vile sneer, his whole countenance exuding hatred, his cigar arrogantly sticking out of
that obscene mouth.

(021-3)

the young, cigar-smoking cop sprinted across the street
charging like a vicious bull, the most vicious and horrifying
look of hatred and contempt on his contorted face, his club
raised, shouting. If hate could kill, that savage's look would
have killed everyone in sight.

(046-9)

The personal, extra-organizational character of police motivation is generalized in lines 060-1:

All the uniformed thugs wanted was someone to vent their
spleen on.

The subordination of expressive demeanor to the expressive
constraints of acting in a representative capacity can be seen thus
to play its part in the conforming of observable actions to the
mandated course of action.

As a total sequence the series of episodes strips away the mandated course of action as a procedure for understanding and legit-
imating what was observed. A shift from implicit to explicit in the
stripping process is marked by a shift in terminology at line 027.

Suddenly two policemen, no, two uniformed thugs....

Thereafter the term policemen is not used in telling the tale.
The representative status assimilating acts to the mandated course
of action is at times dispensed with altogether. The term 'cop' is
used together with such terms as 'huge, strong man' (034),
'uniformed hoods' (037), 'savage' (049 and 053), and 'uniformed
thugs' (060). This terminological shift extracts the police from
their organizational cover and represents them in roles dia-
metrically opposed to those they are mandated to perform, i.e. as
lawless perpetrators of violence. The terminology of police and
policeman is reverted to at the conclusion of the episodes and
when the concluding charge is being made (from line 062).

As a reading experience, then, we see the account located in an 'underground newspaper' and therefore on one side in the struggle. It begins with an explicit linking of what you are now to read as an example of the arbitrary use of force as demonstrated in Chicago and recommended by right-wing leaders identified with Governor Wallace. There follows a description which strips away the police mandate to use force as an interpretive schema applicable to this series of episodes, leaving them standing as a collection of instances of the *arbitrary* use of force by the police. The arbitrary character of the police use of force is produced by this stripping process. The concluding charge then knits these now isolated episodes into a single coherent sequence:

> I herewith state and charge that from all evident appearances the entire fracas had been staged and organized by the police in an obvious attempt to provoke the people there into a confrontation with the heavily armed cops.

(062–4)

THE ORGANIZATIONAL RECONSTRUCTS THE DIRECTLY KNOWN

The incident occurred on 9 September; the Professor's letter was written on 10 September and published in the *Berkeley Barb* on the week of 12–19 September. The Mayor's reply to the Professor is dated 26 September. As a reading procedure, therefore, it is unlikely that most readers would have had both versions before them as we do and be in a position to compare them. At all events, the document B containing the Mayor's response is introduced by an abridged version of the Professor's letter. The work of reconstructing the events of 9 September as properly mandated sequences of police action begins with what has been omitted from the abridged version of the Professor's letter.

Following conversational analysis, the two versions can be seen as an *adjacency pair*, the archetype of which is the 'question and answer' sequence (Schegloff and Sacks 1973). If the first part of a pair of utterances can be heard as a question, the next speaker's turn will be looked to for an answer. The first part of such a pair is specifically incomplete. It is oriented to what is to follow to complete it. In this instance the Professor's letter makes an *accusa-*

147

tion. It is oriented to a response admitting or denying its truth. The effect is to claim what follows from the accused as a response to that accusation. Thus if an accusation has occurred, the absence of response is treated *as a response* – as a virtual admission of guilt. These two versions are locked together in this way.

The agenda of the second is established by the first. The adjacency pair accusation and response is incorporated into the Mayor's account with the printing of an abridged version of the Professor's letter as an introduction to the Mayor's version of events.

The matter at dispute, however, is not strictly a matter of fact. It is rather a matter of how the facts are to be understood as a coherent course of action. The force of the Professor's letter has been to divest the course of police action on a particular occasion from their routine entitlement to have what they do understood in terms of a mandated course of action. An alternative interpretation is supplied. The police used violence with the intention of provoking the crowd. In abridging the Professor's version for inclusion in the Mayor's response, it has in its turn been stripped down in such a way as to remove as far as possible passages intending the alternative to the mandated course of action as an interpretation. The omissions weaken the textual basis of commitment to the alternative interpretation as a method of finding in the particulars a coherent course of action. These are the omissions:[10]

1   The introductory frame which tells the reader what schema to select in locating the underlying pattern for the events she is about to read is gone.

2   Passages describing expressions indicating personal motivations in the use of force have gone. So has the general statement concerning the personal motivations of the police directly involved in the use of force.

3   All references to the Professor's own and the crowd's reactions have gone. Indeed all references to the crowd as present at all have gone.

4   The shift from use of the terms police and policemen to uniformed thugs, cops, savages, etc. is unmarked and with one exception – 'savage' which is integral to a descriptive passage (118) – these terms have been omitted.

5   One sentence of straightforward description is omitted. In

the first episode, the Professor's original letter (A) describes a young man being searched and 'Then he [the policeman] pushed him roughly up the street yelling at him to get moving' (019–20). This part of the description is in direct conflict with the account of police behavior as fully mandated contained in the Mayor's letter of response to the Professor (B).

6   All the charges referring specifically to an excessive and arbitrary use of force are omitted (067–75 and 081–5).

7   The passage locating the Professor as citizen is gone (076–80).

8   Although it is possible to identify as an individual the young policeman who grabs the young man in the first episode, with the young policeman who sprints across the street with his club raised in the last episode, the linkage, lacking the expressive details, is no longer noteworthy. There is no distinction between the four or five policemen who were involved in the action and the others standing around.

The resulting document presents the pared-down particulars supporting the 'charge' that from all evident appearances the entire fracas had been staged... (122–3). The rhetorical effect of the account which communicates the experience of observing the use of excessive force is eliminated. The crowd is no longer an active presence, hence the object of the action with which the Professor charges the police has been removed. The transfer from organizational mandate to personal motivation is not made.

The disappearance of the crowd and the accounts of the build-up of their reaction, coupled with the omission of expressive details constructing a continuous character for one policeman, eliminate the continuity of the episodes as a sequence. This removes some of the support in the particulars for the interpretation of the whole as a course of action – as a systematic attempt to provoke the crowd. The Professor's account dissolves into a collection of episodes or 'incidents' now in conformity with the frame which will be used in redescribing them as instances of proper police procedure.

Then follows the reconstruction, the Mayor's version of the events. It opens by treating the episodes as a collection of 'four incidents'. The reader is provided with an important special instruction with which to work retroactively upon discrepancies between the account she will now read and that which she has just read. It is suggested that the Professor's observations of the incidents were partial (136–7), implying that there is a more complete version to be told. This provides the reader with a method of seeing how to treat the Professor's observations as subsumable by a more complete version to be provided.

The Mayor's reconstruction thus operates not on the original account but on the stripped-down version incorporated into the Mayor's text. Each incident is now redescribed to accord with the mandated course of action. In so doing, the Professor's observations, providing the agenda of the accusation in the adjacency pair, are reconstituted as a partial view of an extended total sequence. Each episode is now treated as an incident complete in itself. Each is constructed in a narrative form such that the slots of the mandated course of action are appropriately filled. The use of force appears as a sub-sequence entitled by the prior occurrence of an offense (hence providing 'because of' motivation) and having as its objective the making of an arrest (hence providing 'in order to' motivation). It is an effect of the documentary method of interpretation that everything need not be said. Hence motivational statements need not be explicit. The reader, commanding the interpretive schema intended by the particulars, knows how to insert them. They are essential to the coherence of the account.

The schema in terms of which the narrative sequence of each episode is written is this:

offense → [use of force] → arrest → charge → court

Each incident as now described conforms to the narrative form of the mandated course of action. Not every cycle is completed through to an arrest and thereafter, but each now includes an offense or suspected offense or some other occasion for police action.

In the first episode, the reading of the Professor's observations is transformed by describing the young man who was grabbed by a policeman and searched, apparently without cause, as a juvenile. He is represented as someone who 'has a record', who is 'known to the police', and of whom, then, there may be grounds for suspicion. Further, this man is now connected, though somewhat awkwardly, with the arrest of two men by the police with which the

Professor's account opens. This overdetermined cycle is sealed by the individual's arrest, charged with being a minor in possession of alcoholic beverages, and his pleading guilty. The last step loops back to confirm the grounds for the initial police move. Essential to this account is the dropping of the Professor's clear and decisively descriptive statement that the policeman pushed the young man roughly up the street yelling at him to get moving (019–20). The conversion of this to 'appeared to be then released' (138) is semantically warranted. It will not subsume the Professor's vivid detail. Once that hurdle is surmounted, the remaining defects are remedied by a purely organizational account lying within the institutional scope of the police and legal processes with no corresponding observational description.

The second incident also replaces the occasion entitling the police to act. The young woman with the child had been 'screaming vile profanity at the police and was agitating the crowd' (144–5). A formally correct sub-sequence of the arrest procedure is described.

> Two officers approached her ... informing her that she was under arrest.
>
> (145–7)

Difficulties were encountered in the course of making the arrest. The woman was with a man. The man locked arms with her. The police are described as acting with caution and restraint.

> The officers attempted to talk to the woman, but she continued screaming and swearing.
>
> (149–50)

One officer reached for the baby intending to give it to the man they thought was the woman's husband (151–2), and

> One of the officers talked to the woman and endeavored to start her toward the patrol car.
>
> (152–3)

The restrained behavior of the police is contrasted with the unrestrained behavior of the woman and the man with her. Far from their use of force being excessive, they decided not to arrest her, rather than risk harm to the baby.

Regarding the third episode, what the Professor witnessed is treated retroactively as some version of a properly mandated sequence involving a young man who has attacked a police officer. A struggle ensues in arresting him and its course; the young woman attempts to prevent the police from making the arrest. Her being on the ground at the termination of this proper sequence is a contingent effect of her attempt to interfere in a properly mandated sequence. That she was beaten by the police is denied.

In the final episode of the beer can, again the narrative reconstructs the incident as a properly mandated course of action. The offense for which a man was arrested was not the throwing of the beer can. Rather, his arrest was occasioned by interfering with the police in their attempt to arrest the man who threw the beer can. He body-blocked the police in their pursuit of the beer can thrower. He was 'subdued', arrested, charged with resisting arrest, and he pleaded guilty.

In two of these cases we can see how the extended organizational sequence in which the actions observed by the Professor are embedded, insert missing pieces of the mandated course of action. When an offense is not visible, it is established retroactively by a charge, a guilty plea, and a sentence. In all the incidents as they have been retold, the basic narrative structure conforms to the 'offense, [use of force] arrest, charge, court' sequence which mandates the particulars. In the new version the reader can readily find particulars intending the interpretive schema which mandates them. There are still discrepancies between this account and that of the Professor. But there are no longer serious obstacles to reading the latter as an imperfect partial account, now understood as the locally situated observation of a course of action which, when grasped from an organizational point of view, is properly mandated.

THE POWER OF THE INSTITUTIONAL IN PUBLIC TEXTUAL DISCOURSE

Document B, the Mayor's version, is not just a rebuttal of the Professor's. It is a process of conversion of one *kind* of account into another, producing a special relation between the two such that the institutional account, that is, the sequence of action described in properly mandated form, embeds and subsumes the observational mode. This operation depends heavily, as I shall try to show by a more detailed analysis of the conversion process in one episode, on the use of a distinctive terminology. It is one which appears to be descriptive, but at a higher level of abstraction than the detailed descriptive passages supplied by the Professor. It is, further, an institutional or organizational language, expressing the organization's mandate, appropriating the actions of individuals to the organization, and, as in the case of the term 'juvenile', presupposing, in many instances, a complex organizational division of labor. It is a language which functions to claim actuality for organizational purposes. Its use commits a description to interpretation in accordance with the mandated course of action. It is one of the practices serving to organize the actual into the forms in which it may be governed by the peculiarly abstracted character of the ruling apparatus of this kind of society. In connection with an earlier discussion of psychiatry, I described it as follows:

Professional and bureaucratic procedures and terminologies are part of an abstracted system. Abstracted systems are set up to be independent of the particular, the individual, the idiosyncratic and the local.... In actual operation ... the abstracted forms must be fitted to the actual local situations in which they must function and which they control. In practice the abstracted system has to be tied into the local and particular. Psychiatric agencies have to develop ways of working which fit situations and which are not standardized, don't present standardized problems, and are not already shaped up into the forms under which they can be recognized in the terms which make them actionable. What actually happens, what people actually do and experience, the real situations they function in, how they get to agencies – none of these things is neatly shaped up. There is a process of practical interchange between an inexhaustibly messy and different and indefinite real world and the bureaucratic and professional system which controls and acts upon it. The professional is trained to produce out of this the order which he believes he discovers in it.

(Smith 1975: 97)

This process viewed here as a property of the operation of institutional processes has its analogue at the level of public textual discourse. Here the terminology of the institutional process is deployed ideologically, to operate on an account of experience in such a way that it can be seen as an expression of, or as documenting, that institutional process. As an experience of reading in which the reader goes from the Professor's account of what he observed, to the institutionally rectified account produced by the Mayor, the passage is also an ideological one in which the personally observed is converted into forms in which it can be appropriated by, and incorporated into, the institution. This process is expressed in Figure 5.1.

The powerful effect of this descriptive strategy is this: once the institutional language has been substituted for detailing, the information it locks in cannot thereafter be recovered. It is a language which is capable of subsuming and claiming an indefinite variety of actual sequences of action, transforming the indeterminate into the determinate, producing them as typical organizational events. Their distinctive local historical character disappears and information relevant to the selection of alternative interpretive schema is no longer available. Clearly the term 'frisk', for example, would provide for many different actual procedures used to search an individual, and hence many possible detailed descriptions of actual sequences. Later episodes not analyzed in Figure 5.1 indicate other pieces of the institutional language (not, incidentally, necessarily formal). 'Struggle' is one example and 'subdue' another. These belong to sub-sequences in the process of making an arrest and expand the scope of what can be described by a language which automatically converts actual sequences into sequences, sub-sequences, or major stages of the mandated courses of action. This is a language which renders actual sequences of action accountable in their 'ideal' or mandated form.[11] Its power derives in part from its capacity to collect and subsume a range of detailed observational accounts like those in the Professor's letter. All that appears to be lost in the substitution of a term like 'frisk' for 'grabbed this young man, rudely spun him

Figure 5.1 Tracking the reader's conversions

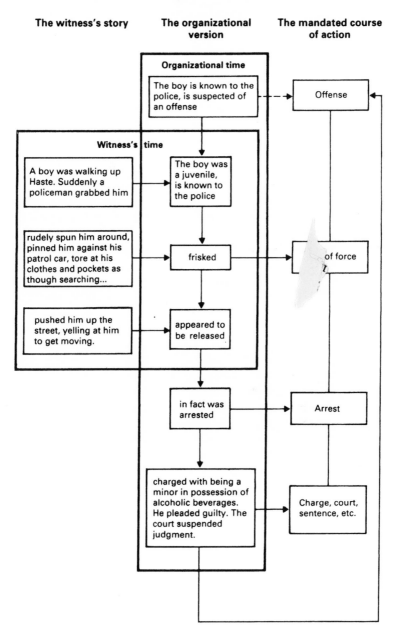

around, pinned him against his patrol car, tore at his clothes and pockets as though searching for something' (016–18) is detail. There is no obstacle to such a redescription in semantic terms. The term 'frisk' appears merely as a summary term for an act which can be detailed as the Professor has done if we need the detail. But in fact using the term bootlegs into the account the connections it sets up, as a constituent of a mandated course of action. The term locates for the reader and pulls into play in her reading, preceding and subsequent moments of the mandated course of action of which it is a proper part. The 'technical' term places the act as a moment in a sequence going from the offense or suspicion of offense which occasioned it toward its proper objective, an arrest.

This conversion is more than a formal shift discoverable on analysis. It is also an experience of reading through which the texts actively organize the social relations in which they are embedded. Stanley Fish has given us the eye to see reading itself as a course of action and the text as unfolding for the reader in such a way that later stages react back upon how we have experienced earlier stages of the reading. The accumulation of experience in reading itself leads the reader into a relation with the text which cannot be equated with what the text says at any particular moment. Thus in his analysis of Milton's *Paradise Lost*, he shows how the apparent anomaly of Milton's heroic treatment of Satan in the first two books is an artful effect. The reader is given the experience of being attracted to Satan by his brilliance, his charisma, and his pathos, becoming, as Blake suggested Milton had become, 'of the Devil's party without knowing it'. The poet's moral intention, however, is to give the reader the experience of being 'surprised by sin'. The reader then has in the course of reading discovered her own susceptibility to temptation and sin and dependence on the redemption of Christ (Fish 1967).

I intend no exact parallels here. But Figure 5.1 is intended to represent a schematic presentation of the operation of the two texts, and particularly, of course, of the work of the second text, upon the experience of reading. I suggest the diagram be conceived not merely as divided between a left and a right but as a movement from left to right in the experience of reading. I want to locate the action or rather interaction of the texts, not as Darrough does as a dialogue, but as a sequence which converts from one version to another, the second reclaiming retroactively the observations of the first as properly mandated police courses of action. I am not, of course, arguing that this is how every reader would take it. There are two sides in conflict and the opposition would not easily be drawn into the second text in a way which would allow it to operate effectively. But given a reader not already committed, the second text has the capacity to work for her in this way.

The movement or sequence from the Professor's letter to its retroactive assimilation to the mandated course of action, is a movement from the observed to the organizational. In the context of the organizational, the observed becomes – even if we have not been told to treat it in this way – a partial observation of an extended course of action to which we have no access. The use of terms such as 'juvenile', 'frisk', etc., specifically expand the time series as do the references to stages of the mandated course of action which occur after the event itself. Embedding the observed in the organizationally extended course of action creates in the course of reading itself different bases of knowledge – that of observation and experience on the one hand, and that founded on an organizational knowledge on the other. These two are not equal, for the observer, the knower, who is confined exclusively to an observational knowledge and does not have access to the full interpretive resources needed to provide the underlying pattern which her experience documents. The Mayor, the Police Chief, and the police are established in different bases of knowledge from she whose knowledge is observational. The mandated course of action which now interprets the observational 'documents' and which has been in the course of reading restored as interpreter of the original observations, embeds the latter as minor sequences in an extended organizational account. The capacity of the mandated course of action (through which an institutional process is given ideological expression) to embed and subsume direct observation, *performs* the superordinate status of the organizational over the experienced. Moving into that relation is provided by the active text in the experience of reading. As the process of correcting the original account with the reconstructed mandated version, the experience of reading carries the reader into a relation wherein her own experience and observations, and those of others, are represented as expressions of an underlying pattern which is organizational in scope. Others represent that organizational relation; others have access to the informational processes; we depend on them to complete the sequences of action we now find have been only partially accessible to us. The documentary method of interpretation here *constructs* the reader's ignorance in an experience of reading.

Eglin tells us that in resolving the problem of reality disjunctures presented to them by these two versions of events on Telegraph Avenue, his students made use of the device organized 'by reference to a membership categorization device (MCD) called K [Sacks 1972: 39], where the author of A has been assigned to the category "layman", and the authority of B (and the police in general) to the category "professional"' (Eglin 1979: 372). The operation of such a categorization device is, I believe, a product of an experience of reading which actually places the reader in this relation to those represented as functioning in a 'professional' capacity. The latter command a privileged access to the organizational processes expressed ideologically in the mandated course of action. As I mentioned earlier, in the conclusion to the complete response from the Mayor, he draws a distinction between the 'sophisticated' and, by implication, the naïve member of the public:

> It is obvious that in an era of instant, capsule news there is an urgency that the public becomes more sophisticated in its viewpoint toward the news, an urgency that the young be educated to get the full story before reaching conclusions, an urgency that the difficulties of law enforcement in a permissive society be recognized.

The lesson to be learned from this experience of reading is that the naïve reader is one like the Professor who has confidence in what he observed actually happen and arrives at an interpretation on that basis. The sophisticated reader is one who has learned an interpretive procedure in relation to her own experience or those of others which suspends confidence in them as a source of understanding of what the police (or presumably others in a like relation to the ruling apparatus) are up to and relies on those organizational representatives whose access to the 'full story' reinstates them as the authoritative interpreters of what was 'really going on'.

Chapter Six

FEMININITY AS DISCOURSE[1]

GENDER AS SOCIAL RELATIONS

Introducing the concept of gender into feminist thought was an important political move. It meant that we did not have to argue our way at every step out of the biological connections implicit in the concept of sex.[2] But the already givenness of 'gender' and 'difference' creates problems for a sociology exploring the social as an ongoing concerting of actual activities, always being brought into being, never concluded. The phenomenon has already been given determination as a discursive entity; it *is* a phenomenon. Difference is already there. The seams, cracks, varieties, and contradictions in the multiple sites and modes of being a woman or being a man are reduced and homogenized. But does it make sense to formulate general statements of women as a social category? As soon as we do so, we encounter the peculiar elusiveness of the 'object' it names. Taking up 'gender' from within, exploring social relations gendering the particular local historical sites of women's experience, means attending to specificities, not gender in the abstract, not as total, but as multiple and sometimes contradictory relations.

In moving away from the already-givenness of gender as a discursive entity, I have learned from the comparable move that Marx made in his critique of Feuerbach in *The German Ideology* (Marx and Engels 1976). Marx was much influenced in his earlier thinking by Ludwig Feuerbach's conception of the species being of humanity as the principle at work in the historical process. But in *The German Ideology* Marx and Engels put in place an alternative ontology that insists on beginning with actual individuals, their activities, and the material conditions of those activities as the ontological basis of inquiry. Nothing else. Only what people themselves bring into being through the work they do and as they work in contexts and are conditioned by what has been laid down for them by the work and activities of others. Statements attributing properties of society to concepts such as species being are to be replaced by explications of the actual social relations organizing and coordinating people's actual activities. In a parallel move, I am exploring here the possibility of replacing statements about gender and gender-differences with explications of (some) social relations that gender. Here gender is explored as a distinctive effect of a complex of social relations specifically defining femininity and organizing, in and across actual local sites of people's lives, the homogeny of gender difference.

In Chapter 4 I described how I have developed the concept of social relations from Marx. I would emphasize again that this is not a special kind of sociological entity calling for investigation in itself. Rather it is a method of analyzing how local sites and activities are organized by and in relations coordinating people's activities in a multiplicity of sites among people most of whom do not know one another and may not know even of one another's existence. I think of social relations not as fixed relations between statuses but as an organization of actual sequences of action *in time.*

The investigation of these relations clearly cannot be restricted to the relations with which Marx was primarily concerned, the relations and organization of the economy.[3] The zones of present life with which we are concerned pass beyond Marx's conception of social relations; they were present only nascently in his time. We are part of a world a major segment of the organization of which is mediated by texts; forms of discourse have emerged that are vested in social relations and organization; reason, knowledge, concepts, are more than merely attributes of individual consciousness, they are embedded in, organize, and are integral to social relations in which subjects act but which are not reducible to the acts of subjects. The strategy of attending to social processes as the ongoing activities of actual people can be extended to phenomena which have formerly been approached as subjective or as cultural phenomena, i.e. as socially given forms of subjectivity.[4] Discourse and ideology can be investigated as actual social relations ongoingly organized in and by the activities of actual people.

This chapter explores femininity as the actual social relations of a discourse mediated by texts in which women are active as subjects and agents. The analysis preserves the presence of women as active subjects. While the focus is on social relations extending beyond the reach of any particular individual, women participate actively in them in a characteristic dialectic: people's actual activities as participants give power to the relations that 'overpower' them. Women's work and activities are an integral part of the overall organization of these relations. Correlatively, the now massive productive apparatus of capital which depends upon, services, and produces the material dimensions of the social relations of femininity, also depends upon and must be responsive to women's active participation. Women are not just the passive products of socialization; they are active; they create themselves. At the same time, their self-creation, their work, the uses of their skills, are co-ordinated with the market for clothes, makeup, shoes, accessories, etc., through print, film, etc. The relations organizing this dialectic between the active and creative subject and the market and productive organization of capital are those of a textually mediated discourse.[5]

The conception of discourse used here originates with Foucault in whose work it defines an assemblage of 'statements' arising in an ongoing 'conversation', mediated by texts, among speakers and hearers separated from one another in time and space (Foucault 1972). The notion of discourse displaces the analysis from the text as originating in writer or thinker, to the discourse itself as an ongoing intertextual process. In the context of Foucault's archaeology, the concept of discourse has some of the same force as structuralism in displacing the subject or reducing her to a mere bearer of systemic processes external to her. Analysis of the extended social relations of complex social processes requires that our concepts embrace properties and processes which cannot be attributed to or reduced to individual practices or intentions. But this does not entail losing the subject. Insisting on preserving the presence of actual individuals does not necessarily commit us to reducing discourse to individual 'utterances' or 'speech acts'. Ongoing organization and relations coordinating multiple sites are produced by actual individuals, but the forms of organization are not intended or fully regulated by any set or sub-set of those individuals. Members of discourse orient to the order of the discourse in talk, writing, creating images whether in texts or on their bodies, producing and determined by the ongoing order which is their concerted accomplishment and arises in the concerting. In preserving the active presence of subjects, I have displaced the central place given by Foucault to the textual, bringing into view the social relations in which texts are embedded and which they organize. Attention moves from the organization of themes and methods of thought to the textual organization of relations and practices. Here is an example of how I want the concept of discourse to work. Recently I got into a cab with two men friends. The ballgame was on the radio. Immediately the cab-driver and my two friends began a conversation indexically structured by the course of the ballgame commentary.[6] Clearly there were understandings about the kind of talk which could go on and the propriety of engaging in conversation without preliminaries among perfect strangers. There is a social organization here. It would be very different were the radio tuned to the news or a political speech or to music. The mass media do not stand in a uniform relation to their 'audience'. They are entered into widely varying social relations. The notion of discourse as it is used here identifies this complex of relations based in texts. It locates a 'field' in which relations and courses of action are mediated by symbolic forms and modes of one kind or another. The practical activities of individuals aim at and accomplish primarily symbolic relations, the radio report of a sports event, the talk among riders in the cab; or in the arena of femininity, the relation between the image in the fashion magazine and the production of a fashionable appearance on a particular woman's body. Such a conception of discourse does not contradict its uses as an analysis of meaning, but addresses it as social relations or social organization, as the organized actual activities of people.

According to this conception, discourse is not limited to the text, though it is organized by and in relation to the text. The textually mediated discourse of sports intersects with and organizes sports as a spectator-activity. Texts are situated in and structure social relations (extended social courses of action) in which people are actively at work. Texts enter into and order courses of action and relations among individuals. The texts themselves have a material presence and are produced in an economic and social process which is part of a political economy.

Textually mediated discourse is a distinctive feature of contemporary society existing as socially organized communicative and interpretive practices intersecting with and structuring people's everyday worlds and contributing thereby to the organization of the social relations of the economy and of the political process. The concept of discourse used in this way transposes the kinds of observations collected by the concept of 'culture' into actual practices which are open to direct investigation. Thus to explore 'femininity' as discourse means a shift away from viewing it as a normative order, reproduced through socialization, to which somehow women are subordinated. Rather femininity is addressed as a complex of actual relations vested in texts.

Social forms of consciousness, 'femininity' included, can be examined as actual practices, actual activities, taking place in real time, in real places, using definite material means and under definite material conditions. Texts, however, must not be isolated from the practices in which they are embedded and which they organize. The reading or viewing of texts, how people organize their activities in relation to texts, and the skills and practices involved and with how relations mediated by texts and textually determined practices operate and are operated, are essential to the investigating of textually mediated discourse. Our investigation focuses on a lived world of ongoing social action organized textually and texts – or their reading or viewing – are moments in, and organizers of, sequences of social action.

In our time to address femininity is to address, directly or indirectly, a textual discourse vested in women's magazines and television, advertisements, the appearance of cosmetics counters, fashion displays and to a lesser extent books. These are constituents of the social relations they organize. Discourse also involves the talk women do in relation to such texts, the work of producing oneself to realize the textual images, the skills involved in going shopping, in making and choosing clothes, in making decisions about colors, styles, makeup, and the ways in which these become a matter of interest among men. It locates the social relations of a 'symbolic' terrain and the material practices which bring it into being and sustain it. Such discourse is clearly articulated to a commercial process and, as we shall see, creates the 'motivational' structures which return the purchaser again and again to the cosmetics counters of department stores, to the fashion boutiques in the malls, to the magazine racks displaying women's magazines. There is then a productive process which creates the symbolic artefact through which the commodity enters discourse – the specialized work of advertisers and the makers of women's magazines, of fashion designers, and so forth. These provide the direct material organization of the discourse which mediates and structures a market for an extensive organization of industry – garment, shoe, fabric, cosmetics, and many other manufacturing enterprises.

A METHOD OF INQUIRY

Central to this approach is the positioning of the inquirer in the actualities of her local everyday/everynight world, the same world in which this text is written and read, and the same world in which the discourse of femininity is brought into being as actual practices (of writing, producing, reading texts, of interpretation, of shopping, of the deployment of skills in producing personal appearance as text, and so forth). We can only know society as insiders, regardless of the sociological artifices constructing social systems and structures as external to the knowing subject. The method of investigation used here takes advantage of this in exploiting our ordinary knowledge of the relations accessed by the concept of femininity. Notice that the procedure does not necessarily dwell on or make an object of women's experience, but goes after the social relations organizing our experience as women investigated and examined from the standpoint of the everyday/everynight sites of our experience and taking advantage of our ordinarily practical good knowledge as practitioners of the world we are part of.

We can begin here, then, with the observation that the notion of femininity deployed as a descriptive category does not locate a bounded class of events, or states of affairs. The most it can produce is an extended collection of instances. The more they are accumulated, the more various and wide-ranging they appear to be. Susan Brownmiller's book on femininity considers it under such topics as 'body', 'hair', 'clothes', 'skin', 'voice', 'movement', 'emotion', 'ambition', but her headings merely collect and do not analyze the phenomenon. Her prologue calls it an 'aesthetic', a 'manner', and a 'strategy', but slides away from commitment to any one characterization, thus enacting the indeterminacy of the concept. It is, she says, 'a slippery subject to grapple with, for its contradictions are elusive, ephemeral and ultimately impressive' (Brownmiller 1984: 19).

The concept itself is implicated in the social construction of the phenomena it appears to describe, assembling a miscellaneous collection of instances apparently lacking coherence other than that it supplies. Its descriptive use relies on our background and ordinary knowledge of everyday practices which are the source and original of these instances. We just know what we are talking about. We can produce examples. There is some ground and some coherence here even though we cannot recover it using definitional procedures. Inquiry, therefore, has to begin with the ordinary and unanalyzed ways in which we know what we are talking about when we use the concept and can demonstrate that competence in how we can recover appropriate instances. That knowledge is grounded in a complex of actual practices and relations (among them that knowledge itself). These are the original ground from which the instances collected by the concept are constructed. Our method of inquiry explores the complex forming that original ground.

This approach treats the topic assembled for our examination by the concept of femininity as an organization of ongoing actual practices of actual individuals among whom are ourselves. We are talking about the same world as we inhabit and our knowledge of it; our share in its ongoing accomplishment is the basis on which we can claim to know and speak of it. The social forms, organization, and relations tapped into by the concept are actively concerted. Its social character is achieved in and through what actual individuals are doing in the everyday settings of their lives. The concepts, categories, and images in which we talk and find 'femininity' are part of those practices. They are embedded in and intelligible only in the context of the complex of which they are part as well as being integral to its organization and accomplishment.

When I was at school, as girls we did not learn natural science. But we did learn 'botany' and 'botanizing'. 'Botanizing' involved going out into the fields and bringing specimens of flowers or leaves for examination and identification. Here an analogous method is used. Instead, however, of specimens, we bring back for examination texts of or about femininity that give us access to the social organization of these relations. Examination and analyses here rely throughout on our, writer's and readers', ordinary knowledge of the relations of femininity and upon the ordinary knowledge of those relations of those writers whose texts contribute particular points of vantage. The social organization and relations of the ongoing concerting of our daily activities are continually expressed in the ordinary ways in which we speak or write of them. Social organization or relations govern how we choose terms and the syntactic arrangements we create among them. In speaking of or in a given form of life, our speech (or writing) is governed by it. In Chapter 4 I wrote about the organization of relations in which terms and usages belonging to an original language-game are entered into the practices of description, knitting a local setting to the social relations of sociological discourse.

> How [terms] mean in the original setting is to be learned as part of the process of learning its organization. It is a familiar experience – the sense of not knowing quite how to speak, quite how to use terms correctly, at the stage when we are only beginners in a setting. The words used are essentially part of the activity which forms a phase of the social relations. The social relations are not a context for the use of the term but the use of the term, how it means there, is part of the activity forming the relation. Thus, learning how to 'mean' with words correctly in that setting is learning how it is socially organized.

In this inquiry we make conscious use of naturally[7] occurring texts that are constituents of or reflect on the social relations of femininity. These are not intended to *illustrate* interpretations. Texts that are constituent of the relations of discourse carry properties of their organization; where people write of experiences of being active in those relations, or write fictionally of them, their texts reflect a tacit knowledge of the organization of the relations of femininity; so too where they write an ideological gloss on femininity. In effect the quotations analyzed in this chapter sample those social relations; they are 'pieces' carrying the social organization of femininity imported directly into the text of this chapter. Inquiry here works from the assumption that texts of or referring to femininity provide points of entry into the social relations that concept gathers for us in this text. This strategy, at this point, enables an exploration focused primarily on the interface of local historical experience and social relations. It opens up the social organization of femininity as it is anchored in and organized by relations that extend beyond into economic and social organization that must be explored differently and more systematically than the method of botanizing. Botanizing provides us with segments of the social organization of local experience embedded in these extended relations, making possible the anchorage of other kinds of exploration to actual local sites of women's experience. To examine the discourse of femininity in this way is to enter and engage with relations organized by a mass media of women's magazines, advertising, television and movie images, romances imaging, imagining, and enunciating femininity; the productive and commercial organization of fashion, cosmetic and garment industries; at the point of women's but also men's local practices of their everyday worlds. The relationship between productive relations and discourse is not conceived on the model of the relationship of superstructure and base. Rather than an image of superstructure balanced over the layers of relations of production rather like the frosting on a cake, the concept of a discourse of femininity, as developed here, envisages a web or a cats-cradle of texts, stringing together and coordinating the multiple local and particular sites of the everyday/everynight worlds of women and men with the market processes of the fashion, cosmetic, garment, and publishing industries.

TEXTUALLY MEDIATED DISCOURSE AS A NEW FORM OF SOCIAL RELATION

The discourse of femininity originates with the emergence of a wholly new order of social relations which resulted from the discovery of movable type and from the organizational and commercial developments which brought about a mass market for books and magazines.[8] I believe we should understand the emergence of a public, textually mediated discourse as a new form of social relation transcending and organizing local settings and bringing about relations among them of a new kind. Textually mediated relations are a distinctive and radically new form. The appearance of meaning in the permanent material form of a text detaches meaning from the lived processes of its making. The text's capacity to transcend the essentially transitory character of social processes and to remain uniform across separate and diverse local settings is key to the distinctive social organization and relations they make possible.

A new kind of public arena emerges in which relations are mediated by objectified extra-local forms – the appearance of 'codes' which have no particular local source. Its authorities and originators are themselves constructs of the media (inscribed in the text). It sets up simultaneous relations among actual local settings so that their local historical processes are mediated and transcended by impersonal and objectified forms.

The nineteenth-century British novelist, Mrs Gaskell, in *Sylvia's Lovers* observes a transition in consciousness linked to the evolution of textual discourse. Reading books of conduct, she suggests, creates a special consciousness of self. People come to know 'what manner of men' they are, 'fully conscious of their virtues, qualities, failings, and weaknesses ... who go about comparing others with themselves – not in a spirit of Pharisaism and arrogance, but with a vivid self-consciousness'.[9] Striking here is how the textual discourse appears as providing a standpoint for the subject from which her own conduct or the conduct of others can be examined. This consciousness of self is the lived moment bringing local settings under the jurisdiction of public textual discourse. Discursive images and statements are constant and standardized across geographically and temporally separated settings and accessible to anyone with the appropriate competences. Thus the gaze from the standpoint of discourse is impersonal and ubiquitous. It is not only an internal reflection, but a shared practice of reflection on others in the light of a common discursive standpoint. These are social relations. They are more than simply an expansion of communication beyond the local. They reorganize relationships among local everyday worlds within them and by relating them to others through common participation in the textually mediated discourse. People scattered and unknown to one another are coordinated in an orientation to the same texts. Public textual discourse creates new forms of social relations.

Our contemporary forms of 'femininity' have been vested in a textually mediated discourse from the beginning. According to Poovey, the ideal of femininity emerges early in the eighteenth-century, culminating in the nineteenth-century paradigm of the Angel of the House (Poovey 1984: x). In her account there is constant reference to the textuality of this emerging discourse. This might go unremarked, since these are the natural sources of the historian. But if we attend to the existence of these texts as locating discursive organization, then her descriptions of the eighteenth-century formulations of femininity can also be seen to exhibit their textual ground.

> During the eighteenth century ... an entire body of literature emerged that was devoted exclusively to this cultivation. Instructions about proper conduct appeared in the numerous periodicals addressed specifically to women, in more general essay-periodicals like the *Spectator* and in ladies' conduct books. This last genre, which consisted of works composed by both men and women, was directed primarily to the middle classes and was intended to educate young girls (and their mothers) in behavior considered 'proper,' then 'natural,' for a 'lady.' Conduct material of all kinds increased in volume and popularity after the 1740s, in keeping with the increased emphasis on domestic education and the growing number of middle-class women readers.
>
> (Poovey 1984: 15)

Again, in delineating 'the Proper Lady' of the nineteenth century, Poovey relies on 'conduct books, popular magazines, novels, and women's memoirs or diaries' (Poovey 1984: xi). Similarly, Gorham's study of the feminine ideal in relation to Victorian girlhood relies on textual materials of the same kind (Gorham 1982). A description of the fashionable forms of femininity of the nineteenth-century United States is also clearly text-based. Banner cites a variety of texts defining the 'fragile and submissive maiden of the Victorian stereotype':

> Nathaniel Hawthorne gave her epic representation in the dovelike Hilda of *The Marble Faun* and the manipulated Priscilla of *The Blithedale Romance*. Poems and stories hymned

169

her praises, and she was the central character in the lyrics of
the parlor songs that constituted the major popular music of
the day. Above all, her dimensions were personified in the
drawings of ethereal maidens that appeared in the
illustrations of fashion magazines like *Godey's Lady's Book* and
in the mass-produced lithographs marketed by firms like
Currier and Ives. One late-century analyst aptly called her the
'steel-engraving lady,' referring both to the lithographic
process by which she was created and to the element of moral
rectitude in her character.

(Banner 1983: 45)

Such references to texts are more than references to sources
through which the culture of a period can be penetrated. Rather
the textuality of the sources traces the textuality of the social
relations of a discourse of femininity and its evolution.

Though in the late nineteenth-century questions of femininity
had been raised to the level of theoretical debate (Steele 1985), it
is the icon, pictured femininity, which is the central medium of the
discourse. Pictures of fashionable clothes and fashionable beauties
circulate early and provide visual paradigms for women's production of appearances reflecting the image and appealing to it as
interpreter and criterion. The curious authority of the nineteenth-
century fashion designers, milliners, and even local dressmakers,
resided in their discursive function as authorities in the making
and transmitting of paradigms to which women everywhere were
oriented. Time, effort, and resources were devoted to their
realization through and on women's bodies at all levels of class
structure (Steele 1985: 79). The citing of texts, the descriptions of
textual materials by such writers, are more than merely an account
of sources of historical information about something other than
themselves. The texts themselves are seen here as constituents and
organizers of social relations unknown to earlier or contemporary
pre-literate forms.

THE BINDING OF APPEARANCE AND DOCTRINE

Textually mediated discourse is more than just a new means of
communicating popular sentiments and values. The printed
image is interpreted by doctrines of femininity; doctrines of

170

femininity are inscribed in printed images. Doctrines and images of feminity are inextricable from the outset. In Rousseau's design of gender, while men are to be educated to be their own man, women are to be educated to be women for men (Rousseau 1979: Pt 5; Okin 1979: 135). Rousseau's moral design is also a design of women's presentation of self. Appearance is integral to his conception of the morality and education of women. Indeed he gives a surprising amount of space to the topic (Rousseau 1979: 361 *et seq.*). General ideological design such as Rousseau's is refracted in books, pamphlets, and eventually magazines, as practical guides to conduct, creating a common code among readers vested in languages and images. It is referenced when people talk, when they reflect on their own and others' actions, and provides that kind of general resource in interpreting behavior and events that builds it into the organization of social reality. Perhaps more importantly, the discourse as a social organization of relations is consolidated in local practices that authorize for its 'participants' the authority of the textually vested image and its doctrinal interpretation. People knew where to look for how they should look or how to look at others. An evolving discourse connected the production and distribution of clothes, furnishings, education, etc., the skills and work (paid and unpaid) of women, and the norms and images regulating the presentation of selves in social circles.[10] The discourse of femininity articulates a moral order vested in appearances to a market and the production of commodities. Images change while fundamental features of doctrinal organization, particularly those suppressing the active presence of women as subjects and agents *vis-à-vis* men, do not.

Ideologies and doctrines of femininity are explicit, publicly spoken and written. They enunciate interpretations of the image and its embodied correlate in women's appearances. The discourse is a matrix of textually mediated relations linking ideologies of women's sexual passivity and subordination to men with the images and icons of the texts, and entered into the organization of the everyday world and its relations through the artful work of women in producing on their bodies the local expressions of the text. Barthes stresses the intimate and necessary relationship between fashion as actual appearance and the writing which constitutes its significations, indeed constitutes it *as fashion*: 'as

171

soon as we observe Fashion, we discover that writing appears
constitutive ... the system of actual clothing is always the natural
horizon which Fashion assumes in order to constitute its significations' (Barthes 1983: xi). The theories or doctrines of the
feminine, often expressed or alluded to in commentary, interpret
the representation or image, supplying its 'underlying meaning'.

Naima Browne and Pauline France's description of the gender
order of a British nursery draws attention to contexts within which
girls learn the relation between appearance and doctrine. A
constellation of adjectival phrases is characteristic: girls are 'sweet
natured', 'neat and tidy', 'docile', 'pretty and domesticated'.
Browne and France note:

> Our obsession with attractive physical appearance in girls
> crops up in conversations between adults and children in the
> nursey. From our tape recordings we have noticed that a
> common opening gambit made by adults to girls concerned
> the clothes they were wearing, for example:
>
> 'You've got new shoes on. They're a nice colour.'
>
> 'That's a pretty dress. You haven't worn that before.'
>
> 'That ribbon matches the red in your dress.'
> (Browne and France 1985: 154)[11]

The distinctively 'feminine' training provided is marked by the
contrast with what boys learn in this setting. The comparable
comments made to boys do not focus on what we could call
'appearance' but on the functionality of what the child was wearing – 'Those shoes look comfortable', 'I bet those shoes are good
for splashing in puddles', 'Those trousers feel warm' (Browne and
France 1985: 155). Rousseau's gender-differentiating scheme of
education provides the prescription:

> Since the body is born, so to speak, before the soul, the body
> ought to be cultivated first. The order is common to the two
> sexes, but the aim of this cultivation is different. For man this
> aim is the development of strength; for woman it is the
> development of attractiveness.
> (Rousseau 1979: 365)

As mass media evolve, image and doctrine become pervasive and invasive. Through the discourse of femininity, the fashion industry coordinates or seeks to coordinate the multiplicity of local sites within which desire is translated into demand for the commodities it produces. It disrupts and displaces orderings founded on other grounds. The following extract from a story by Catherine Texier locates an ideological break between a grandmother on one side and her daughter and granddaughter on the other. Grandmother, Nancine, wants her granddaughter, Chloe, to pursue her school studies; the discipline of study is identified by her with schoolgirl styles of dress that, as we know, are specifically female but asexual. Her granddaughter's dress evokes the sexually suggestive images of the women's magazines, images that are incompatible with the moral commitments of academic success.

> I was having breakfast at the kitchen table, poring over the glossy pages of *Elle*, when Nancine [grandmother] emerged from the basement, an armful of freshly clean laundry held tight against her chest. She leant over my shoulder. 'What are you reading again! When I think that you have studied Latin and Greek! It's these magazines that are giving you these ideas. And these skirts get shorter every season. Look at you. Pretty soon you're going to show your thighs. What a shame! What a shame!
>
> (Texier 1985: 21)

The grandmother's analysis incorporates the components I am explicating here. It is the magazines that give these ideas. But these are not just ideas for Chloe. Nancine formulates a general proposition, 'skirts ... get shorter every season', in which ubiquitous media image and actuality are conflated – is it the skirts-in-the-pictures that are getting shorter or the skirts women are wearing?[12] The injunction 'Look at you' displaces the textual image as criterion summoning a standpoint within an alternative moral order. Short skirts assert a sexuality that a schoolgirl should not display. Nancine's reactions show us discursive images that are more than pictures. They embody doctrines of femininity superseding alternative orderings of gender.

Doctrines of femininity became a political issue for black

women and men during the Civil Rights struggles of the 1960s. The assertion of black masculinity was a political theme of black activism. Black women leaders were displaced by black men in civil rights organizations (Jones 1987: 312). Doctrines of feminine subordination were represented as integral to black struggles for equality. Not all of these participated in the discourse of femininity as these were elaborated in white-centered media. Some, such as black Muslims, located themselves in a counter-discourse, adopting female styles derived from Islamic cultures and associated with marked subordination of women to men theorized differently (Giddings 1984: 318). The black male intelligentsia of that period, however, sought to replicate forms of heterosexual relationships identified as normative in white society.

> Sociologists, psychiatrists, and the male literati accused Black women of castrating not only their men but their sons ... of faring badly when compared to the virtues of White women. Black women were unfeminine, they said; how could they expect the unflagging loyalty and protection of Black men?
> (Giddings 1984: 319)

The doctrines of femininity interpreted in the context of the struggle for equality enjoined a subordination of black women to black men. Were they linked to the emergence of forms of appearance specialized to these doctrines, evoking the styles of femininity established in white-centered media? It is hard to believe they were not.

Doctrines of femininity generate and interpet the visual images of femininity and interpret its embodied correlate in women's appearances. The doctrines of the discourse of femininity are reproduced, revised, updated in popular philosophy, theology, and psychology, in magazines, in books, and as schemata governing the morality of soap operas, sit-coms, TV games shows, and so forth; their interpretive paradigms are commercially produced on television, in movies, in advertising in multiple settings, including packaging, and shop-window and counter displays. Forms of heterosexuality, the ordering of value, relations, agency, subjectivity, practices, are for women vested in appearances, *in what is to be looked at [by men]*. In Texier's story, Chloe reads an interview with a starlet. It illustrates strikingly the binding

174

of image and doctrine in an interpretive circle. In *Marie-Claire,* July 1966,

> Monica Vitti is interviewed. She is gorgeous. Her face full of freckles. Another blond with a pout. She says: A man must be able to create, first and foremost. The woman who helps the man she loves to create better, she is his true woman. The big difference is that I could drop everything for him, including my work, whereas he would drop everything but his work....
>
> (Texier 1985: 21)

Appearance constructs the woman who is desirable, not the woman who desires. Appearance constructs the woman as object 'attractive' to man. The doctrine preserves the essence of Rousseau's design: the man is for himself and the woman is for him.[13]

THE INTERPRETIVE CIRCLE OF FEMININITY

In the organization of discursive relations, the ideality of the textual image establishes a ubiquitous point of reference that is operative for anyone. 'Texts speak in the absence of speakers; meaning is detached from local contexts of interpretation; the "same" meaning can occur simultaneously in a multiplicity of socially and temporally disjoined settings.'[14] The ideality of the text coupled with the ubiquity of print or other media (film or television) standardizes images.

> From all parts of the media the professionally cared-for face of the celebrity (it does not matter in what field the celebrity is famous) beams at us incessantly as the face we must measure against our own. ...the media images we have grown used to are of the young and the extraordinarily good-looking, the exceedingly successful and the remarkably well preserved, whose preservation methods include the finest cutting and sewing that plastic surgery can offer.
>
> (Brownmiller 1984: 165)

The standardization of images, the ideality of the image that is constituted by the text, enter and organize local sites of action and experience. Images distributed through the media are constant for every local site in which they 'occur' in printed form. For women (and men) wherever they are, the normative image is the same as it is for other women anywhere the distribution systems reach. Of course the market is differentiated and images are multiple (though not independently variable). Yet the organization of relations is the same: the ideality of discursive images is a uniform point of reference for women in widely differing settings, in widely differing economic and social circumstances, with different bodies. Regardless of the complexities of the relations that their working lives may create, their relations to one another and to men are mediated by the standardization of visual norms organized by this discourse. Rather than normative organization being expressed in the textually mediated discourse, normative organization is its accomplishment. And it is an organization of discursive relations that corresponds precisely to the organization of a market, with the same impersonality, the same independence of particularized relations, and so forth.

Thus the texts of discourse create relations among discontinuously organized actual local settings. They supply the codes of public settings by providing procedures for reading off the locally produced appearances which Goffman has analyzed as the presentation of self in everyday life (Goffman 1959). Dress itself, hairstyling, makeup, packaging, themselves take on textual properties. They are to be 'read', 'interpreted', not merely seen. Their styles, colors, forms, etc., are codified. For example, I walk up to a display in a shopping mall. It shows custom-made cosmetics. They are packaged in cream colored containers with pale pink tops. They nestle in crumpled pink lace. There are artificial pink and white flowers in the display. This is feminine. The range of colors (the pinks, whites, and creams), the 'softness' (the crumpled lace blurring boundaries and surfaces), the 'delicacy' of the fabrics (the multiplicity of small holes in the lace opposes the solid with the insubstantial), the lack of marked contrast in color and shape (no definite edges or corners) – these code femininity. The terms I draw on to describe them display a knowledge of the code. There is an accomplished correspondence between terms such as 'soft' and the blurring of edges and corners and surfaces which is produced by the arrangement of lace in the display. The display intends a description in the language of femininity. It is one which catches us up into shifting levels of signification in which 'softness' does more than describe. 'Softness' in the discourse of femininity expresses a tenet of its doctrines – the feminine woman is yielding, pliant, and compliant. The structuring of the coded image within the discourse enables its local appearances to function expressively. She who wears the delicate, the floating, diaphanous fabrics (see how the range of adjectives comes readily to us), the pastel colors, presents herself as a text to be read using the doctrines of femininity as interpretive schemata. They are read back into her as the underlying pattern to the 'documents' of femininity she exhibits.

The texts of femininity provide paradigmatic interpretive circles, supplying images, icons, or descriptions of behavior, etc., coupled directly or indirectly to the doctrines of femininity that interpret, and are expressed by, them. It is a 'documentary method of interpretation'. We practitioners of the discourse make local applications of the circular procedure exemplified in the texts. We enter the relation between paradigmatic and local circles of interpretation as practitioners of discourse. This knowledge of how to move from 'display' to its interpretation was already present at the beginning of our inquiry when we posed the problem in terms of the actual practices which the concept of femininity evokes. The capacity of the concept of femininity to find its proper instances exemplifies in practice the operation of the relation between discursive paradigm and discursive practice.

The 'documentary method of interpretation' analyzes the circular procedure which goes from actual appearances or displays to their interpretation in terms of an underlying pattern. The appearances or displays are said to 'document', or to stand as documents of, that underlying pattern. Garfinkel proposes that we enter actively into the social organization of the everyday world through interpretive procedures which treat what is present to us as documenting underlying patterns. According to his account, that pattern is made up of the totality of its appearances (Garfinkel 1967a). The location of features as indices or documents of the underlying pattern accomplish the accountable presence of what is and has been happening, what is there to be spoken of. This is how we can 'read' each new encounter with our families as documenting the underlying pattern of family life. The documents express the pattern: the pattern is made up of its documents.

Garfinkel conceives of this relation as being open-ended – a process in which each next 'document' modifies or even reconstructs the 'pattern' indicated by it. Conceivably it may precipitate a shift into another organization of document and underlying pattern. This interpretive practice is essential to the way in which we organize the speakable and reportable 'reality' of our world. What is there for us arises as accountably what it is in an active process of finding in what we see, hear, or otherwise sense, the evidences of an underlying pattern. Doors, windows, walls, and roof evidence the rest of a whole house lying in back of them; uniform, nightstick, holstered gun, and stance which slot instantly into seeing someone as a policeman.

These practices are our mode of experiencing the world as reality. We do not puzzle over a set of indicators, trying to determine what pattern they might belong to (and in so doing giving them determination). The locking of 'document' and pattern is instantaneous. It gives us the world we know in all its ordinary authority. We open the door of the house and walk in without stopping to determine whether there is anything else behind it. Any particular interpretive circle is built up in the course of experience in which there is a continual play between overall pattern and its 'documents'. The pattern is modified perceptibly or imperceptibly in the succession of subsequent moments.

Garfinkel envisages the underlying pattern as built up from the historical sequence of documents as we experience them. But there is a second mode. There is a documentary method of interpretation organized within textual discourse. It differs from the 'experiential' in one important way. The underlying pattern is not open-ended, shifting as local historical processes add new constituents in the ongoing play between document and pattern. Rather, instead of a shifting pattern, the documents are provided with fixed forms determined by discursive texts. The fixity of a discursively organized interpretive circle is visible in the following account of a girl's changing relation to 'femininity' as she grows.

> At 7 or 8 or 9 identity is something locked away, waiting to be found. For me a feminine self was located in the future. In fantasies I conjured visions of myself at 15 or 16, dwelling on the bright details of appearance: a red drawstring bag, a check-patterned frock; I covered the pages of my drawing books with older 'me's: girls in pony tails and circular New Look skirts, ladies in fish tail evening dresses – all as curvy as

fashion dictated at the time, with nipped-in waists and bulging breasts....

When in my teens, femininity turned into a pressing requirement; something was now expected of me. And this became a reason for shame and disgrace. I never felt, never believed that I looked feminine *enough*. Physically self-conscious even at a younger age, I had still held some of the blithe confidence of anticipation: ugly duckling to swan. But the mirror seemed to deny it as I was confronted with the baleful image of my teenage self. Few others knew the agonies of my predicament: where they were round as women should be, I was skinny and flat-chested. I would become glued to the mirror, contemplating these telling deficiencies of the flesh and, pulling my hair back from my face, I'd be gripped by the horrible certainty that it was *boyish* .... My 16–17-year-old body was an aberration, a freak of nature. Femininity eluded me and without its confirmation I was vexed with questions about who or what I was.

(Heron 1986: 120–1)

The texts of femininity remain, but the girl-growing-into-woman changes her relationship to them. They define the defects of her child's body in different ways from the defects of her adolescent body. Her body as 'document' changes but it is subject to the same paradigmatic interpretive procedure. The ideology or doctrine displaces the open-ended evolution of the underlying pattern as experience accumulates. We may imagine that, in the absence of such an ideological circle, growth and aging would gradually modify how someone's presence would be seen and interpreted. The accumulation of changing 'documents' would be assimilated to the underlying pattern interpreting each new instance. But the ideological circle locks in a fixed relation between the textually given images and interpretive schemata established in the discourse. Her body changes in relation to the texts, but has no power to enter an independent presence into the interpretive process.

The mutually determinative relations between discursive images and doctrine are paradigms for local realization. When women produce their appearances to conform with the textually given images, they summon the doctrine as interpreter. A recent romance novel relies on the paradigms of the femininity discourse in the movement of the story. The woman president of a company, Kalinda Brady, meets with deep-voiced potter and art gallery owner, Rand (randy?) Alastair. As she dresses to go to dinner with him she changes from the tailored style (discussed below) of a professional woman to a definitely feminine style.

> She chose the perfect little summer dress she had brought
> with her, a wrapped and ruffled silk crepe de chine print. It
> was bare, breezy and, combined with strappy little sandals,
> even flirty in a sophisticated way. She left her hair in the sleek
> twist behind her ear and added a gold wire of a bracelet to
> her bare arm.
>
> (James 1982: 18)

Note how Kalinda's participation in the discursive practices of femininity accomplish an appearance communicating an intention that she does not intend. Displaying the coded evidences of femininity summons its doctrines as interpreter. Kalinda does not go out to dinner with Rand with the idea of becoming involved with him sexually; we are told she dresses in the fashion described above to please herself not him, but the description of her dress codes femininity: there is the same blurring of boundaries, lack of definition of borders, as the display of cosmetics in the mall discussed above. The dress is ruffled and wrapped; its material gauzy, semi-transparent. These adjectives also encode a suppressed sexual invitation in the 'wrapped' (rather than buttoned or zippered) dress and the semi-transparency of the fabric. The 'it was', rather than 'she was', 'bare' displaces intentionality from subject to clothing, from Kalinda's intentions as subject to the intentionality of the discourse. The author specifically separates Kalinda's intentions from the intentions vested in her appearance. Though chosen for herself, the dress encodes sexual invitation and submission. Kalinda as a subject who is agent (who chooses what to wear) subordinates herself to the feminine subject-in-discourse who is the object rather than subject of heterosexual desire, who is, but does not choose to be, desirable.

As a device in telling the story this enables the reader to anticipate for Kalinda a feminine sexual submission to Rand's masculinity which she herself does not intend or foresee. Kalinda is allowed this irony of innocence: she does not intend the message her clothes speak for her, but it gets spoken. Women's creation of themselves as instances of the textual image yields their presence to interpretation by the doctrines of femininity.

At the same time, coded references to femininity in a woman's appearance may be deployed to summon that as an interpretive schema modifying a masculinized presentation of self. In James's story, the shift from successful business woman to a woman overwhelmed by her sexual desire for a masterful man is marked, if not levered, by changes in Kalinda's clothing. We have already examined the passage of her first fully sexual encounter with Rand. But at the beginning of the story, the shift from 'masculinized' professional woman to the feminine and desirable Kalinda is foreshadowed in the description of tailored clothing preserving reference to the codes of femininity. This device relies on the reader's competence as participant in the discourse.

> The chic, casual cotton tuxedo shirt she wore was open at the neck to reveal a thin strand of gold around her throat. The shirt was paired with khaki trousers done with a designer's touch. The sophisticated tailoring revealed a slender, supple body. The high breasts were small but firm and gently rounded. The feminine hips flared with a fullness Kalinda had always wished was a little less so but which fairly screamed her femininity from within the confines of the narrow-legged trousers. The short, wooden-heeled sandals which arched her well-shaped feet came from Italy.
>
> (James 1982: 8–9)

Kalinda's coming transformation from business woman to sexually ardent woman is signalled thus: her tailored clothes, perhaps slightly masculine in style, contrast with her body under the clothes which gives a different and a distinctly sexual message.[15]

The feminine fullness of her hips is in contradiction with the masculine tailoring of her trousers. The opening at her neck is marked and given emphasis as an opening by the thin gold chain.

Similarly, the Israeli army sergeant who instructs in tank-warfare can be described as 'feminine even in rumpled fatigues' because in addition to 'the green and black lanyard of an Armored Corps instructor and the badge awarded to graduates of the punishing tank-warfare course, she also wears as much jewelry as rules allow:

181

a pearl pendant, ear-studs, a ring, and a little dog brooch pinned to her cap' (Davis 1985). Her jewelry, and most likely in actuality other aspects of her appearance, her hairstyle for example, reference the coded images of the discourse and hence are interpretable as documents of femininity. Her essential sexual subordination to men is not obliterated. Indeed, it is specifically preserved.

Appearance may be controlled by a woman but its intended meaning is established by discursive texts outside her control. When women enter domains formerly exclusively male, such as business settings, there are problems about locating a style that, like the Israeli sergeant, preserve the signature of femininity (and hence does not challenge male hegemony), while avoiding the signals entering a woman inadvertently into modes of heterosexuality incompatible with her competent presence as business woman. Contexts involving women and men in which women seek to be present as competent agents indicate the selection of appearances that will not summon the doctrines of femininity as their interpreters. Women may, indeed, adopt specific strategies to avoid membership in the discourse of femininity. Orbach reports that women have found that being overweight makes them more acceptable as peers to the men they work with in professional and business contexts.

> When they lose weight, that is, begin to look like a perfect female, they find themselves being treated frivolously by their male colleagues. When women are thin, they *are* treated frivolously: thin-sexy-incompetent worker. But if a woman loses weight, she herself may not yet be able to separate thinness from the packaged sexuality around her which simultaneously defines her as incompetent It is difficult to conform to one image that society would have you fit (thin) without also being the other image (sexy female). 'When I'm fat, I feel I can hold my own. Whenever I get thin I feel I'm being treated like a little doll who doesn't know which end is up.'
> (Orbach 1979: 13)

Being fat breaks with the paradigmatic image of the 'reed thin' woman of the texts of femininity. Breaking with the image also breaks the interpretive circle. The fat woman is not 'read' as feminine. Orbach's informant consciously availed herself of this effect: 'She felt that the only way she could hold on to that aspect of herself that was involved in a career was by having an extra layer covering her femaleness. As she said, "The fat made me one of the boys"' (Orbach 1979: 38).

The experience of Barbara Findlay shows even more strikingly the uses of fatness as a repudiation of the local organization of femininity.

> In high school I was fat and brainy – a double jeopardy. I took a perverse pride in doing well at school, and I got fatter and fatter. As a result I was ostracized. I was weird, a freak, a teacher's pet, and I definitely wasn't socially eligible. But I couldn't have cared less. I wanted no part of the mating–dating scene. I found it humiliating to make a play for the boys. It made me feel cheap to dress and behave for their benefit.
>
> (Findlay 1975: 59)

Being fat specifically excluded Findlay from the circuits of the discourse of femininity. A bodily appearance which contradicted the 'documents' of the interpretive circle also disallowed the doctrines of femininity as its interpreter. She was thereby freed to excel intellectually. Here, as in Orbach's story (her protagonist also a Barbara), being fat opposes the interpretive closure of the discourse of femininity giving her permission to exercise her competence. Escaping the tyranny of the appearance tying her into the doctrines of femininity liberated one Barbara to do well at her job and the other to do well at school. Deviation, no less than conformity, appeals to the texts of the discourse of femininity. Discursive paradigms of femininity also define the range of appearances a woman must choose to avoid feminine interpretations. The management of fashion relies on such paradigms. The 'look' of a particular fashion intends its interpretation. Hence texts which are part of the fashion industry's management of the discourse make specific links between 'look' and interpretation. In the context of a women's movement, they may also be specifically 'political'. Here a writer contrasts the last few years of masculinized styles for women, enhancing shoulders, drawing attention away from hips, to the 'pretty' styles promised for the coming spring. He links this shift to changes in the status of women.

183

What we're seeing in life is women being more comfortable
with themselves than they've ever been, and what we're seeing
in fashion is a reflection of this.

This spring offers clothes for a woman who is glad she is
one, and I think it's one of the most positive directions we've
seen in years, one that you can expect to be around for quite
a while. We're entering the era of 'pretty' clothes, and that
should make a lot of women very, very happy.

(MacKay 1985)

The coincidence of a gender politics and the management of
desire in the interests of the commerce in fashion is even more
visible in this quotation:

From the moderates such as Givenchy and Saint Laurent,
through the staccato stylists Lagerfeld and Montana, to the
cautionless extremists Alaia, Mugler and Gaultier, there has
been no shyness in expressing the newfound mode of
femininity....

The most blatant styles are those of Jean-Paul Gaultier,
whose quilted and elasticized sateen cocktail dresses resemble
grossly drawn cartoons of corsets, circa 1950. However, they
will delight as many rebellious young women as they will
dismay staunch feminists.

(Donovan 1987: 56)

The relation between text and women's appearance treats the
local effects of women's work on their bodies as discursive
instances and hence interpretable by the 'underlying' (i.e. implicit) doctrine of femininity. Textual discourse is not merely in
texts, but in texts situated in social relations which they mediate
and organize. The local settings of feminine discourse appeal to,
express, and are interpreted in relation to the ubiquitous texts of
discourse. Texts among other functions standardize the correspondence between visual codes (the muted yet clear range of
colors, the blurring of edges and surfaces, the submissive styles of
gesture and bearing, etc.) and their interpretation by the doctrines
of femininity (delicacy, sweetness, softness, yielding). The coding

and interpretation of local settings is organized by the textual paradigm which instructs, justifies, interprets, and evaluates local expressions. The icons or images as documents and the written texts accompanying or enunciating the doctrine and its descriptors (which become the descriptors of textual images) create a paradigmatic method of interpretation which anyone can take and apply to the local settings of her everyday life. The 'displays' which are the local accomplishments of women's skill and their work on their bodies intend icon or image as their normative form and doctrine as their interpreter.

DISCOURSE AND THE STRUCTURING OF DESIRE

The discourse of femininity structures desire. From the standpoint of the ideality of the image lodged in its texts, a body is always imperfect, is always still to be brought into a relation of simulacrum to the text. The gap between textual ideality of image and actual appearance generates a movement towards rectification. Its texts provide means of rectification such as cosmetics, styles of clothing, hair shampoos, dyes, rinses, techniques of makeup application as commodities whose textual representation defines the specificities of imperfection in relation to commodified remedies available in retail outlets.

> We have entered an era of cultural life when everyone is preoccupied with a woman's body but few women, whether fat or thin, feel comfortable living inside the body they possess. What else can it mean that in this country alone some three hundred thousand women have had their breasts enlarged, while another fifteen to twenty thousand women undergo a major operation, every year, to have their breasts reduced.
> (Chernin 1983: 35)

This structure is precisely that of textually mediated discourse. The statistics Chernin cites are the surfacing of local effects organized by the discourse of femininity. Discontent with the body is not just a happening of culture, it arises in the relation between text and she who finds in texts images reflecting upon the imperfections of her body. The interpenetration of text as discourse and the organization of desire is reflexive. The text

185

instructs her that her breasts are too small/too big; she reads of a remedy; her too-small breasts become remediable. She enters the discursive organization of desire; now she has an objective where before she had only a defect.

The organization of desire can prevail when the specific imperfection is irremediable. Until the development of beauty magazines, fashion, cosmetics, and hair images for black women, being black confronted the texts of white femininity. A young black woman tells of struggling to make her own hair conform to the textual image:

> A couple of years ago when all this shit was coming out about Lady Di and how shy and pretty she was and all that, I wished I could look like her. I started straightening my hair and trying to get it to sort of flip up and all that. But it wouldn't go that way. I remember crying ... it seems like I was always crying in those days ... wishing that my hair would fall out and grow back in again straight and smooth like they have on TV.
>
> (Lakoff and Scherr 1984: 252)

Toni Morrison's *The Bluest Eye* (Morrison 1969) is the story of Pecola who is black, and, *vis-à-vis* the texts of white femininity, ugly. Her ugliness and her family's ugliness is textually defined.

> They had looked about themselves and saw nothing to contradict the statement [that they were ugly]; saw, in fact, support for it leaning at them from every billboard, every movie, every glance. 'Yes,' they had said, 'You are right.'
>
> (Morrison 1969: 34)

Pauline, Pecola's mother, had tried, like the young woman above, to fix her own hair to reproduce the ideality of the white texts. Her model was Jean Harlow rather than Princess Di, but the relation to the discourse was the same. Pecola wants to have blue eyes. She tries to incorporate whiteness magically by ingesting its texts, drinking her milk from a cup with a picture of Shirley Temple on it and eating candy with the image of a white child on the wrapper.[16]

In the context of the discourse of femininity, a distinctive relation to self arises: not as sex object so much as body to be transformed, an object of work, even of a craft. Participating in the discourse of femininity is also a practical relation of a woman to herself as object. Women's magazines tie the ideality of images to information about how to rectify bodily deficiencies. Different types of magazines locating and structuring different 'publics' present different objectives. Family-style women's magazines, for example, seem to be struggling with the problem of bringing the body imperfect up to an acceptably normal appearance rather than striving for the realization of the ideal. A women's magazine directed at housewives provides detailed instructions on how to make up to conceal the traces of a cold; it recommends a cream to diminish the aging look of drying skin; it shows how to dress to a norm, to 'play up the best of you, camouflage the rest of you'. Recommendations aim at producing a standardized bodily image. The shirtwaist is good for too thin or too heavy figures, or over a full or flat bust, big hips, long or short waist, fat tum or heavy legs. But not if your waist is thick. The drop waist dress hides a thick waist, big seat, protruding tummy, etc. Other media enclaves are less concerned with 'normalization', more with the elaborations of the image. But this is a family-style magazine and the aspirations of its readers must clearly be constrained by the household and maternal responsibilities which are also topics.

The imperfection of the body in relation to the ideality of the textual images is not exceptional. No body is perfect. Even the exceptional woman whose face and body approximate the textual image closely is always imperfect. There is always work to be done. Indeed it is this imperfection which motivates the work. In it, she is situated as subject, she who stands at the beginning of her project. It is defined as she reflects on her self in terms of the discourse, examining her body to appraise its relation to the paradigmatic image, becoming an object to herself.

Susan Griffin's imaginary account of Marilyn Monroe's experience presupposes just this organization generating the perpetual flight from the essential imperfections of the body as object scrutinized by the subject herself from the standpoint of the textual ideal.

Increasingly, as she felt empty, she must have decided that if only she could improve her impersonation of a sex symbol, she might finally find her real *self*. All her life, she had been

led to believe that it was herself and not the pornographic
ideal who was deficient. That she felt herself to be a fraud,
that is to be in reality unlike the image she copied, only made
her try harder and harder to perfect her impersonation.
Finally she became the sex goddess of her age. Now she was
the very image she had hoped so desperately to imitate. Yet,
even *being* this image, she still *felt* empty. Inside this perfection
was the same nothingness and the same numbness she feared.
(Griffin, quoted by Chernin, 1983: 54)

For Monroe, of course, the ideality of the textual image of sex
symbol was a representation of herself.

The 'structure' of the relationship of subject to herself is tripart-
ite: the distance between herself as subject and her body which
becomes the object of her work is created by the textual image
through which she becomes conscious of its defects. This dynamic
relation – a function of the discourse of femininity – appears in
accounts of 'anorexia'. Susie Orbach suggests that some women
identified as anorexic are snared in the permanent imperfections
of the body as it appears from the standpoint of the text.

Many women pinpoint the onset of their anorexia as an
exaggerated response to dieting and teenage ideals of
femininity. As with compulsive eaters, sensing something
amiss at adolescence, they sought the answer in their individual biology. Their bodies were changing, becoming curvy
and fuller, taking on the shape of a woman. They were
changing in a way over which they had no control – they did
not know whether they would be small breasted and large
hipped or whether their bodies would eventually end up as
the teenagers in *Seventeen.*
(Orbach 1979: 167–8)

In the following story from Chernin, the same dialectic can be
seen at work:

a woman writes to me about her experience one autumn
when she discovers that 'the few slacks and shirts she bought
last year to accommodate her increasing girth are tight,
uncomfortable.' She goes shopping and because she knows

that she cannot fit into the new fashions she makes her way to
the shop that 'accommodates the full-figured woman.' But
now, as she looks in the mirror, she sees that everything she
tries on underscores her metamorphosis. Her reflection in
the full-length three-way mirror is more than an embarrassment. It shocks! Who is this stranger? How did it happen?
How, why did she allow it to happen, make it happen? She is
suddenly panic-stricken ... desperate ... unutterably depressed.

(Chernin 1983: 54)

Here the subject is displaced from her body; the mirror provides
the standpoint of the text looking back on her reality in relation to
the textual images of fashion. It is the relationship between her
body and the 'new fashions' which locates her imperfection. As she
goes to work to remedy her defective body, it becomes the object
of her work; she becomes an object for herself to be worked up to
correspond to the textually defined image; she becomes the object
of her project of realizing the textually defined ideal. As Iris
Marion Young in her wonderful article on 'Throwing like a girl'
writes: 'the woman ... actively takes up her body as a mere thing.
She gazes at it in the mirror, worries about how it looks to others,
prunes it, shapes it, molds it and decorates it' (Young 1989: 66).

The mirror offers a simulacrum of the text; a woman can look
in the area and see herself framed as if by the margins of a page
and raised thus to the level of the text; the relation between herself
as text and the ideality of the image is the measure of the gap – 'I
was confronted by the baleful image of my teenage self.' Here are
the symbolic resonances of the mirror image which Judith Williamson argues is a general characteristic of advertising. Although her
elegant analysis of an advertisement for a beauty mask in which a
smiling young girl looks back at the viewer from the mirror is internal to the text, it characterizes exactly the dialectic of women's
relation to the textually inscribed image:

This mirror image involves a separation – between you, 'not
happy with your skin', and the version of you with perfect
skin, shown actually *in* the mirror within the ad: a situation
where your skin smiles back *at* you indicates a gulf between
you and *your skin.* This illustrates the status of an object that
the mirror image has. Your skin becomes a separate thing;

though at the same time, the mirror image's status as *you* is emphasised by the non-youness of the people in the picture in the corner of 'your' mirror – the man is the Other whom you wish to attract. In reality these pictures and the picture of 'your skin smiling back' are equally separate from you. But by representing the mirror within the picture, you are inevitably put in the position of the girl facing the mirror; appropriated by its own structure. And in putting you in front of a mirror like this you are given the possibility of merging with the world of objects in the mirror, since despite the fact that she *is* Other, our spatial position means that we are supposedly able to be united with her.

(Williamson 1978: 67)

It is, perhaps, a mistake to treat the texts of advertisements as self-contained entities, as is done in this example. Advertisements with a 'before and after' theme or other device such as that of woman and mirror mimicking her appearance as ideal, are best interpreted indexically. They contain the coordinates of courses of action, the gap for desire created by the deficiency of the present and actual body in comparison with the ideality of the image now represented as an objective. Here the advertisement creates a space in which the skilled work of the woman as practitioner of discourse is inserted. The coordinates of woman before a mirror, of woman before herself as image in a text, organize an actual course of action involving effort, technical and experiential knowledge of how to produce on her actual body the effects displayed in the mirror object, expenditure of time and money on skilled shopping for tools and materials, and so forth. The ideality of images in the texts of the discourse, advertisements and other representations in magazines, when related to a woman's actual body, organize the gap that generates 'desire'; the same advertisements and magazines have solutions for the problems the image constitutes. The circuit image–desire–shopping is mediated discursively though the mediations may not be apparent. Here the circuit appears in almost reflex form: '"It makes you want to run out and shop," whispered one gala guest midway through the New Designers show on the opening night of the Festival of Canadian Fashion' (Morra 1989: J14). The interplay of images, advice, and advertising in the texts of the discourse, and the correlatively organized retail outlets recapitulating the idealities of the text, presuppose and organize desire arising at the juncture of text and local actualities.

THE FEMININE SUBJECT-IN-DISCOURSE AND THE SECRET AGENT

There is a peculiar organization of the subject in the social relations of femininity. We might think of it as a differentiation of levels within the social relations of discourse. There is, let us say, a surface organization of heterosexual sociality – where women and men meet as feminine women and masculine men. By heterosexual sociality I mean forms of association in which heterosexuality is specifically normative and enforced. Kalinda's encounter with Rand is a romantic idealization of this mode. Here enters the subject-in-discourse, the feminine woman. Hinged beneath and supporting these forms is a second level of relations. At this second level, a subject appears who is active in creating the appearances proper to the subject-in-discourse of her heterosexual presence.

The feminine subject is a disappearing subject, the subject who does not assert herself, who is absent in her own actions as Kalinda is, who is attractive, seen to be sexual, but not a sexual subject. Rousseau prescribes a feminine modesty denying sexual agency to women by a shift of sexual agency to a woman's appearance.

> [Sophie's] adornment is very modest in appearance and very coquettish in fact. She does not display her charms; she covers them, but in covering them, she knows how to make them imagined. When someone sees her, he says, 'Here is a modest, temperate girl.' But so long as he stays near her, his eyes and his heart roam over her whole person without his being able to take them away, and one would say that all this very simple attire was put on only to be taken off piece by piece by the imagination.
>
> (Rousseau 1979: 394)

Doctrines of femininity interpret women as producing themselves for men as extensions of men's consciousness and as objects

of men's desire. Note the typical syntax of a sentence such as 'I
don't think he would find me attractive' that appears in one of the
passages cited below. The passive construction 'he would find me
attractive' is governed by the conventions of the subject-in-discourse, the subject whose appearance is governed and interpreted
by the discourse of femininity. She is to be *found* to be *attractive.*
He is agent; he finds her to be attractive. Even being attractive does
not appear as originating with her. There is an implicit intransitive
structure in 'attractive'. She does not attract him; rather she is or
will be found to be, attractive *to* him. The woman as sexual
predator is the perverse inverse of femininity.

Note also that the displacement of agency is a substitution of the
messages borne by her body and appearance that await interpretation by the masculine other for her active and *present*
intention. This is the organization of the subject-in-discourse corresponding to the bonding of feminine look and doctrines of
femininity described earlier in the section on 'The binding of
appearance and doctrine'. This, I think, is the social ground of
Young's exploration of 'Throwing like a girl'. In her essay she
writes:

> An essential part of being a woman is that of living the ever
> present possibility that one will be gazed upon as mere body,
> as shape and flesh that presents itself as the potential object
> of another's intentions and manipulations, rather than as a
> living manifestation of action and intention.
>
> (Young 1989: 66)

But at another level of the discourse of femininity, something
else is going on. A couple of paragraphs before the passage quoted
above, Rousseau notes that 'Sophie loves adornment *and is expert
at it*' (Rousseau 1979: 393, my emphasis). Sophie does not speak
her desire; Sophie's appearance is not explicitly sexual, but invites
a sexual reading from a man. But though sexual initiative is transferred to the masculine through a feminine practice of appearance, Sophie-behind-the-scenes has calculated just those effects.

In the phrase 'I don't think he would find me attractive' a
similar duality of subjects appears. For while the subject-in-
discourse is denied agency, there is another subject who is here
speaking in her capacity as a knowledgeable practitioner of the

discourse of femininity. She is putting forward her judgement that 'I don't think ... etc.'. Behind the subject-in-discourse is another subject who is also clearly a member of the discourse, but at another level of its organization. We come, then, upon this irony. While the appearance, the presentation of themselves that women seek to create on their bodies, denies and obliterates their heterosexual presence as autonomous subjects, the production of appearance calls for thought, planning, the exercise of judgement, work, the use of resources, skills. Behind appearance and its interpretation is secreted a subject who is fully an agent.

Participation in discourse is indeed a condition of membership in heterosexual sociality, as we see in the following account in which a woman recalls that she began to work on her body and appearance when she discovered as a young woman that she 'would have to look good' if she was to be a member of the social world of heterosexual young women and men.

My involvement with looks started very young. When I was a teenager I thought my girlfriends were far better looking than I was. The boys were very attracted to my girlfriends and I was always ignored and left out of things. It became clear to me that if I ever wanted to attract a man I would have to look good. I dieted until I was reed thin, I tried out all kinds of makeup, I spent hours on my hair, and I pored over fashion magazines.

(Cohen 1984: 18)

'Looking good' was a condition of membership; 'looking good' meant dieting, trying out makeup, spending hours on her hair and poring over fashion magazines. 'Looking good' was/is conditional on and presupposes the organization of relations among the texts of discourse, the market that delivered the images and the product information and the retail outlets giving access to texts, tools, and materials. So 'looking good' contains the connection between the practical organization of activity that the speaker undertook in accomplishing the appearance that would entitle her to membership, and the discursive expertise of both boy and girl friends who know how to operate the interpretive paradigms of femininity. Before she went to work upon herself, the speaker was ignored – she was 'illegible' within the discourse when her appearance fell outside the scope of that interpretive paradigm. Of course, not everything that appears as a defect at the level of appearance, and with reference to the standardized idealities of the text, can be modified. As women age, they cease to be able to conform to the textual image of the body forever youthful and as they become incapable of fully competent participation in femininity, they are excluded from heterosexual sociality.

> My favorite aunt was widowed in her late fifties; her husband died in a terrible car accident. This aunt was stunning as a young woman and extremely popular with men. The last five years have been very difficult for her. I don't mean financially; she is extremely well-off, but she has few opportunities to meet suitable men. She often tells me that she is looking for someone to pay attention to her, to make her feel important again. She desperately needs to be reassured that she is a desirable woman. What she finds is that the men of her age are interested only in younger women.
>
> (Cohen 1984: 21)

Being desirable, being attractive, is a condition of participation in circles organized heterosexually; such circles intersect with the social relations of the discourse of femininity. Being desirable, being attractive, arises as the textual norms of the discourse of femininity provide standardized ideals of what is desirable and hence evaluate a woman's success in achieving desirability on her own body. Accordingly also a woman's desirability may serve to define a man's masculine status with other men.[17]

> [A] boyfriend I had expected me to be dressed to the nines at all times, wearing full face makeup. He became upset whenever I hadn't time to wash my hair or my nails weren't manicured. He noticed almost every detail of my appearance. I was a showpiece that he had on display. I was a pricey, classy item to be shown off and admired.
>
> (Cohen 1984: 20)

Notice here an attention to detail that implies a comparison with the ideality of the textual image. For this man, there must be no traces on this woman's appearance that depart from a strict reading of the text. She must reproduce it word for word.

In these accounts we see the same dual subject, the subject whose appearance enters here on the terrain of heterosexuality as feminine and the subject who speaks from the site of the work behind the appearance. The local realization of the ideality of the images of models, TV and movie actresses, ballet dancers, is the project of women's work. Work and technical skills aim at the image inscribed in the public texts. A woman active in the discourse works within its interpretive circles, attempting to create in her own body the displays which appeal to the public textual images as their authority and depend upon the doctrines of femininity for their interpretation. Eva Szkéley, in her study of the 'relentless pursuit of thinness' of women diagnosed as anorexic, writes of

> thinness [as] an expression of women's striving for today's feminine ideal. A study of the drawings and of the comments ten anorexic and bulimic women made about their depicted ideal bodies suggests that wanting to be attractive to men was on the top of the list of their priorities.
>
> (Székely 1989: 38)[18]

Reading accounts of women engaged in the 'relentless pursuit of thinness' returns us to the interrelations of textual image and the perpetual imperfections of the woman's body as mirrored simulacrum of the text. The orientation of subject to self is not to self as a sexual object. It is an orientation to the self as the object of skilled work, even of rigorous personal discipline.

The appearance of the body as object is a practice learned in childhood. The investigations of how they learned to be feminine by a group of socialist-feminists in Germany disclosed a relation between the objectification of the imperfect body and memories of adult comments on their appearance.

> If for example we remove our clothing, it is possible to see how much too fat or too thin we are, to see our breasts as sagging, overly large or diminutively small, our legs as short, fat and hairy with varicose veins, our hips as too wide, our waistline almost invisible – and so on. Discussions along these lines in the course of our [memory] work immediately triggered memories of the advice with which they were

195

associated: 'show off your best side', 'hold your breath for firmer posture', 'pull back your arms, it looks better that way...'.

(Haug and Others 1987: 30)

Girls may practice this orientation on their dolls. It is as if the girl as body is externalized in the manipulable simulacrum.[19] Dressing the doll is at least as important as nurturing it in play among girls. Doll-play is transferred to the girl-child as object. A young woman in a maternity ward says, 'Mine is a girl but I don't mind *really* because you can dress 'em pretty' (Nairne and Smith 1984: 30). A family-type women's magazine provides instructions for cutting and setting a little girl's hair. A woman remembers her childhood:

My mother wanted me to be her perfect little girl. She enjoyed dressing me in frilly dresses. I wanted to wear trousers and play games with the boys. You couldn't have fun in a dress. As I grew up she wanted me to do something feminine – be a beautician or hairdresser.

(Nairne and Smith 1984: 34)

The production of discursive appearances is a matter of conscious art and technique.

The men I go out with are always reassuring me that they like me as I am, looking natural. What they don't realize is that I work very hard at looking 'natural'; I wear very subtle makeup and I spend a lot of time working on my hair. One of the guys I go out with gets very impatient when we are going out and complains that I spend too much time fussing with myself. But I don't think he would find me attractive if I let myself go and went out with messy hair and a face without makeup. He just thinks he likes the natural look because he has never really seen me looking bad.

(Cohen 1984: 18)

The project is the production of visible self as an instance of the image, this instance being the 'natural' look. It is a project for which the texts of discourse provide objectives.[20] And for some special women, it is a project of producing themselves as sources of the textual ideality. Cheryl Prewitt, a Miss America who is 'slender, bright-eyed, and attractive', followed an arduous regime.

> [She] put herself through a grueling regimen, jogging long distances down back-country roads, pedaling for hours on her stationary bicycle. The bicycle is still kept in the living room of her parents' house so that she can take part in conversation while she works out.
>
> (Chernin 1983: 23)

The same dialectic can be seen in Griffin's account of Marilyn Monroe. In between the image she copied (herself) and the sense of herself as fraudulent (being 'in reality unlike the image she copied') is inserted a work process, as she tried 'harder and harder to perfect her impersonation'.

All texts are indexical, in the sense that their meaning is not fully contained in them but completed in the setting of their reading. Texts are read or seen in context; they are articulated to the readers' relevances and practices of interpretation in definite local settings. The texts of the discourse of femininity index a work process performed by women. Its character as work is not highly visible because it is not paid work nor is it recognizably a hobby. None the less it is consciously planned, takes time, and involves the use of tools and materials and the acquired skills of its practitioners.

The texts of femininity are inserted into the organization of courses of action projected by women. Williamson analyzes a text in which a young woman appears in typical before-and-after images in an advertisement for hair coloring: dull Jane One (appearing in a somewhat smaller image than Jane Two) is transformed into exciting, blonde Jane Two. The analysis treats the image as self-contained and self-referring. The transformation is read as 'magical'.

> In the 'microcosm' inset, 'Jane' seems to be dreaming of the future, of the new self shown below: she is the 'little' that gets turned into 'a lot': 'Bigger eyes, brighter smile – everything about me seemed different, more alive, much more exciting'. Notice that magic helps her to come alive, or 'more alive', just as yeast pack gave 'new life' to your skin. Magic compensates

197

for lifelessness, inactivity. So the 'little' Jane becomes the
'cool, beautiful blonde'.

(Williamson 1978: 147)

Embedding the text in the social relations of femininity means
reading it indexically. Not everything that a text says is in the text.
The missing moments in the transformative process are well
understood by the practitioner of the discourse of femininity. The
work which is presupposed but not represented is that of the
production in local historical settings of simulacra of the textually
imaged ideal.

The background knowledge indexed by the advertisement is
the skills, time, resources, and effort deployed by she who is both
agent and object. The actual subject, the secret agent, who fits
herself to the slot identified as Jane One has done the work or
knows how to do it. At the moment of Jane Two, the feminine
subject, she has done the work of shopping, she has bought the
materials, she has applied them to Jane One's hair to transform
her into Jane Two. This is the local course of action into which the
textual is inserted and it is this course of action which is indexical
to the image. It is taken for granted by a competent participant in
the discourse; it can be 'read into' the text just as I have done. The
transformation is not 'magical' when the text is analyzed indexically. The 'break' in the movement of the advertisement from
Jane One to Jane Two is completed by the reader's know- ledge of
the relevant practices and the stage in a course of action
represented by the two images. The latter do not operate myster-
iously. Image and text are articulated to the *skilled practices and
routines* accomplishing femininity in local historical settings. The
text provides a schematic act, a structuring of desire defining a
point of departure, a means, and an objective. The movement
from Jane One to Jane Two provides textual parameters to a
course of action. The Jane One image identifies for the looker the
criterial state from which she will work towards a production of her
own body as an end-state defined by Jane Two. Jane Two is the
idealized body-as-product, the paradigmatic end-state towards
which work is oriented. The advertisement works by inserting the
particular brand of hair dye into the sequence of action as a means
of getting from One to Two; without the advertised hair dye, Two
could not be attained.

The work of producing the textually given forms upon her body is skilled work. It takes time, resources, thought. Though there are professionals, the amateur is also a member of the craft. The skills involved, practiced, and developed are considerable:

> Putting on makeup well is an exacting craft that requires a sure hand, a knowledge of theatrical effects and an aptitude for composition. Those who appear on camera utilize professional makeup artists as a matter of course, yet the average woman is expected to have skill enough for her daily routine of facial decoration. As street makeup grows increasingly elaborate in imitation of professional techniques, cosmetics companies disingenuously promote the myth of amateur proficiency with color charts, diagrams and fine-point brushes, while those who can afford the expense increasingly rely on the professional salon. The professional-ization of skin care and makeup for women who are not theatrical performers is another indication of the pressures of competitive femininity.
>
> (Brownmiller 1984: 165)

There are sources of advice and training – demonstrations are often available in cosmetics departments; a brand of eye-shadow offers training at makeup salons; store clerks in cosmetics depart-ments are minor experts, providing advice and evaluation; more experienced friends pass on their knowledge. In the discursive organization of local interpersonal relationships, another level of identity and desire is elaborated, bringing girls, young women, and adult women into an active relationship to the market for women's magazines, cosmetics, clothes, and the 'reed thin' body. Shopping for clothes and cosmetics, talking fashion, planning expeditions, evaluating window displays, and showing off the results, are important focuses of social activity among young women. Relations among girls and young women may be organized around these, becoming a focus for friendship and group identity. Women's magazines are a major source of information about changing images, new tools, materials, and instruction. Young women learn both the arts and the doctrines of femininity from such texts, providing the standards and practices of a femininity diversified by age, class, race, and 'style of life'. The various articles and advertisements provide the models to be reproduced, instruction in the skills, and information about means and materials. Magazines educate their readers in the doctrines of femininity as well as in the local production of discursive appearance:

> *Seventeen* taught me how to manicure my nails, how to shave my legs, how to make up my eyes to twice their size, not to mention how to make a tuna casserole, how to let boys win at all tests and sports, how to flirt without making a jerk of myself and how to be FUN for other people to be around.
>
> (Hurst 1984)

Advertisements educate and train as well as inform. They recommend tools, presupposing a reader who is a competent practitioner of the craft. An advertisement in a women's magazine shows the profile of a woman's face with an array of tools, brow and lash comb and brush, a two-tipped applicator, powder puff, lip-brush, large brush for powder, smaller brush for colors, and so forth.

The discourse of femininity has its characteristic forms of inter-textuality. The subject matter of women's magazines and ad-vertising complement one another. Women's magazines in these respects are rather like trade magazines. This analogy is obscured because the discourse of femininity is vested in styles abjuring 'technical' masculine styles. Moreover, preserving the 'amateur' character of the production of femininity is important to its doctrinal interpretation. Appearances must express character or personality rather than testify to the art of the maker. Craft must not be seen as craft; art must not be seen as art if the interpretive circles of the discourse of femininity are to interpret feminine appearance as a document of a woman's inner reality. Appearance indeed must take on the quality of reality. It does not do so when the technical artistry which produces it is visible. But even though they conceal their technical interest for the practitioner of the arts of producing feminine appearances, women's magazines function very similarly to trade magazines. Instructions, recipes, recom-mendations, technical information, etc., are tied into specific products or directly linked to their promotion. For example this series of images and instructions in the art of producing a natural appearance:

How to turn yourself into a natural beauty? With makeup so subtle it's hard to tell it's there. 'Forget about the old-fashioned notion of "the natural look,"' says makeup pro Rich Gillette, who used makeup from Chanel for his artistry here. 'The new way to go natural is with makeup that does not drastically change your looks – just improves them.' Here's how

* 1. Bring your skin to its palest point with foundation thinned with water or a light primer like Blanc de Chanel in Matte.

* 2. To insure a flat matte finish, dust on a fine layer of pale face powder with an oversized brush (here it's Light Translucent Loose Powder).

* 3. Eyelids get a single neutral shade of pale gray shadow – like Glacier – that complements your complexion and adds depth to your eyes.

* 4. A soft shade of Brown mascara, not harsh black, is stroked on, and lashes are brushed gently to separate them.

* 5. Final eye-accentuating touch: liner under lower lashes (this shade is Amazon). Brush it on and smudge softly so it shows up as a shadow, not as a sharp line.[21]

The implied reader is knowledgeable and skilled, already familiar with what the effects referenced by these terms will be and how to produce them. In this 'technical' dimension of the discourse of femininity the subject is far from lacking agency, knowledge, initiative, or judgement. Whereas the doctrines of femininity that her craft aims at constitute a gendered subject whose autonomous capacity as subject is suppressed, who is not her own, the subject of the technical discourse of makeup, clothing, and hairstyles may defer to the knowledge of the expert, but she is addressed as someone who knows what she is doing. The specific effect is to be produced by just these means with just these or similar ingredients. But the woman reader presupposed in this text is no ignoramus. Her technical knowledge of the practices referred to and the terms employed is taken for granted – 'flat matte finish' 'liner', 'smudge', etc. It is taken for granted that she knows how to accent her eyes, to brush on mascara, and what is meant by thinning the foundation with water, etc. The work she is doing will produce the appearance of a gendered subject appropriately entered into local heterosexuality. Planfully and with craft she produces as participant in the discourse of femininity that conflation of appearance and doctrine that can be read as being 'found to be attractive'. The finding is all his; the attraction is for him. There is a secret agent behind the subject in the gendered discourse of femininity; she has been at work to produce the feminine subject-in-discourse whose appearance when read by the doctrines of femininity transfers agency to the man. But she is a secret agent only in relationship to settings of heterosexual sociality. In the settings of her art, of her associations with other women, of talk in the workplace, of sociality organized around shopping expeditions to the mall, she is/we are, active and effective, making decisions, finding pleasure, having fun.

THE DIALECTICS OF DISCOURSE AND THE EVERYDAY: FASHION, FREEDOM, AND OPPOSITION

The discourse of femininity is a medium through which the fashion industry manages the market and its productive relations. We have seen how desire is constructed in the relation between the perfected image in the text and the forever imperfect actuality of the body to be groomed, dressed, and painted. We have seen how advertisements insert themselves into the practical organization of achieving femininity as a presentation of self in everyday life.[22]

We have seen how discourse, both appearance and interpretation of appearance, inserts itself as the normative structure of the everyday. The fashion industry inserts its control over desire and hence demand through texts which structure image and its interpretation. Annually, and seasonally, new 'looks' are created and promulgated in the texts of the discourse. New possibilities and new defects emerge in relation to new images; there are new resources and remedies. A space for desire is opened up in the contrast between last year's clothes and the new images and displays in fashion shows and shop windows. As these migrate to street or workplace in what we see other women wearing, the textual becomes normative in the everyday world. The ubiquity of the image constitutes the tyranny of ideality *vis-à-vis* the body forever imperfect. This is how desire and hence market demand are continually renewed. Last year's cosmetics remain unfinished in the drawer; last year's or the year before's dresses get relegated to everyday wear or the back closet before they are worn out. The economic problem of the eternal renewal of demand is managed through these processes.

The power of the fashion industry to manage desire through the discourse of femininity implicates women as active participants in its discursive relations. Discourse is organized extra-locally; its texts are uniform and ubiquitous; its powers to govern the norms and interpretations of appearances are effective in multiple local sites. Women are caught up in the circle of appearance and inter-pretation established publicly in the discursive texts. Though they can, with the body and resources available to them, choose a 'look', the relation between that look and its interpretation, and therefore how the look they have chosen signifies, are pre-given in discourse. Discourse organizes local social relationships as a relationship to a market selling fashion commodities. The textual mediation of discourse articulates women's desires and practices as its participants to economic organizations using, managing, manipulating, and dependent on it.

Given this organization of relations, it is easy to misconstrue the discourse as having an overriding power to determine the values and interpretation of women's appearances in local settings, and see this power as essentially at the disposal of the fashion industry and media. But the relation between discourse and local practices is not causal. Rather, women are active, skilled, make choices, consider, are not fooled or foolish. Within discourse there is play and interplay. Angela McRobbie shows us a situation in which fashion becomes a resource through which a group of working-class girls assert their independence of the institutional powers of the school and the privileges of class. The discourse of fashion provided them with an alternative and external authority to those of school and class. Make-up, McRobbie tells us, defined their relationship to school; fashion and beauty contributed massively to a feminine anti-school 'culture'. While in school terms they were incompetent, in the discourse of femininity they were 'experts'. They dressed with careful attention to fashions, made up their faces, and did their hair ornamentally. They despised the middle-class girls who wore uniforms to school. 'They wear horrible clothes, I mean they don't know what fashion is. They're not like us at all. They don't wear platform shoes and skirts – mid-calf length.' They contrasted their fashion competence to the incompetence of middle-class girls – 'they don't know what fashion is' (McRobbie 1978: 103). The alternative authority of the discourse gave them room to move within the otherwise exclusive authority of the school.

The 'consumer' is not a puppet of the media. The young women McRobbie describes would be critical, would discuss new products knowledgeably and with discrimination. Though the fashion industry manages the market through the discourse of femininity, it does not control that discourse. Concealed within the ubiquity and apparent uniformity of the texts of discourse and the high skills of their 'manipulations' of the consumer are the resistances, such as Toronto's odd resistance to the color green, or at a major level, the gamble involved in introducing new lines when even major houses have had catastrophic failures, and small innovators have introduced fashion lines that 'catch on' (Mary Quant is the ideal typical instance). The buyer's art is that of knowing intuitively what will go with the customers her store caters for. When the codes and images are viewed as women use, play with, break with, and oppose them, the discourse of femininity appears not as managed construct of the fashion industry manipulating people as puppets, but as an ongoing, unfolding, historically evolving, social organization in which women and sometimes men are actively at work.

More striking are the oppositions arising as specific breaks with the textual idealities of discourse. Black activist resistance to the tyranny of the white texts of femininity and masculinity was realized in the assertion of an independent black identity in African styles of dress — Afro hairstyles, dashikis, and, more recently, the elaborately braided hair. Punk styles irrupt within discourse itself as young working-class women innovate punk styles of hair, makeup, and dress as specific oppositions to public texts of femininity and their underlying class sub-text (Roman 1989). Less striking, but perhaps more pervasive, are new images, some themselves the opening of new paradigmatic interpretive circles. Jean Ehlstain comments on the image projected by Jane Fonda's workout videos of the taut, muscular woman, 'sexualized but curiously defeminized' (Ehlstain 1989). These of course are operations of the same order as those of femininity but bonding different idealities to different doctrines.

Less visibly the discourse is continually undergoing elaboration, contradiction, reworking at the local level among women actively participating in it. Makeup, clothes, jewelry, hairdressing, all yield possibilities for creative elaboration, for art, for fun, for a play of intentions which references the discourse but is not limited by it. Along Bloor West between Bay and Yonge Streets in Toronto, the shop windows are dressed in determinedly feminine styles, but the young women are not. They are cross-gender dressed in black leather or jean jackets with tight jeans, definitely female in hairstyle and revealed hips and crotch, but equally definitely lacking the coding of femininity that appeals to the paradigms of discourse for its interpretation. And not everything is fun, not everything is play. There is strain, anxiety, agonizing over the body that will not meet the textually given conditions of membership in heterosexual sociality.

Innovations from below, styles that catch on from pop or rock stars, oppositional styles, any and all of these signal a potential market. Those who design for the mass markets pick up cues where they can, keeping tuned to what is going on, particularly with young people. The capacity of the industry to incorporate the strikingly oppositional styles of the 1960s, resisting no style in particular but conformity and standardization itself, is perhaps the most dramatic example of its normal feedback processes. New styles are projected textually to renew the image–desire–shopping circuit described above. New computerized methods of production and inventory control enable rapid response to the success or otherwise of a given line in given outlets. There is an ongoing dialectic between women's freedom to express themselves stylistically within discourse, to make choices, among them to choose specifically 'unfeminine' styles, and the strain of the fashion industry and its media towards a controlled and continually changing orthodoxy of both appearance and interpretation which would fully regulate desire as demand. Such closure is never attained.

This investigation of femininity as discourse has disclosed a double subject, a subject-in-discourse who appears as passive, lacking agency, awaiting definition by a man, and a second layer of organization positioning an active and competent subject. While the subject-in-discourse is deprived of agency, the subject-at-work behind her is active and skilled. Here we can see the problematic trap for women of producing an appearance appealing to the ideality of the text through which they represent themselves as other than they are. The alienation of the subject as representation of the text, where her appearance speaks for her but not from her, introduces essential contradictions in her heterosexual relations. Throughout in the accounts we have used of women's work on their bodies we find the recurrent problem that Goffman has described as front and backstage, the problem of masquerade, of falsity, of deceit, of the high artifice in the construction of the natural, in the young man's insistence on a detailed conformity of appearance to text that denies presence to the imperfections of the actual body it conceals. Yet Goffman's account is made from only one viewpoint, that of on-stage and audience. Here we have given presence to an alternative site, generated in the multi-layered organization of discourse, backstage itself. From here indeed we find women at work as active, skilled subjects, enjoying the decoration of their bodies, and while some counterimages emerge from oppositional sites, some at least must emerge from the extrapolation of play, of expertise, of pleasure in the exercise of competence. An alternative discourse begins to emerge in which decorating one's body can be seen as an elaborated expression of who one is, who one might be, who one would like to try on for the evening. The fun of playing with 'vintage' clothes is an instance. The stylistic elaboration of a female sexuality that is rankly invitational, such as Madonna's, is as much at odds with the subject-in-discourse of femininity as any of the earlier puritanisms of feminist dress. The wearer of a 'boy toy' T-shirt is a speaker of her own sexuality. Even though its message may assert sexual subordination, it asserts.[23]

Yet as discourses disrupting femininity as it was laid down first for us in the nineteenth century are elaborated, the organization of desire articulated to the retail sources of its temporary satiation has been preserved. The ubiquitous ideality of the textual image with its power to form the standards under which we are judged and read, and with which we judge and read others, is still at work. This is the medium through which initiatives and countermoves coming from outside discourse and market are claimed, organized, appropriated. The ubiquitous operation of the text in standardizing images, the ideality of the textual image, and the gap between body and image, are still at work as a perpetual desire-creating machine, articulating the competent subject-at-work to retail outlets and magazines. She still goes shopping; she is still consumer. Media work aims at the mass *standardization* of image and desire to coordinate with the mass production capacities vested in textile, cosmetics, and garment manufacturing. Conceiving discourse as actual practices and activities arising in specific local historical contexts and under definite conditions, rather than as bounded by the realm of meaning, leads us 'naturally' to its articulation in a political economy. The concept of discourse allows us to 'magnify' for examination the interface between economic relations and the local sites of women's experiencing that are discursively ordered. 'Femininity' can be explored as a set of relations arising in local historical settings without segregating it from the economic and social relations in which it is embedded and which it both organizes and is determined by.

This chapter has explored femininity as a complex of discursive relations. It has explicated, as linked aspects of this discursive complex, the subordination of women in heterosexual circles, their competence and agency as fashion and cosmetics consumers, the bonding of feminine image and doctrine, and the discursive governing of local presentations of the feminine self through paradigmatic interpretive circles. These and other features of this discursive complex are anchored in, while never reducible to, economic relations. We begin here to open up in quite a new way the relationship of 'consciousness' and economic relations and perhaps, beyond that, to explicate new dimensions of the notion of regime and mode of regulation that contemporary French Marxist economists have put forward as a way of analyzing the relative stabilities of states of an economy (Aglietta 1987; Lipietz 1983). A regime of accumulation stabilizes as a systematic mode of coordinating 'the conditions of production ... and the changing conditions of final consumption' (Lipietz 1983: xvi). A '*mode of regulation* refers to the ensemble ... of institutional forms, networks and explicit or implicit norms which assure compatibility of market behaviour within a regime of accumulation...' (Lipietz 1983: xvi). The analysis of femininity as discourse and discourse as social relations opens the possibility of explicating aspects of a mode of regulating a regime in which the organization of production and markets itself participates in the normative organization that generates desire. The discursive relations of femininity are vested in texts designed for and distributed on a mass market, and the production and distribution of those texts coordinates, differentiates, and regulates the market and production of clothes, cosmetics, etc. The relation between the standardized ideality of the discursive images of femininity and the imperfect body generates that perpetual renewal of desire into which the texts tying desire to commodity are inserted. Women are returned again and again as consumers to the retail outlets that will remedy their ever-renewed textually reflected imperfections. This chapter opens the possibility of grasping the relationship between aspects of masculine domination and capitalism as specific relations organizing and organized by the local practices of women and men as they participate in the discourses of femininity and masculinity.

Chapter Seven

TEXTUALLY MEDIATED SOCIAL ORGANIZATION[1]

The phenomenon with which this book has been concerned is one to which sociology has been extraordinarily blind. It is also ubiquitous – at least in contemporary society. We are constantly implicated in and active in it – indeed this chapter, this book, your reading, are among its manifestations. It is the phenomenon of textually mediated communication, action, and social relations. As intellectuals we take it for granted much as we take for granted the ground we walk on or the air we breathe. Yet it not only constitutes both the arena and the means of our professional work, but permeates our everyday world in other ways. We get passports, birth certificates, parking tickets; we fill in forms to apply for jobs, for insurance, for dental benefits; we are given grades, diplomas, degrees; we pay bills and taxes; we read and answer advertisements; we order from menus in restaurants, take a doctor's prescription to the drugstore, write letters to newspapers; we watch television, go to the movies, and so on and so on. Our lives are, to a more extensive degree than we care to think, infused with a process of inscription, producing printed or written traces or working from them. The omnipresence of these documentary or textual processes is now being entered by the technology of computers. As the textual process is thus radically modified and expanded in its organizing scope, we have become aware of it as a political issue affecting personal privacy.

But sociologists have rarely attended to the documentary or textual process as such. In the study of communication the dominant model has been that of face-to-face communication, even when the object of investigation has been large-scale organization. Or it has been based on the natural scientific model of the communication of information, which takes for granted precisely what, in the context of textually mediated communication, cannot be taken for granted – namely the social construction of the message or information as such.

I am interested here in making documents or texts visible as constituents of social relations, and not in attempting a comprehensive survey of sociological studies of textual materials. It is more important at this stage to expose the potential richness of this field of investigation. As can be seen, it overlaps considerably with a number of other fields, notably with ethnomethodology, in which, indeed, it has its origins. My intention is not to define another exclusive and competing enclosure; it is rather to expand our capacity to investigate a phenomenon which is necessarily, though generally invisibly, present in other areas of sociological investigation. Moreover, there are overlaps with other disciplines, as there must be in any field of sociology concerned with language, notably with the meta-epistemological work of Foucault and with the impressive and rapidly expanding structuralist, post-structuralist, and hermeneutic explorations of literary texts represented by the work of Barthes, Iser, Kristeva, Derrida, and others. I have avoided precise definitions here precisely because investigating the phenomena of textuality bid fair to break us out of our disciplinary enclaves and we cannot yet see what new relations will crystallize in our terminologies.

SOME ELEMENTARY CONSIDERATIONS

The simple properties of the documentary or textually mediated forms of social organization involve their dependence upon, and exploitation of, the textual capacity to crystallize and preserve a definite form of words detached from their local historicity.[2] The appearance of meaning as a text, that is, in permanent material form, detaches meaning from the lived processes of its transitory construction, made and remade at each moment of people's talk. In pre-literate or pre-print societies, the concentration of meaning in a form not subject to the essential temporality of the lived social process was vested in ritual, megalith, and image. In our time, by contrast, extra-temporal modes of meaning are created by the written or printed form.[3] The vesting of meaning in such permanent or semi-permanent forms is routine and commonplace, and has transformed our relation to language, meaning, and each other. Texts speak in the absence of speakers; meaning is detached from local contexts of interpretation; the 'same' meaning (Olson 1977) can occur simultaneously in a multiplicity of socially and temporally disjointed settings (Benjamin 1969). In the distinctive formation of social organization mediated by texts, their capacity to transcend the essentially transitory character of social processes and to remain uniform across separate and diverse local settings is key to their peculiar force (though that transcendence is itself an accomplishment of transitory social processes).

THE ETHNOMETHODOLOGICAL DISCOVERY

The discovery of the text as a significant constituent of social relations must be credited to ethnomethodology. Much of Garfinkel's initial formulation insists that organizational records cannot be understood as objective accounts which can be treated (by social scientists) as independent of their organizational uses and contexts of their production and interpretation. Rather, the sense and rationality of such documentary practices are and must be accomplished in local historical settings (Garfinkel 1967b). Ethnomethodology has insisted on the view that sense, rationality, facticity, etc., are essentially products of, and accomplished in, local historical settings. This has opened the way to the investigation of reasoning, facticity, rationality, and sense-making not as processes going on in people's heads but as social practices. As I pointed out in Chapter 1, these discoveries are grounded in the emergence of forms of social organization which were not characteristic of the societies of a hundred years ago. They are forms that externalize social consciousness in social practices, objectifying reasoning, knowledge, memory, decision-making, judgement, evaluation, etc., as properties of formal organization or discourse rather than as properties of individuals. They are, of course, accomplished only by individuals in everyday local settings, who enter into and participate in objectified forms constituting organizational and discursive relations beyond themselves. Such objectified and objectifying forms are essentially textual.

THE TEXTUAL CHARACTER OF RULING APPARATUS: OBJECTIFIED SOCIAL FORMS

Advanced contemporary industrialized societies are pervasively organized by textually mediated forms of ruling. The organizational processes that execute, control, regulate, inform, and order, in the various sites of governing, management, administration, discursive relations, professional organization, etc., are loosely coordinated as a complex of ruling relations and apparatus. These relations have in general been known in sociology as systems of rational action. They are characterized by a capacity to realize the same forms, relations, courses of action, etc., in the varieties and multiplicities of the local settings in which they operate and regulate. Essential to this capacity are the textual bases that objectify knowledge, organization, and decision processes, distinguishing what individuals do for themselves from what they do organizationally or discursively, thereby constituting properties of formal organization or of discourse that cannot be attributed to individuals.

Let me clarify with an example the notion of objectified social consciousness as a property of organization and its relation to texts. I presented there two accounts of the same event – a confrontation between police and people on the street which took place during the 1960s in the United States (Darrough 1978; Eglin 1979; Chapter 5 of this book). The contrast I want to draw is between the version telling the story from the point of view of a witness to the scene and the version issued by the office of the Mayor and containing the result of the Police Chief's investigation of the affair. The second account is an institutional account. The events are viewed from no particular location. The tellers and their points of observation cannot be identified. Furthermore, and particularly relevant here, the time-frame is of a different order.

In Chapter 5 one episode appearing in both accounts is analyzed in detail. The witness's version described a young man being searched rather roughly by the police. The Mayor's account redescribes this same episode using the organizational and legal category of 'juvenile' – 'the young man was a juvenile' – and tells us that he was later charged with 'being a minor in possession of alcoholic beverages' and found guilty. The latter description lifts us immediately out of the locally observed sequence of events and into organizational time. The continuities of the course of action involved in charging an individual with an offense and of that individual being found guilty is an accomplishment of an extended organizational process. The work of various categories of persons is involved – police, court officials, lawyers perhaps, social workers, probation officers, etc. Coordination is achieved by inscription in a record which makes up 'the record' for this young man, under which his actions on particular occasions can be interpreted. Through the use of this language and these references we are at once located in a temporal structure extending beyond the present of the observer, whereby the local events become an instance, a mere moment, in an extended social course of action. To have a record, to be 'known' to the police, is an organizational accomplishment creating a special character for whoever is located in the records of an organization. This is a form of social consciousness which is a property of organization rather than of the meeting of individuals in local historical settings.

These, of course, were the forms of social relations which Weber analyzed as rational legal forms of domination, focusing in his time particularly upon the bureaucratic process (Weber 1968). For bureaucracy is *par excellence* that mode of governing which separates the performance of ruling from particular individuals, and makes organization independent of particular persons and local settings. Weber saw documents as an essential part of the bureaucratic process. In his time the transfer of functions of social consciousness from individuals to the textual practices of formal organization had not yet reached the degree of technical elaboration attained with the development of the computer. Today, large-scale organization inscribes its processes into textual modes as a continuous feature of its functioning. For example, multiple copies of forms in which entries to a course of organiz- ational action are inscribed exercise a coordinating function sup- planting the older coordinations built into a 'role' structure and sets of (written) rules. Such developments render organizing functions increasingly independent of individuals. The accounting practices of corporations, certified by warranted inspectors (chartered accountants), are the basis on which plans for mergers may be developed. Systems of management are textual systems, including the refinements of piece work rates that organize the textile workers' work and relations on the shop floor. Progressively over

213

the last hundred years a system of organizational consciousness has been produced, constructing 'knowledge, judgement, and will' in a textual mode and transposing what were formerly individual judgements, hunches, guesses, and so on, into formulae for analyzing data or making assessments. Such practices render organizational judgement, feedback, information, or coordination into objectified textual rather than subjective processes.

THE TEXTUAL CHARACTER OF THE RULING APPARATUS: DISCOURSE

In our discussion of the textual practices of the ruling apparatus the term 'discourse' has been used for those forms of communi-cation and interrelation that are mediated by texts – journals, magazines, newspapers, books, television, movies, etc. These are distinctive contemporary forms of social organization which intersect with the largely hierarchical structures of state, business, and other administered formal organizations. They include scientific discourse as well as the public textual discourses of the mass media. Their ideological processes serve to coordinate sites of the ruling apparatus coming under different jurisdictions. When we locate these practices in the social organization of textually mediated discourse, we can begin to specify the actual social practices and relations otherwise conceptualized at the level of meaning as culture or ideology rather than as actual lived activity. Discourse creates forms of social consciousness that are extra-local and externalized *vis-à-vis* the local subject. As Foucault has pointed out, the subject in the texts of discourse 'is a particular, vacant place that may in fact be filled by different individuals' (Foucault 1972). Television advertisements that show the housewife, her gleaming floors, and the floor wax provide an ideological coordination of the social relations of consumers and producers. Whether or not a given housewife 'identifies' with the housewife in the commercial, the textual housewife's floors become a visual standard for her own in terms of which hers may be appraised and found wanting. The discourse of femininity (Chapter 6) is a distinctive order of social relations, knitting together multiple local sites of everyday/everynight practices and constituting a distinctive duality of the subject. Discourse develops the ideological currency of society, providing schemata and methods which transpose local actualities into standardized conceptual and categorical forms. Ideological practices bind the local to the discursive through interpretive circles whereby local instances index the 'text'.[4]

In recognizing how texts function as constituents of social relations or social courses of action my interest is not in tracing back through a given text to the determinations of its meaning structure but in explicating discourse as an active social process. This has been emphasized in my exploration of the discourse of femininity. It means that investigation cannot be confined to the text alone, but must take into account the socially organized practices, including sequences of talk, that are integral to the discursive process. Garfinkel, Lynch, and Livingston's (1981) discussion of a tape recorded sequence leading up to the discovery of a pulsar indicates an essential relation between the lived order of local historicity and the textually mediated discourse. A series of observations as a feature of that lived order has as its intentions the 'possibility that it could become an atemporalized collection of measurable properties of pulse frequency and star location that ... are independent of the local practice' constituting the collection of observations. As has been shown, this movement between the locally historic and the textually mediated discourse is characteristic of many contemporary social forms in addition to science – for example, law, formal organization, the public textual discourse of the mass media. Much of our ordinary language refers to the recurrent accomplishments of their social organization. The notion of 'fact', for example, indicates a recurrent orderliness of movement from locally ordered observations to the textually mediated discourse they intend, the intertextuality of the discourse and further locally historic usages (Latour and Woolgar 1979; Smith 1990).

The movement between the local historical order and textual time is also typical of the public textual discourse of the mass media. It is misleading to treat news, for example, as arising in a simple relation in which information given on one side is received by the other. Rather different kinds of news have different uses and are embedded in (and structure) different kinds of discursive relations. Sports news, for example, enters and is embedded in conversations, mainly among men, and as much between strangers or casual acquaintances as between friends. Similarly, political news can be investigated as a constituent of complex relations of textually mediated discourse and local historic processes (Chua 1979; Chapter 5 of this book).

INSCRIPTION

The process of constructing the objectified forms of social consciousness as textual practices is not best understood as going from a definite initial event or object to an objective record of the event or description of the object. It is better understood as a constitutional work that accomplishes an event or object in the process of its textual inscription. Latour and Woolgar's ethnography of a scientific laboratory describes the appearance of experimental results in computer print-outs (Latour and Woolgar 1979). These textual forms constitute the observables. Lynch's (1983) analysis of 'perception' in the context of scientific discourse demonstrates that the mediation of the text is essential to the standardization of the scientific observable. He describes how the local actualities of observation are geometricized in a series of graphic abstractions made on paper. Each step of the series takes the process a stage further in rendering the object measurable. He argues that this graphic work constructs from the actualities in their raw or savage form those measurable abstractions that are the currency of scientific discourse. Frankel and Beckman have examined the construction of clinical reality in a medical setting, showing how the text-making process – a movement from talk to record taking – influences the production of 'facts' (Frankel and Beckman 1983). Suicide as a legally determinate event does not emerge 'naturally' from the local historical process. Coroner and police intervene to inscribe a particular death in the textual forms that enunciate its final character as suicide (Atkinson 1978; Smith 1990). 'Facts' arise in processes mediated by textual forms.

The process of inscription is of special significance at the boundaries of organization or discourse where 'environing' actualities are converted into the conceptual and categorical order of organizational or discursive courses of action. The production of factual accounts of all kinds is an important part of this process. Facticity itself may well be a distinctive property of textual processes; it certainly plays an important role in the constitution of objectified forms of social consciousness characteristic of the ruling apparatus. We have already noted it as an aspect of the social organization of scientific discourse. In his study of how facts are derived in a welfare agency, Zimmerman (1969) investigates the work of inscription at the boundaries of local actualities and their organizational conversion. He shows how welfare workers assemble factual accounts of their welfare clients' financial status, etc. The welfare worker's investigation is informed by a 'stance' which never takes the client's word but relies on external textual sources (bank statements, birth certificates, etc.) or home visits. Substitution of the 'investigative stance' for the caseworker's subjective judgement is essential to the constitution of organizational facticity. And, although Zimmerman does not describe this phase of the process, it is the accomplishment of the facticity of these accounts that permits them then to be entered into further organizational courses of action leading to decisions about the award of funds to clients.

Discourse and objectified organization acquire their transcendence of local historicities in such inscriptive processes. Ideological practices are an important form of inscription. They begin within the transcendent schemata of discourse or formal organization. An interpretive schema is used to assemble and order a set of particulars – descriptions or instances of actualities. These aim at and can be interpreted by the schema used to assemble them. The particulars become indices of an underlying pattern, corresponding to the schema, in terms of which they make sense. The ordering of events, objects, etc., is thus pre-informed by the schema of discourse or formal organization. This is the ideological process at the boundaries of discourse or formal organization. It is of considerable significance in the exercise of power by the ruling apparatus (Smith 1990).

THE FORMALITY OF FORMAL ORGANIZATION AS TEXTUAL PRACTICES [5]

The investigation of textual practices makes visible many phases of the organizational and discursive processes that are otherwise inaccessible. In particular the formality, the designed, planned, and *organized* character of formal organization, depends heavily on textual practices, which coordinate, order, provide continuity, monitor, and *organize* relations between different segments and phases of organizational courses of action, etc.

Organizational texts order and coordinate the practices of dispersed organizational settings. Hence they will be read and interpreted differently on different organizational occasions.[6] A job description, for example, is misread by the sociologist if she expects to be able to treat it as an account of an actual work process. In fact, its organizational force is in part achieved precisely because it *does not describe any particular work* process but can enter a variety of settings and order the relations among them. It is first of all an element in a set of such descriptions organizing the internal relations and labor market of a large-scale organization. This will have been devised by a personnel department, possibly with the aid of professional managerial consultants. It will have been authorized by the financial department and have passed through whatever other processes are required to establish its organizational warrant. It may then enter in a variety of ways into organizational courses of action. For example, in developing the work organization of a new unit, the person in charge (a textual reference in itself) must operate with a set of job descriptions defining the possible array of positions, relations among them, qualifications of personnel, salaries, etc. Any actual distribution of tasks must be mandated by such descriptions. The question is not whether this job description describes this person or this task allocation, but whether work *can be* described by, or subsumed under, the assigned job description and is thereby organizationally authorized.

When actually hiring, a job description functions as a schema ordering selective attention to an individual's qualifications and experience – themselves textual products. Thus the job description operates as a method of interpreting the particulars of an individual's record. Personnel evaluations are another context in which an analogous procedure is at work. For example, considerable overlap has been observed between the work of executives and their secretaries or administrative assistants in the setting of a government department. But the tasks that accrue to executives as a basis for their further advancement do not play the same role in the career of the secretary. The latter's job description, and the appraisal categories derived from it, define the administrative and executive work which she does as ancillary to, and delegated by, the executive for whom she works; its descriptive categories make the work done by the secretary observable as 'secretarial' rather than as executive or administrative work. Hence, perform- ance evaluations do not build up for secretaries' accounts of their work experience which would establish a basis for advancement to executive positions. Their records show no documented affirmed experience in executive work which does not fit in with the systems of representations ordering the internal labor market of the organization (Reimer 1983). Through such textual practices, organizational processes are coordinated without the direct inter- positions of a chain of command or similar directly communicative process. This is the substance of bureaucracy or objective organiz- ation; the formality of formal organization is an integral feature thereof.

The textual practices constitutive of the formality of formal organization are not idiosyncratic but are embedded in and articulated with those of the extended social relations of the ruling apparatus. Textually mediated discourses interpenetrate and coordinate the schemata, categories, and the conceptual ordering of practices of ruling. The standardization of job descriptions or methods of generating job descriptions across firms facilitates the functioning of extended labor market relations; they are indeed integral to their organization. For example, documented (certi- fied) skills constitute competence as a labor market commodity. They correspond to occupational categories formulated and warranted by government agencies, such as departments of labor. Categories such as mining engineer, mechanical engineer, and so forth specify determinate packages of skills.[7] Such categories are used by formal organizations to articulate their internal division of labor to the external labor market. Increasingly now this textual function is passing from government to management consultants with important accompanying changes in the textual technologies of large-scale management. The person-sized packages of oc- cupational categories are being broken down into standardized dimensions of tasks which can be used to assemble job descriptions rendering jobs widely comparable.[8] This new standardization re- presents the interposition of a professional managerial discourse originating in firms of managerial consultants as well as in universities and can be expected to be increasingly significant for skill certification. But whether we look at the old or the new, standardization and coordination of internal divisions of labor and external labor markets are organized textually. Formal organization is permeated with textual practices tying its internal processes to extended social relations intersecting management and professional organization.

This, however, is only one instance of a very general process in which textual practices tie the internal processes of formal organization to the extended social relations of the ruling apparatus. For example, in organizations concerned with processing people, characteristic forms of co-ordinating work processes focused on individuals are textual. In the psychiatric context, for instance, the notion of individual 'case' refers to a textual practice (Green 1983). Indeed 'cases' as organizational elements exist as continuous (locally accomplished) relations between individuals and their records. The latter include the reports of interviews with physicians, observations by the nurses of the patients' behavior on the ward, records of medications, social workers' investigations of the patients' family situation, etc. Individuals are known as 'cases' under the interpretive aegis of their records. When decisions are to be made their 'current status' is located in the textual traces of their past contained therein. The phrase 'current status' itself refers to this textual order.[9] But the method and categories of the records are not idiosyncrasies of a particular hospital or clinic. Standardized methods of observation and investigation, categories, interpretive schemata and practices, and the like, have been evolved in the discourses of psychiatry and related professions.[10] Professional discourse has in its turn been influenced by the local textual accomplishment of 'cases' and hence incorporates the local textual practices of psychiatric organizations as its presuppositions (Smith 1990). Here, as in the previous example, unveiling the textual process displays relations between the local social order and the larger social structure as practices in language that can be directly investigated.

Making the textual dimension of formal organization visible potentially eliminates the conceptual isolation of organizational process. Though organizational theory has been increasingly interested in how formal organization is embedded in an environment, its conceptual practices preserve the isolation of the organization itself as the primary unit of investigation. The investigation of textual practices enables us by contrast to explicate the extended social relations of the ruling apparatus. Formal organization is no longer seen as isolated but as permeated with relations coordinating it with other phases and forms of the process of ruling.

DIRECTIONS FOR RESEARCH

The foregoing discussion implies an approach to documents or texts which situates them in social relations. It thereby avoids treating as given the very practices of detachment characteristic of the textual mode. It insists also on the materiality of the text and hence on the technologies of its reproduceability and the organized practices of its distribution as fundamental to the relations it organizes. It avoids accepting the conventions of textual time, insisting rather on seeing texts as constituents of the social courses of action in which they become active (remembering, of course, that the activity of a text is a function of its reading). Hermeneutic practices – concepts, categories, codes, methods of interpretation, schemata, and the like – must be understood as active constituents of social relations and social courses of action rather than merely as constituents or indices of that amorphous designate 'culture'. Interpretive practices which 'activate' the text are viewed as properties of social relations and not merely as the competences of individuals (see Chapter 4). Interest in the interpretive moment is not in the idiosyncrasy but in those practices presupposed by the idiosyncrasy which belong in a given discursive or organizational setting and which individuals enter when actually reading. Further, recognizing document or text as a constituent of social relations also means being interested in the social organization of its production as a prior phase in the social relation rather than as the work of a particular author.

I wish to emphasize the linearity and temporality of the concept of social relation. As I have come to use it, it analyzes contexts of texts, speech, or acts not as limited by a time-bound frame – setting, occasion, etc. – but as constituents of a sequential social course of action through which various subjectivities are related. A given locally historic instance is explored as a constituent. It is an analysis which seeks to disclose the non-local determinations of locally historic or lived orderliness. In the first section above, it was pointed out that an important effect of the text is to transcend local historical time. Such possibilities as multiple simultaneous occurrences of a text, or its repeated uses on a number of occasions on which it is treated as 'the same', are to be seen as organizing extra-local relations among the different settings. The replicable or recurrent character, the 'patterning' of the social relations of ruling, depend upon this movement between the textual and the locally historic.

The earlier discussion of inscription has given some idea of the research being done in the conversion of the locally historic into the textual mode. The other central focus of the investigation into textual relations and forms of action must be the reader–text relation. Specialized methods of research are needed. Textual analyses must be a primary but not, of course, exclusive method of investigation. The notion of a social relation or extended social relations as sequential and replicable courses of social action involving more than one individual should not be conceived as subject to examination as such. Rather it offers an analytic procedure enabling local instances to be situated in terms of their role in the movement of such a social course of action. Thus the investigation of the text–reader relation must preserve the movement and sequence of the social relation. Analytic strategies that begin in textual time, treating the text as an internally determined structure of meaning, will not serve this purpose; hence semiotic and structural analyses do not apply. And though very different, the ethnomethodological investigations of Morrison (1981) into textual order suffer from the same limitation. On the other hand, Eglin's (1979) study of how readers resolve contradictions between two versions of a single episode, while it does not situate readers' practices in a specific relation, none the less explicates members' methods of reading a text as an actual social practice. And McHoul's (1982) ethnography of the reader's work in making sense of a news item preserves the text–reader relation. Both the latter, however, isolate the text–reader relation as a unit in itself so that they do not situate the moment of reading, in Eglin's case, in a political discourse intersecting with the social organization of a university course (his analysis is of students' written responses to reading the two versions) or, in McHoul's, in the news–reader relation with its own distinctive properties. The argument here is that the text–reader relation must be explored as a part of a sequence of social action which includes interpretive practices. Hence textual analyses must explain how the text as petrified meaning structures the reader's interpretation and hence how its meaning may be entered into succeeding phases of the relation.

The text does not appear from nowhere. Its detachment from the social relation it organizes is a product of the intervention of the sociologist who wrenches it out of its local context as a collocation of meaning directly available for analysis in itself. This is the basic presupposition of the above methods of analysis. The text, however, should rather be understood as having been produced to intend the interpretive practices and usages of the succeeding phases of the relation. The text–reader moment is contained as a potentiality in the text itself. For example, an analysis of a factual account of someone becoming mentally ill (Chapter 2) shows how the descriptions of the individual's behavior were structured to create normative anomalies which could not be restored to a normal form. Given the reader's competence in the use of mental illness as a schema of interpretation, mental illness could be 'seen' to emerge from the normatively anomalous behavior. To know how to produce an account of mental illness that invokes such methods of reading, and to know how to make such a reading, unites reader and writer as practitioners of an extended social relation of psychiatric discourse (including as it does its extension into public textual discourse). Such interpretive practices are properties of social relations. This does not exclude or invalidate other kinds of interests in a text. But if we are to analyze textual materials for their properties as organizers of social relations, methods of textual analysis are required which explicate the active power of the text as it is realized or activated by the competent reader. The analytical ability to investigate the text and to discover the ways in which it has aimed at its analysis (this provides the methodological grounding for the analysis) depends upon the competence in the practitioner of those relations. Thus the analyst does not have to pretend to withdraw as a member of society in performing analytic work. On the contrary, such analysis depends precisely on such membership; if the analyst does not already command the interpretive method of the relational process being investigated, she will have to learn it.

Insisting on the materiality of the text and on the actual socially organized activities, including writing and reading, articulating texts to social relations, is fundamental to a materialist investigation of knowledge and 'culture'. The study of documentary or textually mediated social relations, as I have envisaged it, is not a distinct field, developing its own theories and methods of research. It is, as I emphasized in the introductory chapter, the extension of a materialism synthesized by Marx into forms of consciousness that are externalized in definite socially organized relations and forms. The analyses of texts, presented in this book, investigate how texts, in their reading, are 'active' in the actual organization of such relations. Textual analysis, as practiced here, explores the ubiquitous and generalizing organization of the ruling relations. Rather than superseding sociological investigations of formal organization, of the state, of mass media, or of other elements of the ruling apparatus, my intention is to rewrite their fundamental ontology. The actual practices ordering the daily relations that regulate contemporary advanced capitalist society, however conceptualized, can be subject to empirical inquiry, to ethnographic exploration, once texts are recognized as integral and 'active' constituents. Uncovering texts as constituents of relations anchors research in the actual ways in which relations are organized and how they operate. The enterprise is indeed grandiose; it is that of transforming our understanding of the nature of power when power is textually mediated.

NOTES

CHAPTER 1 INTRODUCTION

1 For a fuller explication of what is meant by an 'insider's sociology', see my *Everyday World as Problematic: A Feminist Sociology* (Smith 1987).
2 We can, of course, question whether what I learned was the lesson Marx meant to teach. At this historical point, we can already see that what Marx had to teach is refracted in a multiplicity of different sites of reading. But I am claiming only to have learned and not to be making an exegesis.
3 See Derek Sayer's discussion of Marx's view of the 'historicity of concepts' (Sayer 1987: 126–49).
4 This is generally true of Marxist theorizing as well. But most contemporary Marxist analyses do not work with a materialist ontology in the sense in which I have discussed it above.
5 The masculine reference here is conscious.
6 See Marx's discussion of the method of political economy in *Grundrisse* (Marx 1976: 100–2).

CHAPTER 2 K IS MENTALLY ILL: THE ANATOMY OF A FACTUAL ACCOUNT

1 This paper has been published previously as 'K ist geisteskrank. Die Anatomie eines Tatsachenberichtes' in 1976 in E. Weingarten, F. Sack, and J.N. Schenkein (eds) *Ethnomethodologie. Beitrage zu einer Soziologie des Alltagslebens*, Frankfurt: Suhrkamp.
2 This sentence is lifted directly from Austin's paper on 'Pretending' (Austin 1964: 113), but I have modified the wording and therefore supply it without quotes.

CHAPTER 3 THE SOCIAL ORGANIZATION OF SUBJECTIVITY: AN ANALYSIS OF THE MICRO-POLITICS OF A MEETING

1 The document is transcribed from a tape recording made at one of a series of semi-public meetings. The meeting was the last of four which met to discuss the state of the university. The second meeting of the series had been a panel discussion which included an active leader of the student movement from another university, the then president of the University of British Columbia, a minister from the city, and two faculty members. I was in the audience on that occasion. The session which I analyze was the one which followed that on the evening of the same day. The chair of the meeting was a graduate student, its speaker a member of the faculty. Among those who discussed the paper he presented were the same active members of the student movement who had been present at the panel discussion earlier. What was said into the microphones available at the meeting was taped and transcribed by a steno-graphic firm.

The transcript was made up for distribution in a bound volume but it includes no additional information about the occasion other than that which the title-page and transcription provide. I do not know how many people were present. The transcript presents us with a chair, a speaker, and some members of an audience, in all some seven or eight people, but the chair's approach to organizing the meeting, including situating the mikes, suggests the presence of a fairly substantial audience. The chair refers to microphones distributed among the audience and this electronic facility means that discussion of what the speaker said was effectively recorded and is available on the transcript.

The transcript includes only what was voiced through microphone and hence only what participants intended to make public as part of the meeting. Thus the technical provision for the transcription served as part of the actual procedures which constitute what, for the public textual record, happened on that occasion. The transcript does not include the asides, the mutters, the coughs, the sniggers, or the like. It does not include what was said in the break for beer which intervened between the end of the speaker's reading of his paper and the beginning of the publicly recorded discussion. Clearly either at the point of transcription or as part of the recording procedures, decisions were being made about what was part of the meeting and should be recorded and what was not.

I do not know what kind of editorial work was done. Gaps in the transcription where the stenographer could not make out what was said have been left in the text as gaps. There are errors in spelling ('Herbert Marcoust' clearly should be 'Herbert Marcuse'). There are points at which a sense is not recoverable from the text without reconstruction. I judge therefore that while there has been considerable accidental editorial work on the part of the typist making out as best she could the unfamiliar material, the editorial work at the point of transcription has otherwise been slight. I have not supplemented it myself. When I quote I reproduce the text of the transcription. Thus the occasion as we have it is mediated to us by the social and technical organization which produced the text. This includes those aspects of what was done at the meeting which were directed towards the making of such a text; the actual recording and transcription procedures (including therefore, decisions made about when the recording equipment should be started and stopped) and so forth.

This mediating organization is not the topic of the chapter but the status of the analysis cannot be properly evaluated without taking it into account. This is a moment in the social relation or socially organized course of action mediating between the world as it happens and the world inscribed in texts as it becomes available to us as data. Our work as sociologists has characteristically the form of a doughnut in which the hole turns out to be part of the same space which encloses the surface which constitutes the hole. The infinite regress that some sociologists worry about or decide not to worry about is not really an infinite regress, it is a doughnut.

2 Letters in square brackets refer to the passage from the transcript presented in the next section, 'The social organization of the occasion', p.61.

3 A quotation from the paper as it was transcribed.

4 Numbers in brackets after extracts from the transcript refer to page and line numbers in the original document.

5 'Mr Robinson' read the original version of this paper. He dissented from only one passage, which has been removed.

6 From the transcript of Mr Robinson's paper as read on that occasion.

7 The concepts of 'because of' and 'in order to' motives are Schutz's (Schutz 1962b).

8 The passage from which this is taken is quoted more fully on p. 74.

9 Of course edited out by the mechanics of the recording procedure and transcription.

10 This representation must not be taken as an account of all that the speaker said about the development of student uprisings. It is that aspect which is specifically constitutive of the episodic structure that I have isolated.

11 From the transcript of the meeting.

CHAPTER 4   ON SOCIOLOGICAL DESCRIPTION: A METHOD FROM MARX

1 This paper was originally presented by invitation at the Department of Sociology of the University of California at Santa Barbara during May 1977. I am very much indebted to the department for the

opportunity to develop this work and discuss it with them. I should like also to make special acknowledgement of the advice and encouragement of Tom Wilson and Don Zimmerman. The research on which this work is based was funded by Canada Council Grant Number S73–1457.

2 Nancy Jackson's research resulted in a valuable methodological study, 'Describing news: towards an alternative account', that formed her MA thesis in Sociology at the University of British Columbia (Jackson 1974).

3 A useful model of the relation between the organization of local settings (of production) and the extended social relations of (a capitalist) mode of production is provided by Marx in a chapter that was not in the end included in *Capital.* He is working through the ways in which the subordination of productive organization to the relations of capital changes its internal relationships of 'supremacy and subordination' (Marx 1977: 1027) without any change of technology. Among other examples, he spends some time analyzing the shift in productive organization from the master–journeyman–apprentice mode in which the authority of the master is based upon his mastery of his craft.

> He is an artisan in the first place and is supposed to be a master of his craft. Within the process of production he appears as an artisan, like his journeymen, and it is he who initiates his apprentices into the mysteries of the craft. He has precisely the same relationship to his apprentices as a professor to his students. Hence his approach to his apprentices and journeymen is not that of a capitalist, but of a *master* of his craft, and by virtue of that fact he assumes a position of superiority in the corporation and hence towards them.
>
> (Marx 1977: 1029)

The subordination of such organization to capitalist social relations transforms the internal structure of the productive organization. 'The master now ceases to be a capitalist because he is a master, and becomes a master because he is a capitalist' (Marx 1977: 1031).

The analytic power of this concept of social relation for sociology lies, in my view, precisely in its capacity to examine the local organization of settings, occasions, work, the ordinary stuff of sociology, as they are coordinated with and determined by the extended social relations coordinating the multiplicity of actual local sites of people's activities and experience.

4 By 'normal positivism' I do not mean an explicit methodological commitment to a positivist epistemology. I am referring rather to those taken-for-granted practices of most social scientific discourses that treat the 'objects' of which discourse speaks as existing in a non-problematic way 'out there'. This is particularly striking in economics and political economy. I am suggesting here that this

normal positivism is grounded in the co-occurrence of the same terms in the 'original' setting in which they are part of a working vocabulary and in the discourse. It seems likely that the ordinary cogency and hence unproblematic character of such textual practices for a given social scientific discourse depend upon the possibility of incorporating into discourse what is already known in an unexplicated way of the operations of the term in its original site. This is another way of addressing a part of what ethnomethodology has addressed as indexicality.

5   Here I am using the term 'original' to speak of that which the description intends. So we can think of the relation between description and its original as a grammatical relation. Each term arises in relation to the other and implies the other. The original comes into being as what has been described and the description implicates the original.

6   We shall in this context be thinking mainly in terms of instances of sociological description. I have not attempted to ensure that these explications of descriptive practices are generalizable to all cases, though I shall claim implicitly that they are not restricted to sociological description.

7   See Tuchman's interesting paper on telling stories (Tuchman 1976).

CHAPTER 5   THE ACTIVE TEXT: A TEXTUAL ANALYSIS OF THE SOCIAL RELATIONS OF PUBLIC TEXTUAL DISCOURSE

1   This was originally presented as a paper at the World Congress of Sociology in Mexico City in 1981.

2   A deeper problem arises with the multiple levels of interpretation involved in the reading of a text – there are, for example, the fundamental operations of syntax which are presupposed in an analysis of the kind projected here. Some of the differences in analysis in the literature cited at the beginning of the chapter result from differences in the level at which analysis goes on. For example, in addition to differences in how the two texts investigated in this chapter have been thematized in studies by Darrough and Eglin, there appear to be differences in analytic level. Darrough's analysis is at the level of social process; Eglin's addresses the devices used by readers to handle the discrepancies between the two accounts. The level of Darrough's analysis would appear to presuppose that of Eglin's; and mine in this chapter is presupposed in both. We are not yet able to address the problem of levels systematically, to lay out the logic of their relations and hence to begin to determine whether levels correspond to methodical properties of the phenomenon or are merely the contingent effects of different angles of approach. The problem of levels as opposed to alternative angles of approach is also posed by the work of McHoul and

Morrison, whose micro-analyses of textual work address a level presupposed in the kind of analysis presented here.

3 These texts originated with William Darrough and I am indebted to him for their use. He has analyzed them in the context of problems in the relations between public and police, resulting, he suggests, from public misconceptions about the nature of the police mandate (Darrough 1978). Peter Eglin's more recent work on the same texts addresses the issue of the 'reality disjunctures' presented by them, working with students' written discussions of them. (Eglin 1979).

4 Personal communication, William Darrough.

5 My source here is Darrough (1978).

6 Darrough – personal communication.

7 The numbers in parentheses after quotations refer to the numbered lines in the texts reproduced later in the chapter.

8 I have adopted Eglin's lettering and numbering of the lines to facilitate comparison and cross-reference. I have made two modifications. One is that, in addition to lettering the versions A and B, I have described A as the Professor's letter and B as the Mayor's response. It helps to keep things straight without referring back to the texts themselves. Second, the numbering in Eglin's version skips a line between 165 and 166. This has been corrected so that from lines 166 on, my numbering is one ahead of Eglin's.

9 I am indebted to Charles Goodwin for this observation.

10 Many of these are noted, in a different interpretive context, by Darrough (1978).

11 I have described a similar effect in a discussion of the structure of the account of the months leading up to Virginia Woolf's suicide in Clive Bell's biography. See Smith (1990).

CHAPTER 6   FEMININITY AS DISCOURSE

1 This paper has been published previously in a rather different and abridged form in Leslie G. Roman and Linda K. Christian-Smith (eds) (1988) *Becoming Feminine: The Politics of Popular Culture*, London: Falmer Press 37–59.

2 Though it also creates problems in exploring the relationship between biological and social or cultural sex.

3 For a marvelous explication of labor as an ontological category, see Lukács, *The Social Ontology of Being: Labour*. Lukács, however, is working with 'labor' as the primary theoretical category of historical materialism. In Marx's own work, the status of labour is quite ambiguous. It is given such primary theoretical formulation, including mind and thought, e.g. in *Capital*, vol. I. At the same time labor is also a category foundational to the superstructure of thought and governing that is conceived as outside labor as directly productive activity. This problem is, I think, the product of the historical setting of a work at a point in time when the textual and

extra-local organization of the superstructure had scarcely developed and therefore the possibility of exploring thought, knowledge, reasoning, as practical activities was no more than adumbrated in Marx's thought.

4   I have developed this method (see Smith 1987) from a conjunction of the materialist method developed by Marx and Engels (1976) and Garfinkel's ethnomethodology (Garfinkel 1967a). Both of the latter ground inquiry in the actual ongoing activities of actual individuals. For Marx and Engels, society and history come into being only as the ongoing actual activities of individuals and the material conditions of those activities and not otherwise. Though there are of course important divergences. In particular, Garfinkel's work opens up the site of concerted social activities and practices in the textually mediated organization of management, professional work, government agencies, etc. to inquiry conforming to the stipulations of a materialist method which require a focus on actual ongoing practices in definite actual settings. It is this aspect of his method and thinking which I have brought into relation to Marxist materialism as I have interpreted it and which I have developed in my work in the social organization of knowledge.

5   The conceptualization of these phenomena as 'culture', as well as the older tradition going under the title of studies of the mass media, makes the texts the central focus and treats the audience as derivative (responding to, influenced by, implied by, etc.).

Recent approaches have attempted to revise the earlier exclusively textual focus. The new approaches to media studies introduced by the Birmingham Centre for Cultural Studies have broken with 'the passive and undifferentiated conceptions of the "audience"' of traditional research.

> We began to replace these too-simple notions with a more active conception of the 'audience', of 'reading' and of the relation between how media messages were encoded, the 'moment' of the encoded text and the variation of the audience 'decodings'.
> (Hall 1980: 118)

But the revised approach still takes the text as central; the audience is a derivative of the text; the central audience activity of 'decoding' is a textual activity ascribed to audience to complete the textual function.

6   For the purposes of this commentary, I am treating the radio broadcast as a text. Although it lacks some of the properties of the text proper in that it has not been given a permanent form enabling reader or hearer to return to it again and treat it as a meaning-event outside the temporal course of the lived world, none the less it is inserted into interaction in a characteristic textual fashion. It is *there* for them to orient to but not to interact with.

7   That is, texts that were not designed for these analytic purposes.

8 For a general account of the significance of print in the reorganization of communications and culture in Europe, see Eisenstein (1979).

9 The complete passage reads as follows:

> In the agricultural counties, and among the class to which these four persons belonged, there is little analysis of motive or comparison of characters and actions, even at this present day of enlightenment.
>
> Sixty or seventy years ago there was still less. I do not mean that amongst thoughtful and serious people there was not much reading of such books as *Mason on Self-Knowledge* and *Law's Serious Call*, or that there were not the experiences of the Wesleyans, that were related at class-meetings for edification of the hearers. But, taken as a general rule, it may be said that few knew what manner of men they were, compared to the numbers now who are fully conscious of their virtues, qualities, failings, and weaknesses, and who go about comparing others with themselves – not in a spirit of Pharisaism and arrogance, but with a vivid self-consciousness, that more than anything else deprives characters of freshness and originality....
>
> To return to the party we left standing on the high-raised footway that ran alongside of the bridle-path to Haytersbank. Sylvia had leisure in her heart to think 'how good Hester is for sitting with the poor bed-ridden sister of Darley!' without having a pang of self-depreciation in the comparison of her own conduct with that she was capable of so fully appreciating. She had gone to church for the ends of vanity, and remained to the funeral for curiosity and the pleasure of the excitement. In this way a modern young lady would have condemned herself, and therefore lost the simple, purifying pleasure of admiration of another.
>
> (Gaskell 1964: 64)

10 Similar discursive forms standardized household and family health and socialization practices, hence progressively articulating household and family to changing retail, medical, and educational practices.

11 Of interest also is the indication of a special focus on 'newness' – new shoes, a dress not worn before.

12 Can her phrasing be interpreted as expressing, and located in, the social relations of the textually mediated discourse, as I have formulated them to embrace both texts and practices of subjects?

13 In North America and Britain the Second World War created doctrinal clashes between the doctrines of 'femininity' and those of patriotism. How to justify, for example, the purchase of a new lipstick in the context of a morality of austerity and of women's work in distinctly non-feminine jobs. A Tangee advertisement finds

an ingenious synthesis of the doctrines of femininity and patriotism. 'A Tangee advertisement showed two women in overalls, one taking over the controls of an airplane; Lipstick, it said, is "an instrument of personal morale that helps her conceal heartbreak or sorrow; gives her self-confidence when it's badly needed..." (Gaine 1985: 43).

14 Chapter 1.

15 The second theme is Kalinda's wealth – her casual clothes are chic, the strand round her neck is gold; the khaki trousers show a 'designer's touch'; her sandals are Italian. The description of clothes clearly relies on the reader's knowledge of contemporary styles of dress, and the indicators of wealth.

16 Eventually she seeks an impossible transformation from a black soothsayer and goes mad.

17 In Toni Morrison's story, Pecola Breedlove's schoolmates ridicule one boy merely by suggesting that he associates with her (Morrison 1969: 39–40).

18 The reference is to Székely and Morris, 1986.

19 The black narrator of Morrison's *The Bluest Eye* (Morrison 1969) tells of destroying the 'blue-eyed, yellow-haired, pink-skinned doll[s]' she was given as a child.

20 Note that the images are various – magazines like *Bazaar* or *Mademoiselle* display a multiplicity of images, contained within stylistic boundaries characteristic of the magazine and defining the textually mediated community into which it is inserted and which it serves to organize.

21 Unfortunately I've lost the reference for this quotation and have not been able to locate it. It dates from 1983 (I think) and possibly appeared in *Mademoiselle*. Of course, I would appreciate hearing from anyone who happens to locate it.

22 This sentence quotes the title of Erving Goffman's book, *The Presentation of Self in Everyday Life* (Goffman 1959).

23 See John Fiske's marvellous essay 'Madonna' (Fiske 1989: 95–113).

CHAPTER 7   TEXTUALLY MEDIATED SOCIAL ORGANIZATION

1 This article has benefited greatly from discussions with Nancy Jackson.

2 The conception of local historicity is to be found in Garfinkel *et al.* (1981). It expresses the localized and irreversible movement of the social process as it is lived.

3 See my discussion of 'document time' in Smith (1974b). It is a concept which analyzes the fixity of the text as a social accomplishment.

4 This is a special case of Garfinkel's 'documentary method of interpretation' (Garfinkel 1967a). Garfinkel's use of the term 'documentary' in this phrase does not refer to documents or texts in the sense that is used in this chapter. It refers to the relation

between instances which 'document' or index an underlying pattern, where that pattern is a cumulation of all such 'instances'. The notion originates in Mannheim (1971).

5 For the content of this section, I am very much indebted to discussions with Marguerite Cassin.

6 Cassin's term. Cassin's organizational study of textual processes is reported in a Ph.D. dissertation in progress in the Department of Sociology in Education, Ontario Institute for Studies in Education.

7 This example was given to me by George Smith and is based on his researches into the governmental production of occupational categories and their role in the organization of the labor market. This is reported in a Ph.D. dissertation in progress in the Department of Sociology in Education, Ontario Institute for Studies in Education.

8 I am indebted here again to Cassin and also to Nancy Jackson for this observation.

9 Similar processes are observed by Cicourel and Kitsuse (1963) in the context of a high school

10 I have explored the conceptual practices of psychiatry in *The Conceptual Practices of Power*, Boston: Northeastern University Press, 1990.

BIBLIOGRAPHY

Aglietta, Michel (1987) *A Theory of Capitalist Regulation: The US Experience*, London: Verso.

Atkinson, J. Maxwell (1978) *Discovering Suicide: Studies in the Social Organization of Sudden Death*, London: Macmillan.

Austin, J.L. (1962) *How to do Things with Words*, London: Oxford University Press.

Austin, J.L. (1964) 'Pretending', in Donald F. Gustafson (ed.) *Essays in Philosophical Psychology*, Garden City, New York: Doubleday Anchor Books.

Banner, Lois W. (1983) *American Beauty*, Chicago: University of Chicago Press.

Barthes, Roland (1983) *The Fashion System*, New York: Hill & Wang.

Bartky, Sandra Lee (1988) 'Foucault, femininity and the modernization of patriarchal power', in Irene Diamond and Lee Quinby (eds) *Feminism and Foucault: Reflections on Resistance*, Boston, Mass.: Northeastern University Press.

Benjamin, Walter (1969) 'The work of art in the age of mechanical reproduction', in W. Benjamin *Illuminations*, New York: Schocken Books.

Browne, Naima and France, Pauline (1985) '"Only cissies wear dresses": A look at sexist talk in the nursery', in Gaby Weiner (ed.) *Just a Bunch of Girls*, Milton Keynes: Open University Press.

Brownmiller, Susan (1984) *Femininity*, New York: Simon & Schuster.

Caplow, Theodore (1968) *Two Against One: Coalitions in Triads*, Englewood Cliffs, NJ: Prentice-Hall.

Chernin, Kim (1983) *Womansize: the Tyranny of Slenderness*, London: The Women's Press.

Chua, Beng-Huat (1979) 'Democracy as a textual accomplishment', *The Sociological Quarterly* 20: 541–9.

Cicourel, Aaron V. (1969) *The Social Organization of Juvenile Justice*, New York: John Wiley.

Cicourel, Aaron V. and Kitsuse, John I. (1963) *The Educational Decision Makers*, Indianapolis: Bobbs-Merrill.

Clausen, John A. and Yarrow, Madeleine (eds) (1955) 'The impact of mental illness on the family', *Journal of Social Issues*, Special Issue, II (4).

Cohen, Leah (1984) *Small Expectations: Society's Betrayal of Older Women*, Toronto: McCelland & Stewart.

Darrough, William D. (1978) 'When versions collide: police and the dialectics of accountability', *Urban Life* 7 (3): 379–403.

Davis, Helen (1985) 'Women moving up in the Israeli army', in *Globe and Mail*, Toronto, 31 August.

Donovan, Carrie (1987) 'Paris Shapes', *New York Times Magazine*, 25 January: 56–9.

Durkheim, Emile (1960) *The Division of Labor in Society*, Glencoe, Ill.: The Free Press.

Eglin, Peter (1979) 'Resolving reality disjuncture on Telegraph Avenue: a study of practical reasoning', *Canadian Journal of Sociology* 4 (4): 359–75.

Ehlstain, Jean (1989) In Ian Angus and Sut Jhally (eds) *Cultural Politics in Contemporary America*, New York: Routledge.

Eisenstein, Elizabeth L. (1979) *The Printing Press as an Agent of Change: Communications and Cultural Transformation in Early Modern Europe*, Cambridge: Cambridge University Press.

Findlay, Barbara (1975) 'Shrink! Shrank! Shriek!', in Dorothy E. Smith and Sara J. David (eds) *Women Look at Psychiatry*, Vancouver: Press Gang.

Fish, Stanley E. (1967) *Suprised by Sin: The reader in Paradise Lost*, New York: St. Martin's Press.

Fiske, John (1989) *Reading the Popular*, Boston: Unwin Hyman.

Foucault, Michel (1972) *The Archaeology of Knowledge*, New York: Harper Colophon.

Frankel, Richard M. and Beckman, Howard B. (1983) 'Between physician and patient: the medical record and the construction of clinical reality', paper presented at the Annual Meetings of the Society for the Study of Social Problems, Detroit.

Gaine, Jane (1985) 'War, women and lipstick: fan mags in the forties', in *Heresies: A Feminist Publication on Art and Politics* 5 (2) issue 18: 42–7.

Garfinkel, Harold (1967a) *Studies in Ethnomethodology*, Englewood Cliffs, NJ: Prentice-Hall.

Garfinkel, Harold (1967b) 'Suicide, for all practical purposes', in *Studies in Ethnomethodology*, Englewood Cliffs, NJ: Prentice-Hall.

Garfinkel, Harold (1968) In Richard J. Hill and Kathleen Stones Crittenden (eds) *Proceedings of the Purdue Symposium on*

Ethnomethodology, Institute Monograph Series no. 1, Institute for the Study of Social Change, Purdue University.

Garfinkel, Harold, Lynch, Michael, and Livingstone, Edward (1981) 'The work of a discovering science construed with materials from the optically discovered pulsar', *Philosophy of the Social Sciences* 11: 131–58.

Gaskell, Elizabeth (1964) *Sylvia's Lovers,* London: Dent.

Giddings, Paula (1984) *When and Where I Enter . . . The Impact of Black Women on Race and Sex in America,* New York: William Morrow & Co.

Goffman, Erving (1959) *The Presentation of Self in Everyday Life,* New York: Doubleday Anchor Books.

Goffman, Erving (1961a) *Asylums: Essays on the Social Situation of Mental Patients and Other Inmates,* Garden City, NY: Doubleday Anchor Books.

Goffman, Erving (1961b) 'The moral career of the mental patient', *Asylums: Essays on the Social Situation of Mental Patients and Other Inmates,* Garden City, NY: Doubleday Anchor Books.

Goffman, Erving (1963) *Behavior in Public Places,* New York: The Free Press.

Gorham, Deborah (1982) *The Victorian Girl and the Feminine Ideal,* Bloomington, Ind.: Indiana University Press.

Green, Bryan S. (1983) *Knowing the Poor: A Case Study in Textual Reality Construction,* London: Routledge & Kegan Paul.

Hall, Stuart (1980) 'Introduction to media studies at the centre', in Stuart Hall, Dorothy Hobson, Andrew Lowe, and Paul Willis (eds) *Culture, Media, Language: Working Papers in Cultural Studies, 1972–9,* London: Hutchinson.

Harré, Rom (1961) *Theories and Things,* London: Sheed and Ward.

Haug, Frigga and Others (1987) *Female Sexualization: A Collective Work of Memory,* London: Verso.

Heron, Liz (1986) *Changes of Heart: Reflections on Women's Independence,* London: Pandora.

Holland, Norman (1975) *The Dynamics of Literary Response,* New York: W. Norton & Co.

Hurst, Lynda (1984) *Sunday Star,* 19 April.

Jackson, Nancy S. (1974) 'Describing news: towards an alternative account', M.A. thesis, Department of Anthropology and Sociology, University of British Columbia.

James, Stephanie (1982) *Corporate Affair,* New York: Silhouette Books.

Jones, Jacqueline (1987) *Labor of Love, Labor of Sorrow: Black Women, Work and the Family, from Slavery to the Present,* New York: Vintage Books.

Jules-Rosette, B. (1978) 'The politics of paradigms: contrasting theories of consciousness and society', *Human Studies* 1: 92–110.

Kitsuse, John I. (1962) 'Societal reaction to deviant behavior', *Social Problems* 9 (3) winter: 247–56.

Lakoff, Robin Tolmach and Scherr, Raquel L. (1984) *Face Value: The Politics of Beauty*, London: Routledge & Kegan Paul.

Latour, Bruno and Woolgar, Steve (1979) *Laboratory Life: Social Construction of Scientific Facts*, New York: Sage Publications.

Lemert, Edwin M. (1962) 'Paranoia and the dynamics of exclusion' *Sociometry* 25: 2–20.

Lipietz, Alain (1983) *The Enchanted World: Inflation, Credit and World Crisis*, London: Verso.

Lukács, Georg (1980) *The Ontology of Social Being: 3. Labour*, London: Merlin Press.

Lynch, Michael (1983) 'Discipline and the material form of images: an analysis of scientific visibility', paper presented at the meetings of the Canadian Sociology and Anthropology Association, Vancouver, BC.

Lyons, John (1963) *Introduction to Theoretical Linguistics*, Cambridge: Cambridge University Press.

McHoul, Alasdair W. (1982) *Telling How Texts Talk: Essays on Reading and Ethnomethodology*, London: Routledge & Kegan Paul.

MacKay, John (1985) 'We're entering era *[sic]* of "pretty" clothes', *Toronto Star*, 24 January.

McRobbie, Angela (1978) 'Working class girls and the culture of femininity', in Women's Studies Group, Centre for Contemporary Cultural Studies, *Women Take Issue: Aspects of Women's Subordination*, London: Hutchinson & Co.

Mannheim, Karl (1965) *Ideology and Utopia*, New York: Doubleday Anchor.

Mannheim, Karl (1971) 'On the interpretation of *Weltanschauung*', in K. Wolff (ed.) *From Karl Mannheim*, New York: Oxford University Press.

Marx, Karl (1971) *A Contribution to the Critique of Political Economy*, London: Lawrence & Wishart.

Marx, Karl (1976) *Grundrisse: Foundations of the Critique of Political Economy*, New York: Random House.

Marx, Karl (1977) *Capital: A Theory of Political Economy*, vol.I, New York: Vintage Books.

Marx, Karl and Engels, Friedrich (1973) *Feuerbach: Opposition of the Materialist and Idealist Outlooks*, London: Lawrence & Wishart.

Marx, Karl and Engels, Friedrich (1976) *The German Ideology*, Moscow: Progress Publishers.

Mead, George Herbert (1934) *Mind, Self and Society: From the Standpoint of a Social Behaviorist*, Chicago, Ill.: University of Chicago Press.

Mechanic, David (1962) 'Some factors in identifying mental illness',

Mental Hygiene 46, January: 66–75.

Morra, Bernadette (1989) 'New designers fashion festival', *Toronto Star*, 6 April.

Morrison, Kenneth L. (1981) 'Some properties of "telling-order designs" in didactive inquiry', *Philosophy of Social Sciences* 11: 245–62.

Morrison, Toni (1969) *The Bluest Eye*, New York: Washington Square Press.

Nairne, Kathy, and Smith, Gerrilyn (1984) *Dealing with Depression*, London: The Women's Press.

Okin, Susan Moller (1979) *Woman in Western Political Thought*, Princeton: Princeton University Press.

Olson, David (1977) 'From utterance to text: the bias of language in speech and writing', *Harvard Educational Review* 47 (3).

Orbach, Susie (1979) *Fat is a Feminist Issue: A Self-Help Guide for Compulsive Eaters*, New York: Berkley Books.

Polanyi, Michael (1967) *The Tacit Dimension*, New York: Doubleday Anchor Books.

Pollner, Melvin (1974) 'Sociological and common-sense models of the labelling process', in Roy Turner (ed.) *Ethnomethodology*, Harmondsworth, Middx: Penguin Books.

Poovey, Mary (1984) *The Proper Lady and the Woman Writer: Ideology as Style in the Works of Mary Wollstonecraft, Mary Shelley, and Jane Austen*, Chicago: University of Chicago Press.

Reimer, Marilee (1983) 'The organization of a gender-differentiated work force: the case of clerical work in the public sector', paper presented at the Annual Meetings of the Canadian Sociology and Anthropology Association, Vancouver, BC.

Roman, Leslie G. (1989) 'Intimacy, labor, and class: ideologies of feminine sexuality in the punk slam dance', in Leslie G. Roman and Linda K. Christian-Smith with Elizabeth Ellsworth *Becoming Feminine: The Politics of Popular Culture*, London: The Falmer Press.

Rousseau, Jean-Jacques (1979) *Emile or On Education*, introduction, translation and notes by Alan Bloom, New York: Basic Books.

Rubin, I.I. (1973) *Essays on Marx's Theory of Value*, Montreal: Black Rose Books.

Sacks, Harvey (1963) 'Sociological description', *Berkeley Journal of Sociology* 8: 1–16.

Sacks, Harvey (1972) 'On the analyzability of stories by children', in John J. Gumperz and Dell Hymes (eds) *Directions in Sociolinguistics: The Ethnography of Communication*, Holt, Rinehart & Winston.

Sayer, Derek (1987) *The Violence of Abstraction: The Analytic Foundations of Historical Materialism*, Oxford: Basil Blackwell.

Schegloff, Emmanuel and Sacks, Harvey (1973) 'Opening-up closings', *Semiotica* 8: 289–327.

Scheff, Thomas J. (1964) 'The societal reaction to deviance: ascriptive elements in the psychiatric screening of mental patients in a midwestern state hospital', *Social Problems* 11 (4) spring: 401–13.

Scheff, Thomas J. (1966) *Being Mentally Ill: A Sociological Theory*, Chicago: Aldine Press.

Schutz, Alfred (1962a) 'Commonsense and scientific interpetations of human action', in Alfred Schutz *Collected Papers*, vol. 1, The Hague: Martinus Nijhoff.

Schutz, Alfred (1962b) 'On multiple realities', *Collected Papers*, The Hague: Martinus Nijhoff.

Searle, John R. (1969) *Speech Acts: An Essay in the Philosophy of Language*, Cambridge: Cambridge University Press.

Silverman, David (1972) *Reading Castenada: A Prologue to the Social Sciences*, London: Routledge & Kegan Paul.

Smith, Dorothy E. (1974a) 'The ideological practice of sociology', *Catalyst* 8 Winter: 39–54

Smith, Dorothy E. (1974b) 'The social construction of documentary reality', *Social Inquiry* 44 (4): 257–68.

Smith, Dorothy E. (1975) 'The statistics on mental illness: what they will not tell us about women and why', in D.E. Smith and Sarah David (eds) *Women Look at Psychiatry*, Vancouver, BC: Press Gang.

Smith, Dorothy E. (1978) 'K is mentally ill: the anatomy of a factual account', *Sociology* 12 (1): 25–53.

Smith, Dorothy E. (1979) 'How settings determine descriptions of settings', unpublished paper.

Smith, Dorothy E. (1983) 'No one commits suicide: textual analyses of ideological practices', *Human Studies* 6: 309–59.

Smith, Dorothy E. (1984) 'Textually-mediated social organization', *The International Journal of Sociology* 36 (1): 59–75.

Smith, Dorothy E. (1987) *The Everyday World as Problematic: A Feminist Sociology*, Boston, Mass.: Northeastern University Press.

Smith, Dorothy E. (1988) 'Femininity as discourse', in Leslie G. Roman and Linda K. Christian-Smith (eds) *Becoming Feminine: The Politics of Popular Culture*, London: The Falmer Press.

Smith, Dorothy E. (1989) 'Sociological theory: writing patriarchy into feminist texts', in Ruth Wallace (ed.) *Feminism and Sociological Theory*, New York: Sage.

Smith, Dorothy E. (1990) *The Conceptual Practices of Power: A Feminist Sociology to Knowledge*, Boston, Mass.: Northeastern University Press.

Steele, Valerie (1985) *Fashion and Eroticism: Ideals of Feminine Beauty from the Victorian Era to the Jazz Age*, Oxford and New York: Oxford University Press.

Székely, Eva (1989) *Never Too Thin*, Toronto: Women's Press.

Székely, E. and Morris, N. (1986) 'Anorexia Nervosa: A psychometric investigation of hospitalized patients', unpublished paper.

Texier, Catherine (1985) 'Nancine, Lili and Chloe', *Heresies: A Feminist Publication on Art and Politics* 5 (2) issue 18: 20–1.

Tompkins, Jane P. (1980) *Reader-Response Criticism: From Formalism to Post-Structuralism*, Baltimore, Md.: Johns Hopkins University Press.

Tuchman, Gaye (1973) 'Making news by doing work: routinizing the unexpected', *American Journal of Sociology* 79 (1).

Tuchman, Gaye (1976) 'Telling stories', *Journal of Communication* 26 (4) autumn: 93–7.

Turner, Roy (1974a) 'Introduction', in R. Turner (ed.) *Ethnomethodology*, Harmondsworth, Middx: Penguin.

Turner, Roy (1974b) 'Words, utterances and activities', in R. Turner (ed.) *Ethnomethodology*, Harmondsworth, Middx: Penguin.

Weber, Max (1968) *Economy and Society*, Guenther Roth and Claus Wittich (eds), New York: Bedminster Press.

Whyte, William Foot (1955) *Street Corner Society*, Chicago, Ill.: University of Chicago Press.

Williamson, Judith (1978) *Decoding Advertisements*, London: Marion Boyars.

Wilson, Thomas P. (1970) 'Conceptions of interaction: a focus of sociological explanation', *American Sociological Review* 35 (4) august: 697–710.

Wittgenstein, Ludwig (1953) *Philosophical Investigations*, New York: Macmillan.

Yarrow, M. R., Schwartz, C. A., Murphy, H. S., and Deasy, L. C. (1955) 'The psychological meaning of mental illness in the family', in John A. Clausen and Madeleine R. Yarrow (eds) 'The Impact of Mental Illness on the Family', *Journal of Social Issues*, Special Issue, II (4): 12–24.

Young, Iris Marion (1989) 'Throwing like a girl: a phenomenology of feminine body comportment, motility, and spatiality', In Jeffner Allen and Iris Marion Young (eds) *The Thinking Muse: Feminism and Modern French Philosophy*, Bloomington, Ind.: Indiana University Press.

Zimmerman, Don H. (1969) 'Record-keeping and the intake process in a public welfare agency', in Stanton Wheeler (ed.) *On Record: Files and Dossiers in American Life*, New York: Russell Sage Foundation.

Zimmerman, Don H. and Pollner, Melvin (1971) 'The everyday world as phenomenon', in Jack Douglas (ed.) *Understanding Everyday Life: Towards the Reconstruction of Sociological Knowledge*, London: Routledge & Kegan Paul.

NAME INDEX

242

SUBJECT INDEX

account/s: authorization of 24–5; factual 13, 86, 104, 117, 216; fictional 104; social organization of 22, 49, 51
adjacency pair 147, 148, 150
authorization: rules 36, 39, 43, 47–49; of version 24

background knowledge of social structures *see* social structures, background knowledge of
botanizing 165, 167
bureaucracy 6, 8, 122, 213, 219

capital 161
capitalism 7, 208; social relations of 115
capitalist society, advanced 224
class 8; ruling 8; class structure 170
cognitive domain/s 54, 58–60, of scientific theorizing 83
consciousness 9–10, 160, 207; a materialist ontology of 6; of self 168; social forms of 7–8, 163; social relations of 4, 7; *see also* social consciousness
consciousness-raising 2
contrast structure/s (c-structure/s) 33–4, 36, 38–9, 47–8
conversational analysis 147
culture 8, 163, 185, 221, 224

definition/s of situations 42–3, 48
deictic categories 55
deictic locking devices/procedures 56–8, 62, 73, 77
deictic order 57–8, 60–2, 64–6, 71,

83–6; of the meeting 81, 84–5; of the text 81, 85–6
deictic procedures 56, 62, 80, 83
deictic system 56, 62
deixis/es 56, 67, 78, 83
description/s 76, 84–9, 97–8, 100–1, 103–8, 111, 117, 119, 134, 166; categories of 116, 117; language-game of 104–6, 111, 114, 117; literal 89–90, 114, 116; paradox of 89; sociological 87, 91, 97–8, 103, 116, 119
descriptive method of reading 106
descriptive procedure/method 110–11
deviance: categorizations of 26; as legitimation 25
deviant behavior 34
deviant categories 15
discourse/s: 72, 159–64, 167, 169–71, 214–17; bureaucratic/professional 117; cultural 6; femininity as 6, 159, 163; of femininity 164, 167, 170–2, 174, 176, 179, 182–3, 185–6, 188, 192, 194, 197–8, 200–4, 208, 214–15; material organization of 164; order of 161; professional 122, 220; professional managerial 219; psychiatric 220, 223; public textual/textually mediated 123, 125, 133, 167–8; schema/ta of 125, 217; scientific 6, 122, 217; social relations of 161, 166, 170; sociological 166; standpoint of 168; technical 6; textual/textually mediated 1, 4, 7–8 71, 139–40, 161, 163, 167–8, 170, 178, 184, 214–15, 219
discursive courses of action 216

Printed in the United Kingdom
by Lightning Source UK Ltd.
134716UK00001B/169/A

9 780415 102445